Creating the New Economy

This book is in memory of Norman Sarkisian (1931-2000), an entrepreneur in the best tradition and a loyal and loving friend.

●

It is dedicated to my children, Maya and Elias, and my wife, Gina Higgins – who give me a faith in the future that makes every day a celebration.

Creating the New Economy

The Entrepreneur and the US Resurgence

R.D. Norton

Sarkisian Professor of Business Economics
Bryant College
Smithfield, RI, USA

Edward Elgar

Cheltenham, UK • Northampton, MA, USA

Published by
Edward Elgar Publishing Limited
Glensanda House
Montpellier Parade
Cheltenham
Glos GL50 1UA
UK

Edward Elgar Publishing, Inc.
136 West Street
Suite 202
Northampton
Massachusetts 01060
USA

A catalogue record for this book
is available from the British Library

Library of Congress Cataloguing in Publication Data
    Creating the new economy : the entrepreneur and the U.S. resurgence / R.D. Norton.
    p. cm.
    Includes bibliographical references and index.
    1. Entrepreneurship—United States.   2. Technological innovations—Economic aspects—United States.   3. United States—Economic conditions—1993.   I. Title.

    HB615.C74   2000
    338'.04'0973—dc21   00–042695

ISBN 1 84064 448 6
Printed and bound in Great Britain by MPG Books Ltd, Bodmin, Cornwall

Contents

PART V WHAT WENT RIGHT?

Figures

Tables

Acknowledgments

This book has been written with Carla Scott, my friend and co-worker for 15 good years. No one could have been a better workmate. Of late she has been assisted by Jamie Nielsen, to whom I am also grateful.

Friends and colleagues who have helped include Don Peppers, Moses Abramovitz, Andrew Calvert, Gregg Carter, Andrea Celenza, Brian Ceh, Ben Chinitz, Marc Cunningham, Karen Cunningham, Pamela Devenney, John Duca, Chip Elitzer, Bruce Embry, Larry Farrell, Guldem Gokcek, Niles Hansen, Fred Harwood, Tom Hehir, Robert Heilbroner, Brian Holly, Mike Lahr, Mike Lawlor, Scott Loveridge, Brett McKenzie, Ron Miller, C. Edgar Murray, Mita Natarajan, Bruce Norton, John Rees, Luis Suarez-Villa, Doug Wooldridge, and Allen Holland.

Thanks also to Christopher Burke for his inspired opening cartoon, which appeared in the April 2, 1999 *Chronicle of Higher Education* (p. B3).

The Regional Research Institute at West Virginia University, the American Institute for Economic Research, and the US Department of Defense have provided financial and other support for some of the work that appears in the book. I thank them.

I am indebted to Alan Sturmer and to Edward Elgar for helping this book happen. Anyone seeking a creative entrepreneur need look no further than Edward. Also on the English front, I am grateful to John Le Carre, whose warmth, grace, and humor have to be experienced to be believed.

Portions of the book have appeared elsewhere in different form. Chapter 19 has been adapted from my article, 'The Changing IT Roles of the American States 1986-1996,' Copyright 2000, in *Regional Science Perspectives in Economic Analysis* (edited by Michael L. Lahr and Ronald E. Miller), with permission from Elsevier Science. Thanks for reprint permission go also to the *Journal of Economic Literature* for material from Norton (1986) appearing in Chapters 7-10.

I owe a special debt to the Regional Research Institute, which published earlier, on-line versions of Chapters 1-6, 14-18, and 20 and 23 in my chapter, 'The Geography of the New Economy.' Under Scott Loveridge, the RRI at West Virginia has launched an innovative web-based textbook in regional science. Readers may find the RRI Web Book of Regional Science on-line at http://www.rri.wvu.edu/regsweb.htm.

As the dedication page says, Norman Sarkisian was a steadfast and generous friend for the last 16 years and I will miss him.

Words cannot express the debt I owe to Gina Higgins, but that won't stop me from trying to tell her: Thank you.

Preface: geographies of creation

This book has three premises. First, the New Economy is real. Second, its emergence around networked PCs propelled the US resurgence in the world economy during the 1990s. Third, the PC revolution itself can be traced to entrepreneurs from the western half of the US.

The central theme is the vital role played by newcomers, acting as entrepreneurs, to overthrow the old order and blast through the deep tendencies toward stagnation that afflict advanced, affluent economies.

The context is the record of Japan, Europe, and the US in the information-technology (IT) race of the 1980s and 1990s. Japan and western Europe both have impressive educational systems and some of the most accomplished large companies in the world, as evidenced by widespread predictions in the late 1980s that they would overtake the US.

But when it came to computers and the Internet, most established leaders bit the dust in all three countries from about 1985 on. The reason the US defied the odds and regained the lead in IT was the ability of younger, initially smaller firms – especially in the American West – to win in global markets at the PC and then the Internet game.

The questions raised by this historic episode shape the agenda for the book.

What is the mystery that makes people in some nations (and within them, in specific places or regions) entrepreneurial, when in most times and places entrepreneurship is hard to find? Why do large corporations, often with huge R&D budgets, so often stumble in the face of genuinely new technologies? Why did the PC revolutionaries within the US operate in and typically hail from the western half of the country?

Above all, what was it about the US that rendered it more open than, say, France, Germany, or Japan to the creativity of newcomers, acting as entrepreneurs?

The explanation to be developed here invokes America's continental geography and the interplay of its regional economic cultures. Economic progress will be said to depend not only on the organization of production, but also, crucially, on its location.

Perhaps the main economic theory of entrepreneurship is that of the Austrian-born economist Joseph Schumpeter (1883-1950). Schumpeter's doctoral dissertation was published in 1911, when he was 28, and was later translated as *The Theory of Economic Development* (1934). The book advances the idea that the entrepreneur disrupts the circular flow of money and production by introducing a new product or process into the economy.

One consequence is the cyclical rhythm of booms and busts, expansions and declines – short and long. Later, *Business Cycles* (1939) and *Capitalism, Socialism, and Democracy* (1942) would expand and develop this theory of economic change. A 1947 paper, 'The Creative Response in Economic History,' restated and synthesized his views on the matter.

For Schumpeter the entrepreneur is defined by 'the doing of new things or the doing of things that are already being done in a new way (innovation)' (Schumpeter 1947, p. 151). This notion of the entrepreneur excludes most small and new businesses. But he adds that the innovation need not be cosmic in its scale or consequences to merit the term entrepreneurship.

His capitalism is a system that, for all its instability, doubles living standards about every 40 years. In a famous paradox, however, Schumpeter agreed with Marx that capitalism could not survive – for reasons having more to do with its successes than its shortcomings. (Chapter 9 recounts the reasoning.) In his view, what would bring creative capitalism to an end was precisely the disappearance of the classical entrepreneur.

This conclusion can be traced to the then dominant role of banks in the financial system (Chapter 21). Schumpeter died in 1950, when the phrase 'venture capitalism' had yet to be coined. In a world in which new businesses must depend on banks, any number of daring experiments will fail to find financing. That was the world he knew. Hence his view in the 1940s that the main engine for economic change had become the managerial corporation – an engine that would eventually run out of fuel.

As things turned out, the US followed a different trajectory, one shaped and energized by newcomers (to be stylized in what follows as 'geeks, freaks, and immigrants').

The book traces this outpouring of entrepreneurial energy to America's cornucopian geography. The US can be understood as a continent-sized nation of country-sized regions. In turn, such 'regional nations' have distinct economic cultures, reflecting the historical roles they played in the nation's development.

The upshot is that different places in the US display differences in the 'spirit' of capitalism – that value-set Max Weber saw as the source of the original entrepreneurial revolution in eighteenth-century Britain.

What it comes down to today is a tendency toward originality and rejuvenation from the provinces. The point has been made eloquently about Seattle by someone in a position to know, the *New York Times*' former Washington, DC, bureau chief, R. W. Apple Jr. Except for New York, Los Angeles, and perhaps the nation's capital, he writes,

> It's difficult to think of any city . . . that has shaped modern living in the United States as much as this one. Nordstrom, Boeing, Microsoft, Starbucks, Amazon:

all innovators, all based here in the Pacific Northwest, off in a remote corner of the nation, far from the main centers of population. Yet they play a central part in daily life across this continent and beyond. (Apple 2000, p. E29)

In turn, the far-flung geographical sources of America's creativity and innovation have helped to redeem Schumpeter's claim for capitalism. The periodic doubling of living standards has held true for every 40-year interval in the US since 1920 (Chapter 24). Accordingly, in the year 2000 US per capita income is about seven times as high as it was in 1900.

Yet the question of inequality remains wide open. It is not a question I address directly in this book. In the end, there is no getting around the realities of a vital and creative capitalism: it is vulgar, messy, unstable and in many ways unfair. How to remedy its defects without killing the goose is the philosophical point at issue as between Europe and the US.

But the US approach – the arrangements, geography and culture that have given birth to the dynamism of the New Economy – has done a great deal to reduce the worst form of American inequality.

That, of course, is slavery's legacy, black poverty. From the inability of the framers of the Constitution to address slavery, through the Civil War, the assassination of Lincoln, and the persistence of institutionalized racism down through the 1960s and beyond, the 'American Dilemma' (as the Swedish economist Gunnar Myrdal aptly described it in 1944) has been the contrast between egalitarian ideals and racial realities.

I wrote a book on the subject that appeared in 1979. The urban black poverty that book addressed intensified in the 1980s, owing to the nightmarish confluence of crack and AIDS in declining northern cities. The rapid gains in black-poverty rates in the 1960s faded from memory.

In that light, perhaps the chief claim to be made for the New Economy is a 10-point reduction in black poverty in the 1990s. The accompanying timeline documents the pace of the improvement – and the contrast from the grim days of the 1970s and 1980s. As the exhibit shows, the incidence of black poverty in 1992, 33.4 percent, was as high as it had been in 1969.

But from 1992 to 1999 it fell by some 10 percentage points, to 23.6. That cut the poverty rate from a third of the African-American population to less than a fourth. At over twice the national rate, this is still far too high. But until the 1990s, the black poverty rate had never fallen below 30 percent.

In a nutshell, then, the theme of the book is that entrepreneurs from the provinces, acting as individuals, not as 'organization men,' have infused the US economy with a dynamism that has restored the American dream.

That the social progress generated by economic growth is an old-fashioned theme, I grant you. But then, this is the motif that pervades what follows. Everything old becomes new again, if things go right.

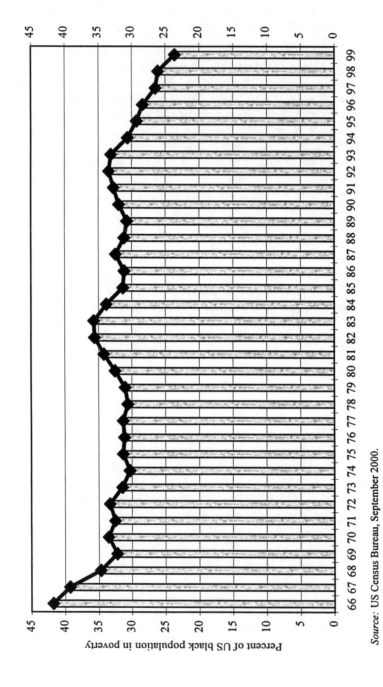

Source: US Census Bureau, September 2000.

Exhibit 10-point reductions in the black poverty rate: the late 1960s and the 1990s

The United States has remained young very long, partly because the geographical distribution of her resources has been such as to tempt men of strong character to move to new scenes, in which their enterprise has been further stimulated.

Alfred Marshall 1919 (p. 141)

PART I

Three conceptions of the New Economy

1. What is the New Economy?

> A new economy has emerged in the last two decades on a worldwide scale.
> (Castells 1996, p. 66)

A magazine solicitation from the Harvard Business School begins, 'Please join other pioneers in the new economy and take advantage of this Charter rate.' I am delighted to be recognized as a pioneer in the New Economy, especially by the Harvard Business School. But which 'New Economy' am I a pioneer in? People (and business magazines) are referring to 'the' New Economy all the time now, but they seem to have different models in mind.

There is a *macroeconomic* version, able to keep on growing rapidly without inflation. There is a *microeconomic* version, apparently driven by a new kind of firm. There is the *digital* version, likely to be identified with an Information Age. Then there are variants that focus on management, labor relations, sustainable development, and other topics as well.

What most New-Economy approaches have in common is the idea that computers and in particular networked PCs have changed things in a fundamental way. That is the common denominator we shall encounter as we look at the macro, micro, and digital versions of the New-Economy hypothesis in turn.

I conclude that there really is something new about the economy, as tends to happen every 50 years or so. Also, *the New Economy is in some relevant sense a 'reborn' economy*. That is, it has successfully weathered what could be termed a maturity crisis (or, as the British call it, a 'climacteric') and defied the predictions a decade ago of inevitable US economic decline. What has helped all this along is the nation's unique regional geography, a product of its continental scale.

But you do not have to arrive at these same conclusions to get something out of the grand tour we are about to take in Part I.

FASTER GROWTH, LOWER INFLATION

The crux of the macroeconomic version of the New Economy is the idea that information technology (IT) creates higher productivity growth, which in turn permits faster growth in output without a rise in the rate of inflation. Despite doubts from skeptics, this view became increasingly plausible in 1999, as strong productivity growth continued and the expansion headed for a record ninth year.

Federal Reserve Board Chair Alan Greenspan himself seems to believe that things have changed dramatically. In testimony of February 24, 1998, he observed,

> [O]ur nation has been experiencing a higher growth rate of productivity – output per hour worked – in recent years. The dramatic improvements in computing power and communication and information technology appear to have been a major force behind this beneficial trend.

Indeed, in a recent report, *The Emerging Digital Economy* (1998), the Department of Commerce presents a graph that shows IT reducing the rate of inflation by one full percentage point over what it would be in the absence of IT.

There is no question that the macroeconomic picture has been a thing of beauty in recent years. A useful indicator to show the improvement is the *misery index*, the sum of the inflation and unemployment rates. It used to be said there was an inescapable tradeoff between the two, a tradeoff portrayed in the Phillips Curve. In the late 1990s, however, with unemployment down to 4.5 percent and inflation below 3 percent, the index for the US looked better than in three decades (see Figure 1.1).

Generalizing, Bernard Weinstein (1997) offered the following list of New-Economy attributes:

- An economy that grows without apparent threat of recession.
- An economy that continues to expand without a pickup in inflation.
- An economy constantly restructuring itself for greater efficiency and productivity.
- An economy replenishing and revitalizing itself through new technology and capital investment.
- An economy that functions without excessive debt, either public or private.
- An economy that maintains a balanced budget.
- An economy that is increasingly globalized and export driven.

Professor Weinstein concludes, 'Not to suggest that inflation is dead, the business cycle extinct, and the stock market destined to rise forever. But, with good macroeconomic management, we believe the economy can grow virtually without interruption for the foreseeable future.'

Mark Zandi of Regional Financial Associates, a forecasting firm, described the New Economy at a Boston conference in May 1998: 'The new economy adjusts more quickly to exogenous shocks, and it does not generate an environment that leads to recession.' In his view, (1) globalization, (2) faster technological change, (3) securitization, and (4) deregulation have together introduced new variables that have yet to be included in conventional forecasting models of the economy (Miara 1998).

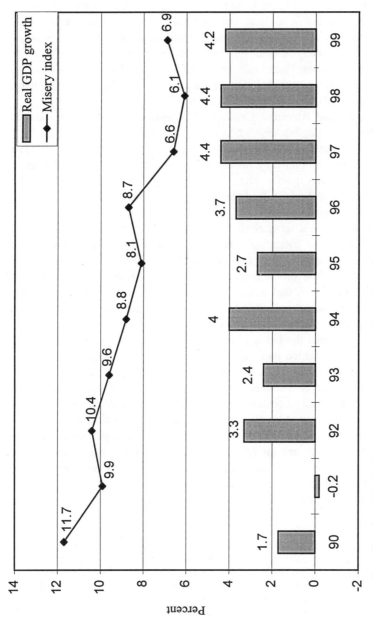

Note: The misery index is the sum of the unemployment and CPI inflation rates.

Figure 1.1 Breaking the speed limit in the 1990s

TRIUMPHALISM?

Zandi (1998) offers a fuller treatment in 'Musings on the New Economy.' There he describes it as 'part real and part surreal.' Many economists would conclude in a similar vein that the improvement in the misery index is as much as can be said for any macroeconomic version of a New Economy. For example, an exchange in the May/June 1998 issue of *Foreign Affairs* turns on whether America's long expansion in the 1990s signaled a true restoration of the nation's bygone glory.

In 'A Second American Century,' Mortimer Zuckerman (a real-estate developer and publisher) contends that the US triumph reflects 'deft managers, technological innovation, and a culture that values rugged individualism – all fueled by finance capital that can nimbly meet the needs of a globalized, rapidly changing economy' (p.1). Accordingly, he concludes, the present US lead relative to Europe and Asia will if anything increase in the next century.

Paul Krugman's rebuttal in the same issue, 'America the Boastful,' views all this as a triumphalist caricature. As background, Krugman has long since declared the new economy dead. Here he points out in a lucid analysis that while productivity growth may be faster than the official measurements show, that has always been true. Technically, he says, the growth of real output is limited by the sum of (1) the increase in employed workers plus (2) the rate of growth of productivity, or output per worker.

Instead he sees the US ascendance as the result of a sustained cyclical expansion here, which looks all the better next to difficulties in Europe, Japan, and emerging Asia. Everything could change once the US has another recession, and economies elsewhere revive. 'Future historians will not record that the 21st century belonged to the United States' (p. 45).

In a related vein, Alan Blinder speaks of 'lucky shocks,' as the reason for the reduction in the rate of inflation while the unemployment rate also falls. Among them are lower prices for oil and for imports generally, a slowdown in the rise of health costs, and – last but for our purposes not least – the relentless fall in computer prices (Uchitelle 1999, p. C2).

A similar dismissal of the macro version of the thesis appeared in a Silicon Valley magazine, *Red Herring*, whose editor concludes,

> [T]he argument for a new economy does not make sense. Digital technologies have not dramatically increased productivity; international competition doesn't have much effect on prices; and the economy cannot grow by more than the sum of the increase in productivity and the increase in new workers (Jason Pontin, 'There Is No New Economy,' *Red Herring Magazine*, on-line, September 1997).

2. The US resurgence

> The intriguing question here is whether there is a peculiarly English disease . . .
> or whether its experience is the reflection of more deeply rooted forces that will
> inevitably assault all countries at some sufficiently advanced stage of industrial
> maturity.   (Rosenberg 1982, p. 283)

More generally, Krugman chides New Economy advocates for a lack of
historical perspective. His point is that there is nothing new about
technological change. Now, Krugman knows what he is talking about on
these questions. Of particular interest to us at this point is 'Requiem for the
New Economy' (from way back on 10 November 1997).

But economic history yields an alternative view as well. In hindsight, we
could say that there were two great economic questions of the twentieth
century. One was about the effectiveness of communism as an economic
system. That was answered decisively with the collapse of the Soviet Union
after 1989.

The second great economic question of the twentieth century has been
the adaptability of what might be termed 'mature capitalism'—above all as
practiced in the largest mature economy, the US. The big question was
whether the US had to endure the decline that afflicted the world's first
industrial nation, Britain, at the end of the nineteenth century.

INDICATORS OF A US COMEBACK

In that light, it is precisely Britain's historical precedent that makes the US
comeback in the world economy such an unexpected event.

The Swiss Competitiveness Ranks

Consider, for example, the annual press releases from Davos, Switzerland,
where an organization called the World Economic Forum publishes ratings
of the world's economies in terms of their 'competitiveness.' Any single
index of competitiveness is bound to be in part arbitrary, and this one has
met its share of criticism. But in the past couple of years Jeffrey Sachs and
Michael Porter of Harvard have helped refine the measure.

What it shows in each recent year is a ranking for the US (third, after
Singapore and Hong Kong) higher than for any other major economy. And
by the subjective appraisals of business executives polled by the Forum, the

US actually ranked first in both 1997 and 1998. (See Table 6 of the *Executive Summary*.)

Industrial Output

One reason for the business leaders' view may be that the US manufacturing sector has surged in the 1990s. This is not always understood, partly because downsizing and layoffs still occur and indeed accelerated in 1998. In addition there is a lingering 'post-industrial fallacy,' which in one version measures the sector's role by employment – or in another uses current instead of inflation-adjusted dollars to track manufacturing output as a share of gross domestic product (GDP).

An example of the fallacy is a recent *New York Times* column: 'The Economy Grows. The Smokestacks Shrink.' There we read, 'Manufacturing has been losing momentum for decades, with its share of the gross domestic product dwindling to just over half of what it was in 1953' (Uchitelle, 1998, 3:4).

In real terms, manufacturing's 1996 share of GDP reached its highest value in a generation, 19.1 percent compared with previous peak values of 18.3 percent in 1989 and 18.7 percent in 1979. (See Table 1231 of the *Statistical Abstract of the United States 1998*, and the corresponding tables in earlier editions.)

At over 3 percent a year since 1975, manufacturing's productivity growth is much faster than in the rest of the economy. (As Table 689 of the *Abstract* shows, output per hour rose 65 percent from 1980 to 1997, compared with 21 percent in the non-farm private sector as a whole.) Therefore manufacturing output can grow rapidly over time without adding more workers – or even with fewer workers, as in agriculture in the early twentieth century. Faster productivity gains also mean costs and prices rise less rapidly in manufacturing than in other parts of the economy. For that reason, when measured in current dollars, manufacturing as a share of output lags. But the shrinkage is an illusion of prices.

US productivity levels in manufacturing are the highest in the world. While the Netherlands and Sweden come close, and other countries have higher levels in specific sectors (for example, cars in Japan), the aggregate US lead remains. In 1996, output per hour worked in manufacturing was half again as high as in Canada or the UK, and a third again as high as in Japan. (That is, the index values relative to 100 in the US were 68 for Canada, 67 for the UK, and 74 for Japan. See Tables 1374 and 1375 of the *Abstract*.)

The US share of world exports in manufactures rebounded from a 10.7 percent share in the late 1980s to 11.5 percent in 1995. Faced with the rapid expansion of exports from China and the Asian newly industrializing countries (NICs: Hong Kong, South Korea, Singapore, and Taiwan) other advanced economies lost ground. The former West Germany's share fell from 14.6 to 12.2 percent, and Japan's from 12.4 to 11.4 percent. (Table 1244.)

What all this adds up to is that the US has had a faster expansion in industrial output since 1980 than any other advanced economy. Figure 2.1 tells the story, tracking the percentage growth in output for manufacturing, mining, and electric and gas utilities. The US increase of 56 percent exceeded Japan's 51 percent, virtually all of which occurred in the 1980s. Mexico and Canada are not far behind, with Europe's major economies trailing.

In short, it is not obvious that the US has been deindustrialized, or that its manufacturing sector is shrinking relative to the rest of the economy, or that it has lost its industrial competitiveness.

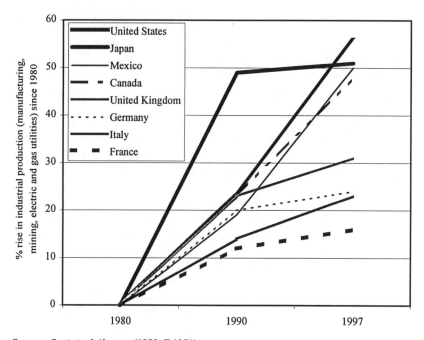

Source: Statistical Abstract (1998, T 1371).

Figure 2.1   US industrial growth leads Japan and Europe, 1980-1997

LIVING STANDARDS

As a result of its economic revitalization, the US continues to have the world's highest average living standards. Economists compare living standards across countries by output per person, assuming that the more output is produced per year, the more will be available for consumption by the population. The usual measure of output is GDP, defined as the market value of currently produced final goods and services during one year. For any given year, then, a country's average living standards are gauged by per capita GDP.

For the US in 1997, this figure, $28,740, equals a GDP of $7.7 trillion divided by a population of 268 million. These numbers may be found in Table 1 of the statistical appendix to the World Bank's *World Development Report 1998/99*.

Comparing per capita GDP across countries requires one more step. Except for the Euro group, which rallied around a single currency on January 1, 1999, each country has its own currency whose value depends on supply and demand in world markets. Therefore an adjustment must be made for something called 'purchasing-power parity' (PPP). The adjustment corrects for any discrepancy between a currency's domestic purchasing power and its exchange rate, to give a more accurate index of living standards.

The benchmark value in the World Bank's Table 1 is the US figure in 1997 of $28,740. That placed it a close second to tiny Singapore's $29,000. The US figure was, for example, 23 percent higher than No. 6 Japan's $23,400 and 31 percent higher than No. 10 Canada's $21,860.

To be sure, any such average value says nothing about income distribution, which is becoming more unequal in the US and in other industrial economies. In addition, there are various other measurement and quality-of-life issues that make per capita GDP a crude yardstick at best.

The UNDP Human Development Index

For skeptics, the United Nations Development Program provides an interesting alternative measure of well-being. Their Human Development Index (HDI) factors in not only per capita GDP but also life expectancy at birth and average educational levels. As the UNDP explains, 'a composite index, the HDI thus contains three variables: life expectancy, education attainment (adult literacy and combined primary, secondary and tertiary enrolment) and real GDP per capita (in PPP$).' By this score the US ranks No. 4, behind Canada, France, and Norway. (France had lower education and output values, but a higher life expectancy, 78.7 versus 76.4 for the US, in 1995.) Japan ranked No. 9, the UK No. 14.

Revising Real Growth Upward

How does all this square with the view that US living standards have not improved much over the past quarter-century? Much has been made of the fact that after about 1973, productivity growth and the rise in living standards slowed.

But it turns out that the official numbers have given too pessimistic a picture. The distortion stems from the way the year-to-year changes in output and income are adjusted for inflation. According to the Boskin Commission (chaired by Michael J. Boskin and including the luminaries Ellen Dullberger, R.J. Gordon, Zvi Griliches, and Dale Jorgenson), inflation rates have been overestimated by about 1.1 percent a year for some time. The technical reasons inflation has been measured at too high a rate come under four headings: product substitution, retail outlet substitution, quality, and new-goods biases.

Thus about 1 percent too much has been subtracted from each year's measured per capita GDP for perhaps the past two decades. Living standards, thought to be stagnant, may actually have risen by something closer to 2 percent a year. That would still not be as high as before 1973, but it is respectable for an economy that already had the world's highest absolute productivity levels.

For perspective, let us view the change in terms of the 'rule of 72,' which says that the time it takes an amount growing at compound growth rate r percent to double can be found by dividing 72 by r. Living standards would thus double in 36 years at 2 percent a year, compared with 72 years at 1 percent.

Labor-force Outcomes

A look at labor-market conditions may be found in a recent on-line report from the Progressive Policy Institute, a Democratic Party think-tank. The report (*What's New about the New Economy?*) organizes a variety of indicators. In combination, the findings (some of which are quoted directly below) suggest a less-secure economy – but one teeming with opportunity:

1. Low-wage jobs are growing, but higher-wage jobs are growing even faster.
2. Manufacturing has not disappeared, it has been reinvented.
3. In the last 9 years, three million new managerial jobs have been added.
4. Fewer workers are unemployed and under-employed.
5. The increases in worker displacement remain modest.

6. The wage premium for skilled jobs is growing.
7. Increases in contingent (part-time, contract, temp) work are also modest.
8. Workers experience less job stability.

In a similar analysis, Michael J. Mandel, economics editor of *Business Week*, observes that since March 1991, 'real wages have risen at an annual rate of 1 percent,' a big improvement over the 0.2 percent average for the expansion of the 1980s. Mandel also provides a chart on page 9 of his 1999 report showing that over two-thirds of the new jobs created in the economy between 1995 and 1998 are 'good jobs,' in managerial, professional, and skilled-production occupations. As he puts it, 'The benefits are especially apparent for young people graduating from college, who are coming into a world of soaring salaries rather than [the] dim prospects many had expected.'

THE JOB MACHINE

Not that it is new, but we should make explicit another feature of the US economy that is familiar enough by now that we tend to take it for granted.

Since 1980, the US has experienced net employment growth of over 30 million new jobs. What puts this achievement in perspective is the fact that over the past generation, the major industrial economies of Europe have had next to no job growth (see Figure 2.2).

From one point of view, the national economy spawns large numbers of new jobs of all types because of the rapid growth of the South and West— not only Florida and Texas, that is, but also Arizona, North Carolina, and Washington.

Putting it another way, a decisive difference between the US and most other advanced economies is America's continental scale.

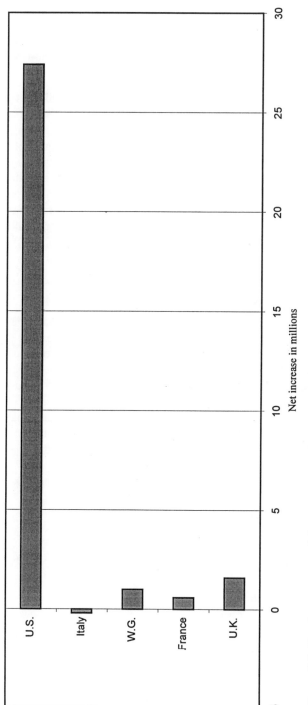

Figure 2.2 Employment growth by country, 1980-1996

3. Regional wellsprings

[T]he Western scenario is one of sheer *growth of numbers*; the Southern scenario is one of *industrialization*; the Northern scenario is one of *adjustment to adversity*. (Chinitz 1984, p. 300)

Geographically, the US is a continent-sized nation of country-sized regions. The origins of the New Economy derive largely from the actions of entrepreneurs from younger regions, especially the West. This chapter provides an introductory look at the 'ages' of US regions—and notes that sharp contrasts in regional job growth may finally have come to an end.

THE MANUFACTURING BELT AND THE PERIPHERY

Economic geographers see the historical development of the nation's regional structure in terms of an industrial core and a less-developed periphery. To say more, it helps to draw on some official definitions.

The Census Bureau designates four main 'regions': the Northeast, Midwest, South, and West, as shown in Figure 3.1 (adapted from the map that appears on the inside front cover of the *Statistical Abstract*). There are then nine component 'divisions':

- Northeast: *New England* and *Middle Atlantic* divisions
- Midwest: *East North Central* and West North Central
- South: South Atlantic, East South Central, and West South Central
- West: Mountain and Pacific divisions

The three italicized divisions industrialized before the others: New England, the Middle Atlantic, and the East North Central (or Lakes or Upper Midwest) divisions. These were the matrix for America's nineteenth-century industrial revolution before and especially after the Civil War.

Accordingly, historians and geographers define the *Manufacturing Belt* as the super-region from Boston to Baltimore to St. Louis to Milwaukee. In this book, the Manufacturing Belt will be approximated for data purposes by the New England, Middle Atlantic, and East North Central divisions.

The other six divisions constitute the South and West, a label masking enormous diversity. Though an approximation, this core-periphery approach has proved useful. Such variables as city growth, attitudes toward unions,

15

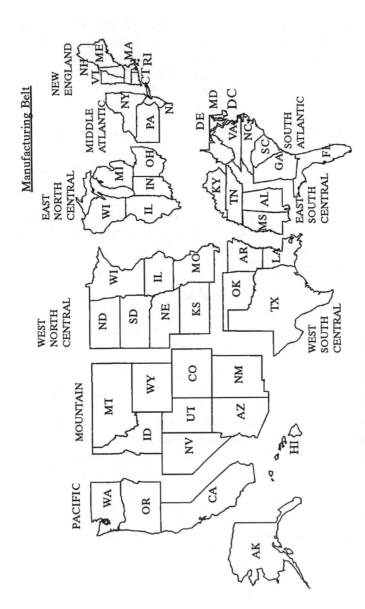

Source: Statistical Abstract of the United States.

Figure 3.1 The nine divisions and the Manufacturing Belt

and ethnicity display contrasting values as between the old industrial core and the periphery.

Table 3.1 ranks the nine divisions by 'age,' that is, by the timing of their industrialization. Then, as recently as 1980, a standard measure of state business climates aligned closely with the age variable. Similarly, of the states with 'right-to-work' laws that forbid union shops (requiring workers to join unions at unionized job sites), all 20 are in the five 'younger' divisions. Not one is in the four divisions that industrialized earlier, including now the Pacific Division along with the Belt. (We return to this topic in Chapter 9.)

Table 3.1 Regional maturity and business climates

Regional maturity as ranked by population share in manufacturing	Age rank	Business climate rank from averages of 1980 state scores (Grant Index)	No. of states with right-to-work laws
The Manufacturing Belt			
New England	9	8	0
Middle Atlantic	8	9	0
East North Central	7	6	0
The South and West			
Pacific	6	7	0
South Atlantic	5	5	5
West North Central	4	1	5
East South Central	3	3	3
Mountain	2	3	4
West South Central	1	2	3

Source: Norton (1986, p. 21).

Partly as a result of such political and institutional variables, manufacturing employment in the core has declined steadily since the late 1960s (see Figure 3.2). The core had 10.8 million in 1970, but only 7.7 million in 1997. Offsetting much of that decline, the South and West gained two million jobs over the interval, most of it by 1980. For the US as a whole, the count peaked at 21.0 million in 1979 and has dropped by one million in the 1990s, from 19.7 to 18.8 million.

All in all, the US has fared far better on this score than Europe (which has lost over five million manufacturing jobs). Judging by evidence to be presented later (in Chapter 11), the reason is the job growth in new manufacturing activities in the South and West.

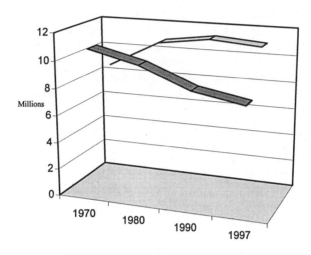

	1970	1980	1990	1997
☐ MFG BELT	10.8	9.9	8.4	7.7
☐ SOUTH &WEST	8.9	10.8	11.3	11

Figure 3.2   Manufacturing employment tilts South and West

THE LATE 1990S: ALL BOATS RISING

Hidden from these sweeping comparisons is a remarkable industrial resurgence in the Upper Midwest. During the 1990s, after a generation of painful adjustment, the Lakes states have displayed an impressive comeback. It is based on the division's traditional cluster of 'heavy-metal' and vehicles – and on another staple activity, agriculture. The effects are less evident in manufacturing than in total employment.

In terms of total (non-farm) payroll employment, the triumph of the resurgent Midwest is that it added jobs at about the national rate during the 1990s. Figure 3.3 reports an increase of nearly three million jobs for the division between 1990 and 1998.

The divisions hit hardest in the first half of the 1990s were New England and the Mid-Atlantic. As the figure shows, the Northeast lagged far behind the rest of the US in job growth in the 1990s. In the early part of the decade, the traditionally slow-growing Northeast was hit especially hard by (1) defense cuts, (2), corporate downsizing (which rocked the region's

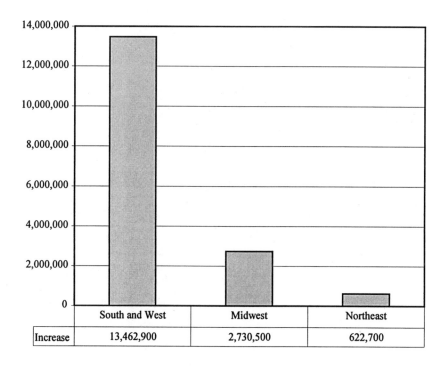

	South and West	Midwest	Northeast
Increase	13,462,900	2,730,500	622,700

Figure 3.3 Seventeen million new jobs, by region (non-farm payroll employment, January 1990-September 1998)

headquarters complex in New York City, New Jersey, and Connecticut), and (3) the rapid shift of American computing to the West.

Nevertheless, by the beginning of 1997 the state and regional job picture had reached a new stage, in which, for example, Massachusetts would add employment at about the national rate. By that point the Northeast had ridden out its various shocks, and the region's strengths in finance, health care, software, and other services gave it a new lease on growth.

In the meantime, however, enduring regional legacies still shape the political landscape. A case in point is the 2000 presidential campaign, which finds each of the two major candidates coming from the South or West – just as in every presidential election since 1964.

This is the point of departure for the next chapter.

4. New politics (as usual)

In the Information Age political power will rest on the ability to compete in the marketplace of ideas. (Galston and Kamarck 1998, p. 10)

When it comes to the politics of the New Economy, a good place to start is demography. By demography I refer not so much to generational or ethnic conflicts, familiar and important as they are. Instead, the initial focus now is on the location of population growth.

The redistribution of the US population to the South and West and the suburbs has had any number of subtle effects on the nation's marketing, media, culture, and politics. We can begin by noting a more direct impact: the link between population growth and the home states of recent presidents (see Figure 4.1).

YANKEE NO

No one from the Manufacturing Belt has been elected President since John F. Kennedy defeated Richard Nixon in 1960. That was 40 years ago. At the time of this writing, in 2000, either George W. Bush of Texas or Al Gore of Tennessee will be the seventh elected president in a row, spanning the last ten elections, from the South or West.

The explanation is that 90 percent of the nation's population growth since 1970 has taken place outside the North. That makes presidential candidates from the South and West more attractive to the two major nominating parties. It also tends to give such candidates a powerful regional base. The reasons have to do with the Constitution and the technicalities of the Electoral College.

The Constitution mandates that political representation reflects the distribution of the US population. Each state has two US senators, of course. But the state-by-state shares of the 450 members of the House of Representatives are variable. By the doctrine of 'one man, one vote,' the Constitution requires *reapportionment* of the House of Representatives every ten years to reflect the changing distribution of the population.

Both regional and city-suburban shifts thus require a congressional redistricting after every decennial census. The states and localities that have the most population growth receive an added number of representatives, and those with least growth lose seats. The effect is to redistribute power from older cities and from the Manufacturing Belt.

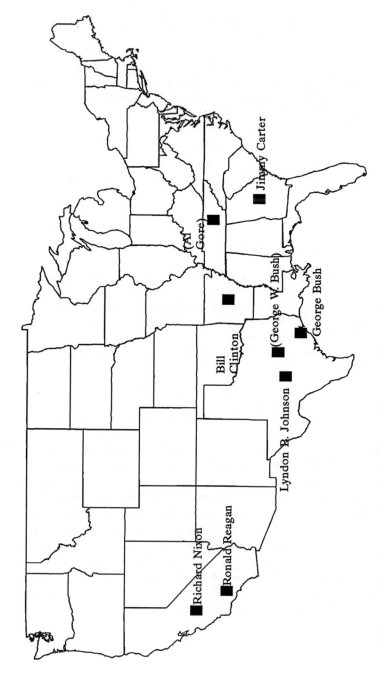

Richard Nixon

Ronald Reagan

Al Gore

Bill Clinton

(George W. Bush)

Jimmy Carter

George Bush

Lyndon B. Johnson

Figure 4.1 Home states of all elected presidents since 1964

Redistricting also alters the number of votes states have in the Electoral College – which technically determines the outcome of a presidential election. The more representatives a state has, the more electoral votes, and the more important the state to a national presidential campaign strategy.

The 1980 delegation from the North in the House of Representatives was 225 (or 50 percent of the 450). It fell to 208 in the 1980s, and again to 193 after the 1990 census. After the 2000 census and reapportionment, it is likely to approach 180, which would leave the South and West with about 270 seats.

In the span of barely a generation, the balance of power in the House will thus shift from 50-50 to 40-60, in favor of the South and West. Regional weights in the Electoral College have tilted apace, which seems to set the regional origins of American presidents for some time to come.

But why should that matter, beyond the home addresses of would-be presidents? The answer, not surprisingly, is that the regional shift in population and power maps out ideologically as a tilt to the right.

POWER SHIFTS

Most states in the South and interior West are more conservative than most states in the North, the Manufacturing Belt. As noted in the last chapter, the South and interior West were historically less urban and industrial. Today they tend to retain more rural and conservative values. In general, new residents not only add to a growing state's electoral count but also tend to acquire the local political coloration.

As President Clinton's impeachment demonstrated, virtually every major House Committee was chaired in the late 1990s by a Republican from the South or West. Such an outcome was predicted as early as 1969, when the Republican theorist Kevin Phillips titled his book on electoral demographics, *The Emerging Republican Majority.*

By 1975, President Nixon's resignation in disgrace was seen by Kirkpatrick Sale as the surface of a conspiratorial struggle between 'cowboys' and Yankees – power-brokers in a dying 'eastern establishment.' Even at the time, the argument seemed overheated. Still, Sale was on to something.

In a prescient glimpse of the Reagan Revolution still to come, Sale wrote that the US was experiencing its fifth fundamental political Power Shift (Sale 1975, p. 152). Quoting him directly, the sequence ran as follows:

1. the consolidation of federal control at the turn of the eighteenth century,
2. the introduction of Jacksonian democracy in the early nineteenth century,
3. the expansion of Northern industrialism after the Civil War . . .

4.   the establishment of Rooseveltian welfarism in the 1930s.
5.   [t]he rise of the Southern Rim marks a fifth.

In retrospect, the power shift was neither to the Republican party *per se* nor even necessarily to the 'Southern Rim,' unless that includes California. What subsequent elections would reveal was not a Republican lock on the presidency, but a regional (and ideological) lock-out.

For the job of president, no one from the North, and no New Deal liberals (for example, Mario Cuomo or Bill Bradley), need apply. Jimmy Carter or Bill Clinton could get elected President as Democrats. But as southerners they were also 'new Democrats,' just as Tony Blair in the UK is a new or 'third way' Labour Prime Minister.

All this, while now familiar, flows from the subtle and gradual interplay of America's political institutions and geography. Over time, the geography of growth combined with a decentralized and flexible federal system to alter Americans' collective consensus on what government should do. By 1995, President Clinton could conclude that the 'era of big government is over' (Gross 2000, p. 8).

SUBURBS AND SKEPTICS

Population shifts are also reshaping the political process on another axis, from cities to suburbs.

In 'Five Realities that Will Shape 21st Century Politics,' William A. Galston and Elaine C. Kamarck view the future of the Democratic Party through the prism of demographic and geographic change. The five tendencies emphasize not so much regional as city-suburban tensions.

The Rising Learning Class

The New Economy holds new realities for party politics, away from class-based legacies of the New Deal. The key determinant of economic position now is family structure. Unions have shrunk so much that they are no longer pivotal. 'In the Information Age political power will rest on the ability to compete in the marketplace of ideas' (Galston and Kamarck 1998, p. 10).

A Generation of Skeptics

Whereas the New Deal generation saw government as a solution, and Baby-Boomers have mixed emotions based on Watergate and Vietnam, the formative Generation-Xers are just plain skeptical. They have come of age in a time of economic insecurity, in which government seems as much a problem as a solution. In their view, 'large-scale politics is a blunt and ineffective instrument for addressing key social problems' (p. 13). But they can be recruited to programs for education and the environment.

Power to the Suburbs

Twenty-five years ago, 'there were roughly equal numbers of urban, suburban, and rural districts in the US House of Representatives. Today, suburban districts outnumber urban districts by more than 2 to 1, and rural districts by almost 3 to 1' (p. 14). If the Democrats want to find a demographic power-base comparable to the cities in the New Deal, it will have to be the suburbs, where relevant issues will be education, crime, sustainable development, and the environment (p. 16).

Family Structure

The paradox of changes in family structure is this: 'The needs of children will be increasingly central . . . but the percentage of families with minor children will continue to shrink' (p. 17). There will be an empathy problem on the part of the majority of the electorate.

Identity Politics

Whereas the old politics were about black/white divisions, immigration is changing the picture. From an immigrant low-point in the 1960s, *today 11 percent of the population is Hispanic and another 3 percent Asian by birth.* (This combined share of the foreign-born exceeds the African-American share of 12 percent.) Such tendencies are likely to accelerate. The challenge will be to appeal to the American Dream as a unifying message to offset the divisive politics of ethnic identities.

THE DEMOCRATIZATION OF MONEY

Another approach to the politics of the New Economy is to ask what ever happened to class conflict. A prerequisite, of course, is to ask what defines 'social class' in the US at the Millennium. The answer, not to mince words, is unclear. Still, two recent books on the topic are suggestive.

In *Bull Run: Wall Street, the Democrats, and the New Politics of Personal Finance*, Daniel Gross draws a telling contrast between the 1980s and 1990s. In his view, the 1990s saw a profound change: the democratization of money. The phrase refers to the doubling of stock ownership in the 1990s, from 23 to 46 percent of the US population. When combined with indirect ownership via pension funds, the result was that a majority of Americans had a stake in Wall Street by the end of the 1990s (Gross 2000, pp. 4-5).

In his view, the public now distinguishes between 'arrogant capital' (symbolized by excessive CEO pay and abuse of stock options) and 'modest capital,' as represented by Warren Buffett. Modest capital and its practitioners earn respect and admiration, as distinct from the disdain most people felt for the new plutocrats of the 1980s.

Combined with the Newt Gingrich phenomenon (the takeover of the Republican Party by anti-Wall Street populists from the South and Mountain West), the outcome is a partial reversal of party alignments. In the 1990s, the Democratic Party became the trustee of the vast middle and upper-middle class who owned stock. And the Republicans shunned their traditional alliance with Wall Street.

A still more iconoclastic view is David Brooks's *Bobos in Paradise: The New Upper Class and How They Got That Way*. 'Bobos' is an acronym for 'bourgeois bohemians.' As such it conflates the traditional opposites of wealth and cultural rebellion. The point, part tongue in cheek, is that the proverbial 1960s legacy (filling the void of the long-lost WASP aristocracy) has turned out to be a new moneyed class that sees itself as rebelling against obsolete cultural constraints.

The result for party alignments, as Daniel Gross puts it (p. 16), is that 'It's more hip to be a Democrat if you're loaded than it was in the 1980s. And it's more hip to be loaded if you're a Democrat.'

One reason for the increased legitimacy of 'modest capital,' perhaps, is the prominence of self-made entrepreneurs among America's richest people. This topic gets the next chapter started.

APPENDIX 4A: POPULATION GROWTH IN THE 1990S

A good overview of state population growth in the 1990s appeared in two recent Census Bureau maps. Posted on the last day of 1998, the maps show population changes by state for 1990-98 and the one-year change for 1997-98.

The 1990-98 map shows most of the states in the South and West growing faster than the US average of 8.7 percent. Most of the states in the Northeast and Midwest are growing more slowly. The slow-growth region sweeps from Maine to Oklahoma and up to North Dakota, which (like Connecticut and Rhode Island) actually declined. Anomalies are slow-growth Louisiana and brisk New Hampshire.

For 1997-98, relative to the US average (a convenient 1.0 percent), the regional pattern was unchanged. But now Alaska, Washington, and Oregon were closer to the average, and California surged ahead. On the downside, Pennsylvania and West Virginia lost population.

California aside, these tendencies are broadly similar to the prior two decades, the 1970s and 1980s. From 1970 to 1997 the US population grew by 64.3 million, an increase of 32 percent (*Statistical Abstract of the United States 1998*, Table 29, p. 31, 'U.S. Resident Population, by Region and Division: 1970 to 1997'). Less than 10 percent of the increase took place in the Manufacturing Belt.

In short, and as noted at the outset, over 90 percent of the increase in the US population between 1970 and 1997 occurred in the South and West.

MIGRATION, THE LEVER OF POWER

Why do most states of the South and West typically add population faster than those elsewhere? In practice, domestic migration has for a long time tilted the population increasingly away from the Northeast and Midwest. That this tendency continued to operate in the 1990s can be seen via comparisons among the nine divisions. By way of background, we can take a quick look at the definitional components of population growth.

For the US as a whole, population growth is equal to the *natural increase* (births - deaths) + net *immigration*. The US adds nearly a million people a year through legal (and illegal) immigration. This, plus higher birth-rates among recent immigrants (especially Hispanics), is what gives the US higher rates of population growth than Japan or Europe.

For states and regions, we have to add domestic *migration*. To see why a state or region is growing at a higher or lower rate, we need to find the natural increase (births - deaths) and then add the two migration entries. The first, as for the US, is NIM (net international migration). The second is NDM (net domestic migration).

These definitions provide a handle on regional population changes in the 1990s (see Figure 4A.1). To begin with, every division had a positive natural increase, births - deaths. But four of the divisions lost migrants to the rest of the US, as indicated by their 'below-the-line' bars in the chart.

We can compare two divisions on the East Coast that had offsetting flows of domestic migrants. The Middle Atlantic division attracted 1.5 million net foreign migrants but lost 2.3 million people to other US regions. Its natural increase, 1.5 million (= 4.5 million births - 3 million deaths), was therefore reduced by over 0.8 million net migrants out of the region. All in all, its net increase in population was less than 700,000, for a population growth rate of only 1.8 percent. Had it not been for immigrants, in other words, the Mid-Atlantic division would have lost 800,000 residents.

In contrast, the South Atlantic (which includes Florida and North Carolina) added 5.4 million people, for a rate of 12.3 percent. The increase consisted of a natural gain of 2.3 million, plus net foreign immigration of 1 million, plus 2.2 million in-migrants (job-seeking and sun-seeking both) from other parts of the US.

In the far West, a similar contrast can be seen for the Pacific Division, dominated by the flight from California in the early 1990s, and the Mountain states. Visually (as with the Mid-Atlantic and South Atlantic divisions), the number of domestic out-migrants from the Pacific was matched by the number of domestic in-migrants to the Mountain states.

This brief sketch can suffice as a first look at the pivotal role played by domestic migration. We return to the topic in Chapter 23, in relation to some ten 'magnet metros' occupying a zone from Seattle to Atlanta.

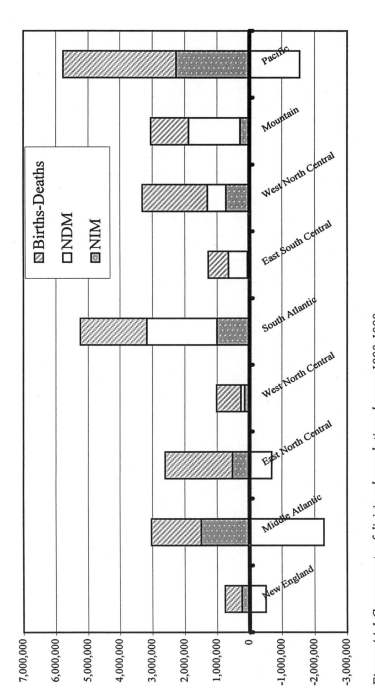

Figure 4A.1 Components of divisional population change, 1990-1998

5. New firm?

Networks are the fundamental stuff of which new organizations are and will be made. (Castells 1996, p. 168)

To sum up our exploration so far: the macroeconomic debate over a New Economy is about changes in growth-inflation tradeoffs in the economy. A number of skeptical economists (Paul Krugman, Alan Blinder, or Brad DeLong, for example) hold fast to what might be termed the 'Casablanca Rule': 'The fundamental things apply, as time goes by.' On the other hand, Fed Chairman Alan Greenspan, no fad-chaser himself, is a proponent of the idea of a New Economy.

FROM ROBBER BARONS TO CYBER BARONS

Our topic now is the microeconomic version of this thesis. As background, we can take a light look at the 1998 *Forbes Magazine* list of the 400 richest people in the US (see Table 5.1). This list is mainly a creature of stock-market valuations at any given month or year, since truly monumental for-

Table 5.1 Forbes Magazine's estimates for the 15 richest Americans in 1998

1. William H. Gates III	$58 bln.	Microsoft	Bellevue, Washington
2. Warren E. Buffet	29	(Independent)	Omaha, Nebraska
3. Paul G. Allen	22	Microsoft	Mercer Island, Wash.
4. Michael Dell	13	Dell	Austin, Texas
5. Steven A. Ballmer	12	Microsoft	Bellevue, Washington
6. Alice L. Walton	11	Wal-Mart	Rogers, Arkansas
7. Helen R. Walton	11	Wal-Mart	Bentonville, Arkansas
8. Jim C. Walton	11	Wal-Mart	Bentonville, Arkansas
9. John T. Walton	11	Wal-Mart	Durango, Colorado
10. S. Robson Walton	11	Wal-Mart	Bentonville, Arkansas
11. John W. Kluge	10	Metromedia	Charlottesville, Va.
12. Barbara C. Anthony	7	Cox Coms.	Honolulu, Hawaii
13. Anne Cox Chambers	7	Cox Coms.	Atlanta, Georgia
14. Gordon Earl Moore	7	Intel	Woodside, California
15. Sumner M. Redstone	6	Viacom	Newton, Mass.

Note: Corporate affiliations have been added by the author.
Source: Quinones (1998).

31

tunes (the ones denominated in billions) in the US nearly always reflect ownership of large corporations. The 1998 list appeared in the October 12 issue, when the stock market was in a temporary slump. Still, and allowing for these and other vicissitudes in the wealth estimates, the top ranks of the list tell quite a story about the American economy in the late 1990s.

For one thing, the top 14 people on the list all live outside the Manufacturing Belt. In general, there are no old-fashioned smokestack industrialists among the top 15 (and not many among the top 50). True, the 15th member of the list, Sumner Redstone, is from Newton, Massachusetts, but he is a media magnate (his Viacom owns Paramount, CBS, MTV, and Blockbuster Video), not an industrialist or denizen of Route 128. Except perhaps for John Werner Kluge (founder of Metromedia and developer of the nation's largest cell-phone network in the 1980s), the top 14 appear to live in the regions where their fortunes originated. (Barbara Cox Anthony's came from Cox Communications, an Atlanta media company; she lives in Honolulu.)

With the possible exception of Warren Buffet, these fortunes emanate from IT, Wal-Mart, and media. Five of the top 15 are high-tech entrepreneurs, from Seattle, Austin, and Silicon Valley. Five are members of the Arkansas Walton family; their vast wealth derives from founding-father Sam Walton's controversial innovations in the organization of retailing. Four (Kluge, Redstone, and the Cox sisters) owe their fortunes to media empires of one kind or another. And one (ranked second with $29 billion) is Warren Buffett from Omaha, a financier.

While far from definitive, this list would seem to be consistent with the thesis of a New Economy. What are its implications?

1. The growth sectors of the US economy – as perceived and valued by Wall Street – have shifted to new activities.
2. There is at least a preliminary suggestion here of heightened entrepreneurial performance in younger regions.
3. It appears that firms (Dell, say, or Wal-Mart) can spring up from nowhere and catapult to great size within the span of a generation or two.

What no such list can tell us is whether something has changed about the firm, that is, about the organization of production. Beyond management consultants' jargon about re-engineering, core competencies, and so on, is there a 'new firm' spearheading the New Economy?

CORPORATE AMERICA, DUAL ECONOMY

For context most of the millions of companies in the economy are proprietorships, 99 percent of them engaged in monopolistic competition. Because firms in this category are subject to competition from new entrants, profits seldom get too far above the amount required to cover the opportunity cost of capital, that is, to keep the firm afloat.

But what about the other representative category, not small business but 'Big Business'? One way to put big business in perspective is to look at the profit (net income) figures, which are dominated by a relatively small number (fewer than 5,000, say) of oligopolistic corporations in (1) manufacturing, and (2) finance, insurance, and real estate (FIRE) (see Figure 5.1). In 1994, the most recent year available, these relatively few corporations had over two-thirds of the $550 billion in total business profits in the US.

The upshot, as a first approximation, is that *we live in a dual economy of millions of small firms (a relative handful of which will become large) and a few thousand large and often highly profitable corporations.*

Beyond that, what can be said at this point is that companies of all sizes and in all locations are going through changes that reflect breakthroughs in communication technology.

THE GOSPEL ACCORDING TO MANUEL

Perhaps the most influential guru of the New Economy among scholars (and especially among non-economists) is Manuel Castells, a Berkeley sociology professor born in Barcelona in 1942. Following a book published in 1989, *The Informational City*, Castells has written a massive trilogy between 1996 and 1998 on *The Information Age: Economy, Society, and Culture.* Volume one is *The Rise of the Network Society.* It lays out a worldview and describes 'the information technology paradigm,' and it contains long chapters on 'the network enterprise' and 'the space of flows' (that is, as distinct from 'the space of places').

Castells' logic and rhetoric are traditional, though not quantitatively analytical. (In other words, the numbers are used to illustrate, but they do not purport to prove anything.) Without claiming to do justice to the range and ambition of Castells' magnum opus, we may sketch out the main lines of his argument on the new firm here.

In a nutshell, *the new firm is the networked firm.* As such, it is neither small nor large, neither start-up nor corporate, neither digital nor industrial.

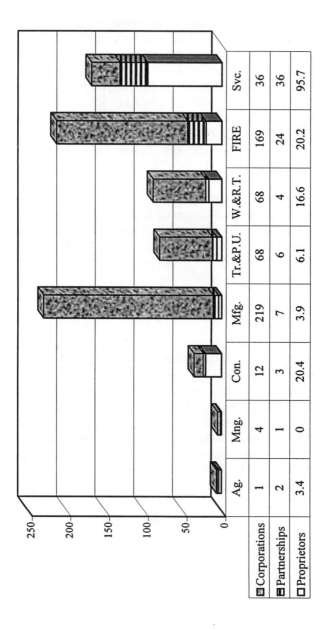

	Ag.	Mng.	Con.	Mfg.	Tr.&P.U.	W.&R.T.	FIRE	Svc.
Corporations	1	4	12	219	68	68	169	36
Partnerships	2	1	3	7	6	4	24	36
Proprietors	3.4	0	20.4	3.9	6.1	16.6	20.2	95.7

Figure 5.1 Business profits (billions of $) by sector, 1994

Instead, it can be any combination of the foregoing, provided it uses computer networks to adapt and compete.

The Information Technology Paradigm

Castells, a former Marxist, offers a framework for 'the material foundation of the informational society' (p. 61). The key features he lists refer not to all the influences the new technologies exert upon society, but only to economic factors, 'the material foundation.' Five characteristics define the information technology paradigm:

1. In contrast to earlier technological revolutions, this one is about technologies that 'act on information.'
2. Since information is a part of all human activities, all aspects of life are affected.
3. Any system or organization using information technologies has a network logic, a logic which in turn has become more powerful because of computers.
4. The paradigm is accordingly based on the flexibility that networks provide. As Castells puts it, '*Turning the rules upside down* without destroying the organization has become a possibility, because *the material basis of the organization can be reprogrammed and retooled*' (p. 62, emphasis added).
5. The fifth property is the technological convergence of such formerly separate sectors as computers, telecommunications, and biology.

The information-technology paradigm, writes Castells, is informed by (but not the same as) 'complexity theory.' The descendant of the 'chaos theory' of the 1980s, the complexity school is centered in the Santa Fe Institute, which derives from the nuclear laboratories at nearby Los Alamos, New Mexico. One hallmark of complexity theory is its focus on how simple systems in nature and in the economy generate spontaneous order, that is, operate as self-organizing systems.

Putting it differently, a broader school of thought links not only (1) complexity, but also (2) fractals (self-replicating geometric patterns in nature, as in the leaves of a tree), (3) self-organizing systems, and (4) emergent computation. In any case, as a perspective for understanding diversity, complexity theory has a part in Castells' paradigm – whose defining qualities he lists as 'Comprehensiveness, complexity, and networking' (p. 65).

By way of distancing himself from the morality of the new information technologies, Castells concludes this discussion of his organizing framework with Kranzberg's Law, a maxim from the technologist Melvin Kranzberg. "'*Technology is neither good nor bad, nor is it neutral*'" (Kranzberg, 1985, p. 50, quoted in Castells, emphasis in Castells, p. 65).

The Network Enterprise

Castells also posits a 'new organizational logic.' This he sees as common to all organizations, whereas their contexts may vary with circumstances and cultures. In his view the 1980s saw a 'recapitalization of capitalism' (p. 85) that restored the preconditions for investment that capitalist economies require for growth.

One hallmark was the much-heralded 'transition from mass production to flexible production, or from "Fordism" to "post-Fordism"' (p. 154). Another is the 'crisis of the large corporation, and the resilience of small and medium firms [SMEs]' (p. 155). A third is a new style of management, most evidently around the Japanese practices that reduce uncertainty by opening up communication between workers and management, and between suppliers and customers.

In addition, three other sets of arrangements that give firms new flexibility derive from networks. One concerns a variety of networked relationships among SMEs. Another encompasses the various practices large corporations use to subcontract and license production to smaller firms. Finally, a sixth arrangement is the 'intertwining of large corporations in . . . strategic alliances' (p. 162).

From all this emerges the horizontal corporation. The organizational innovations just listed can be understood as a response to the crisis of the bureaucratic, hierarchical corporation – the corporate dinosaurs decried in the late 1980s and early 1990s. Nor is the horizontal corporation necessarily 'lean and mean,' since it became clear in the 1990s that 'large corporations had to become primarily more effective rather than more thrifty' (p. 164).

Instead, the meaning of the horizontal corporation within what Castells terms the informational/global economy is as a 'network enterprise.' Following the French theorist Alain Touraine, Castells distinguishes here between static and evolving organizations. The first type has as its goal self-reproduction. In the second type, the organization's goals lead to endless structural changes. 'I call the first type of organizations *bureaucracies*; the second type *enterprises*' (p. 171, emphasis added).

All this may sound hopelessly abstract. What we need now is a more specific version of the story, the digital version.

6. Digital Millennium

> What is new to the Information Age is the ability to do things in a digital way.
> (Byrnes 1998)

As noted in Chapter 2, many economists have believed that a developed capitalist economy tends to slow down and even stagnate over time. In that context, a 'new' economy becomes a welcome thing. In hindsight, however, it turns out that new economies have emerged in the US and Europe about every half-century or so. Today's New Economy, in other words, is one of a progression of new economies over the past two centuries, beginning with the high Industrial Revolution in Britain in the late 1700s.

What does this New Economy replace? What was the Old Economy? We might jot down a working list of some of its stylized features:

- The vertically integrated corporation, mass-producing goods within the US.
- Political party coalitions forged in the New Deal.
- A core Manufacturing Belt, shipping goods to other US regions.
- After 1950, a mainframe culture: big computers in big organizations.
- A military-industrial complex.

And we might assign it a life-span of 50 years, from the beginning of World War II in Europe (1939) to the end of the Cold War (1989).

A COLD-WAR ECONOMY?

A diverse tradition in the history of economics concluded that advanced capitalist economies inevitably tend to stagnate. Stagnationists like the Marxists Paul Baran and Paul Sweezy and the Keynesian Alvin Hansen (who all witnessed the transition) may well have viewed post-World War II America as a case in point. From 1939 to 1989, military spending justified both Keynesian budget deficits and an implicit technology or industrial policy. Pump-priming there was, along with any number of infrastructure and R&D projects justified in the name of national security, including epochal infrastructure projects like the Interstate Highway Program and ARPAnet, the forerunner of the Internet.

The Cold-War economy was without question a new stage of American economic development. For example, President Eisenhower was elected in 1952 on a pledge to end the Korean War – which he did in July 1953. But the arms budget grew relentlessly anyway through the 1950s. Alarmed by this unprecedented 'peacetime' build-up, Eisenhower uttered a famous warning on leaving office in 1961:

> The conjunction of an immediate military establishment and a large arms industry is new to the American experience . . . In the councils of government, we must guard against the acquisition of unwarranted influence . . . by the military-industrial complex. The potential for the disastrous rise of misplaced power exists and will persist. (Dwight David Eisenhower, January 17, 1961, in Augarde 1991, p. 73)

Hence stagnationists might well have concluded that the Great Depression of the 1930s marked the end of the private economy's capacity to grow steadily on its own.

And it is true that today we tend to forget the shock to the economic system that ensued with the end of the Cold War. After the post-Vietnam retrenchment, the Reagan arms build-up of the mid-1980s had given new life to the military-industrial complex. Then, between 1987 and 1995 the US lost nearly two million defense-related jobs: nearly one in two. But by the mid-1990s the transition was complete. The proof? Unemployment rates below 5 percent in every region (see Chapter 12).

What happened to make the economic exit from the Cold War relatively smooth? A partial answer is that *the private economy was more resilient than many had thought.* In particular, a new core sector had been forming for some time, one capable of driving the economy to a subsequent basis for expansion.

INFORMATION GOODS AND THE NEW ECONOMY

In 1989 Robert Heilbroner, perhaps the best-known American historian of economic thought, declared the stagnation thesis dead. 'The long-term process of expansion has bypassed saturation by discovering or creating new commodities' (as quoted in Schlefer 1989, p. 33).

What were these 'new commodities,' so powerful that they could swamp any tendencies the economy had toward stagnation? Today, of course, the answer is obvious.

They were information goods, old and new, that can be digitized. Information goods typically (1) display economies of scale in their production, often with negligible marginal costs; (2) are 'experience goods' that may need to be tried out before they are bought; and (3) may need to conform to a technology standard – such that 'network economies' are likely to come into play (Shapiro and Varian 1999).

But how have such information goods become so prominent in the economy? The answer entails three landmark events: the invention of the microprocessor in 1971, the introduction of the IBM PC in 1981, and the commercialization of the Internet in 1994.

For purposes of understanding the transition of the 1980s, in which the old economy expired and the new one gathered its forces, we can focus on 1981.

THE PC REVOLUTION

Before that year there were three major technology industries: mainframe computers, electronic components, and medical instruments. These, plus a few other activities employing high proportions of scientists and engineers, used to constitute the 'high tech' sector of the economy. The market for computers *per se* had only two components. Fortune 500 companies used big computers to compile databases for customer billing and employee records. The federal government was the other. There the Defense Department and the National Aeronautics and Space Administration relied on mainframes and supercomputers for military and space programs and the Census Bureau kept counting.

The IBM PC broadened the market from corporations and the federal government to include all manner of businesses, large and small, and households as well. The definition of IT changed accordingly:

> Today, due in large part to that one significant product introduction in 1981, virtually every person, company, and government is a customer for technology products. The definition of technology industries has expanded from large computers to include personal computers, software, semiconductors, semiconductor equipment, communications (both telecommunications and data communications), and medical technology (biotechnology and medical devices). (Murphy 1998, p. 47)

In this view, the IT sector today has seven components:

1. large computers,
2. personal computers,
3. software,
4. semiconductors,
5. semiconductor equipment,
6. communications, and
7. medical technology (biotech and instruments).

What was so revolutionary about the personal computer? The microprocessor, as put to use in the Apple II and then the IBM PC, carried the world from an analog to a digital mode of representing ideas (language, numbers, images and sounds). Five basic ingredients in this change are:

- *Digitization*, through which all information (text, numbers, images, and sounds) can be reduced to 0's and 1's, or on-off states on a transistor.
- *Moore's Law* (from Gordon Moore of Intel), which states that the amount of information that can be stored on a microchip doubles every 18 months (while in Joy's Law, which is similar, it is the speed of the processor that doubles).
- *A law of increasing bandwidth* (also known as Gilder's Law), a tendency for telecommunications carrying capacity to double periodically as speeds gradually approach fiber-optic or near light-speed transmission.
- *Metcalfe's Law* (after Robert Metcalfe, a founder of 3Com), which says that costs of adding a user to a network increase linearly, while benefits in the form of access points expand with the square of the number of users.
- *Packet-switching* as a digital transmission technique of the kind used on the Internet, in which messages sent from one point can be broken up into many different packets, each of which is sent individually at higher speeds, to be reassembled upon delivery.

'What is new to the Information Age,' in other words, 'is *the ability to do things in a digital way*.' (This elegant formulation is explained in *The Big Picture*, a web site and CD-ROM that provides a tutorial on the digital revolution.) Today, for example, we can sample CDs or videos on the Internet before paying for them, again on the Internet. Why? Because the sounds and images are digitized.

For such generalized purposes, mainframes and minicomputers were all but irrelevant, tools from the era of mass production, automation, and top-down bureaucratic management. The coming of the PC thus rendered anything and everything subject to the power of the computer, while retaining the crucial dimensions of human scale, decentralized decision-making, customized design, and creativity.

In that light, it is striking to find that US Commerce Department data on IT's share of corporate investment in business equipment show sharp jumps after both the PC and the Internet. In *The Emerging Digital Economy* (Figure 6), the IT share jumps from about 10 percent in 1979 to 25 percent in 1985 and again with the Internet from about 33 percent in 1994 to 45 percent in 1996[1] (Department of Commerce, 1998). It would then surpass 50 percent by 1999.

LONG WAVES AS NEW ECONOMIES .

And yet, to repeat, this is not the first or even the second or third new economy. On the contrary, and from one point of view, world development unfolds through a succession of 'new economies.' The roughly 50-year rhythm of the sequence can be seen in Table 6.1. The table is based on a review by Nobel-Prize-winner Simon Kuznets of Joseph Schumpeter's 1939 book, *Business Cycles: A Theoretical, Historical and Statistical Analysis of the Capitalist Process.*

The waves labeled 'Kondratieff' refer to Nikolai Kondratieff, the great Russian economist of the early twentieth-century who first posited and explored such 50–55-year cycles – and died at the hands of Stalin. (Kuznets, 'the father of national income accounting' in the US, was also Russian-born.)

Table 6.1 Long waves of creative destruction

---

1. Industrial Revolution (1787–1842): cotton textiles, iron, steam power

2. The Bourgeois Kondratieff (1842–97): railroadization

3. The Neo-Mercantilist Kondratieff (1897–1939): electricity, automobiles

4. *The Cold-War Kondratieff* (1939–89): defense, TV, mainframes

5. *The Information Age* (1989–) PCs, telecommunications, entertainment

---

Source: Adapted by the author and updated (in the italicized items) from Kuznets (1940, p. 257).

The first was the beginning of the Industrial Revolution and the factory system, the second had as its symbol the railroads, the third electricity and automobiles, and the fourth (for the US, at least) the military-industrial complex of the Cold War. The fifth wave, the Information Age, is today's New Economy.

The series of five 'new economies' corresponds in its logic to Schumpeter's theory of creative destruction. In *Capitalism, Socialism, and Democracy* ([1942] 1962, p. 83), he wrote that innovation 'incessantly revolutionizes the economic structure from within, incessantly destroying the old one, incessantly creating a new one. This process of Creative Destruction is the essential fact about capitalism' (p. 83). In a footnote, he points out that the years of 'comparative quiet' can make us miss out on the longer rhythm:

> These revolutions are not strictly incessant; they occur in discrete rushes which are separated from each other by spans of comparative quiet. The process as a whole works incessantly, however, in the sense that there always is either revolution or absorption of the results of the revolution, both together forming what are known as business cycles. (p. 83)

Strictly speaking, not many economists today view such long waves as technically measurable. Numerous attempts to quantify and measure price and output fluctuations to validate more formal Kondratieff cycles have proved unsatisfying. But then the same thing is true of 'business cycles' of any duration: economists have come to doubt any regular cycle of business fluctuations over time.

In any case, in this softer version, as labels for distinct technology regimes through the stages of the Industrial Revolution, long waves seem useful constructs. By this I mean that they can provide a framework for understanding other seemingly autonomous (that is, seemingly independent or free-standing) changes that catch our attention.

Consider, for example, globalization. One of the organizers of the World Economic Forum in Davos, Switzerland, sees globalization as the hallmark of the 1990s. In turn, globalization in her view awaited the end of the Cold War. When the USSR was dissolved in 1991, she says, 'That unleashed all the capital and energy that had previously been locked in this global power struggle' (Maria Livanos Cattaui, in Henriques 1998, p. C3).

Fair enough. Globalization seems on the surface to be 'what the 1990s were all about' (my phrase, not hers). But what was it in the 1990s that stepped up the pace of global communication? As a commentary in *Newsweek* put it in September 1998, 'Globalization has become the decade's most overused word. But at its heart, it embodies a real truth: technology has made this a planet of shared experiences' (quoted by Stevenson 1998).

Here we have it. In the 1990s, 'technology has made this a planet of shared experiences.' The technology in question is digital.

I conclude from all this: there is a New Economy. Part macro, part micro, and all digital, it has provided a gradually building shockwave that has renewed the US economy and restored it to global leadership.

For perspective on the comeback, we turn now to the twilight of the old economy, the 1980s.

NOTE

1. Other indicators in the report show similar shifts in the economy toward digitized products and processes. For a quick introduction to the Commerce Department report, *The Emerging Digital Economy*, go to Chapter 1, 'The Digital Revolution,' and see Figures 1-5.

PART II

Requiem

Roadmap:

This section of the book explores a 'maturity hypothesis' of advanced economic development.

Chapters 7-9 pursue the topic as an episode in the history of economic thought. Chapter 11 profiles offsetting changes in manufacturing employment among older and younger US regions.

A shortcut for readers more interested in the main thread is to go directly now to chapters 10 (on Europe), 12 (on downsizing defense), and 13 (on the role of the entrepreneur).

7. Only yesterday:
the industrial-policy debate

> Industrial policy is one of those rare ideas that has moved swiftly from
> obscurity to meaninglessness without any intervening period of coherence.
> (Reich 1984, p. 32)

Looking back, the industrial policy debate of the late 1970s and early 1980s
can be understood as an attempt to make sense of a 'maturity crisis' that
afflicted both the US Manufacturing Belt and much of Europe. The idea of
a maturity crisis will be explored in the rest of Part II. In this chapter we
highlight the pivotal issue in the industrial-policy debate – the inherent
contradiction between holding on and moving on.

For the record, in Europe industrial policy gave up the ghost in the late
1980s. As the *World Development Report 1999/2000* observes, 'The 1980s
saw the demise – at least in Europe – of top-down industrial policies and
their spatial correlate, regional economic development policies. By the early
1990s not a single national industrial policy initiative could be identified in
Europe' (World Bank 2000, p. 137). Perhaps the one great exception is the
multi-government consortium that would make Airbus the only formidable
rival to Boeing as a supplier to the world's airlines.

In the US, a formal national industrial policy also turned out to be an
idea with a brief career, as the opening quotation from one of its chief
proponents, Robert Reich, suggests. Nevertheless, industrial-policy issues
have continued to reappear under diverse labels:

- Its immediate US descendant was *competitiveness policy*, as housed in the
  Department of Commerce, the Pentagon's DARPA (the Defense Advance
  Research Projects Agency), and later in NIST (the National Institute of
  Standards and Technology), where it still flickers anachronistically as
  industrial-policy-in-waiting.
- As an *export-led growth strategy* it flourished in Japan, at least until the
  financial and real-estate bubble popped in 1990. Elsewhere in East Asia it
  has been used to promote national IT roles. According to a recent study, its
  success there has depended on the quality of local companies and on the
  ability of companies and policy-makers to adapt local strategy to the
  emerging 'global production network' in IT, a function in turn of 'the
  changing international division of labor' (Dedrick and Kraemer 1998, pp. v
  and vi). In other words, no single industrial-policy approach can be cited as
  a general model.
- As *cluster theory*, it would become the theoretical rationale for much state
  and local economic development policy in the 1990s (see Chapter 20).

PLAYERS AND ACRONYMS: AICS, LDCS, NICS, OPEC

To understand the intensity of the original debate, it helps to recall the painful dislocations the rich economies went through from about 1965 on. About that time, 'the international economy began to turn on its head' (Lewis 1978a, p. 35). The advanced industrial countries (AICs) of the West experienced rising trade competition from a select group of less developed countries (LDCs) dubbed newly industrializing countries (NICs).

The NICs' export-led growth reflected their comparative advantage (from low labor costs) in mature, standardized goods in a world economy newly unified by breakthroughs in transport and communications. The correlate was a loss of manufacturing employment, notably in mature industries, in Europe and from the US North to the South and West.

After 1973, rumors of deindustrialization were compounded by the OPEC oil price shock, the quadrupling of the price of crude in the space of a few months time. On all three fronts – the NIC challenge, the regional tilt south and west, and the energy price revolution – rapid adjustment became the order of the day. It was painful. Not surprisingly, it was resisted.

The debate in the US turned on the following points:

1. A dichotomy marked industrial policy's goals. 'Modernizers' like Lester Thurow wanted to boost international competitiveness; 'preservationists' such as Felix Rohatyn were more concerned with saving jobs in industries that were losing out in international competition.
2. On either count, most economists rejected the argument for an industry-specific or targeted industrial policy (Krugman 1983).
3. The modernizers notwithstanding, there was no general decline in US trade competitiveness in the 1970s; the exchange rate fell by enough to maintain it (Branson 1981).
4. When the exchange rate rose sharply under the Reagan administration, the 'deindustrialization' that resulted had macroeconomic causes; industrial policy was beside the point (Lawrence 1984).
5. Insofar as industrial policy proposals fronted for regional relief, much of the debate ran at cross purposes; economists rejected 'preservation' as inefficient, whereas advocates made their case in terms of equity (Eads 1983).

We focus now on the contradiction between the preservationists and the modernizers because it points up the challenges posed by the forces of Creative Destruction. In a US context, modernization also meant conflict between older and younger regions. As a result, the question of national renewal was hopelessly intertwined with the clash of regional interests.

THE PRESERVATIONISTS VERSUS THE MODERNIZERS

Thurow had not used the term 'industrial policy'. But in that direction, and as a means of raising productivity growth, he did call for an updated version of the Reconstruction Finance Corporation of 50 years earlier. Contending that '*disinvestment is what our economy does worst*' (Thurow 1980, p. 77), he saw a role for 'the national equivalent of a corporate investment committee to redirect investment flows from our "sunset" industries to our "sunrise" industries' (p. 95). In this view, the problem was that market forces failed to shift capital to growing industries fast enough.

In contrast, *Business Week* would soon call for targeted sectoral policies to counter – not to accelerate – market forces. In a special issue on America's restructured economy *(Business Week* 1981), the case was made that the US economy had 'evolved into five separate economies [old-line and high-tech manufacturing, energy, agriculture, and services] that no longer act as one' (p. 56).

This approach to the economy's evolving structure seemed mystifying, at least until the policy punch line. The policy problem, in this view, was that without targeted sectoral policies, 'the market will continue to steer all funds' to the energy and high-tech sectors of the South and West, thus further weakening the old-line manufacturing sector and the North. Therefore 'government policies will have to be carefully targeted to meet special needs. . . . The government needs a new set of fiscal policies aimed at bringing out capital and channeling it in the right directions' (p. 100). So market forces worked to hurt the basic industries of the North – and should be countered.

This dichotomy would prove characteristic of proposals for targeted industrial policies. On the one hand, the modernizers like Thurow (and Reich and Frank Weil) argued that without an industrial policy, the US would suffer a further relative decline within the world economy. Meantime, others argued for the restoration or at least support of declining industries and places – a preservationist strategy.

The distinction between modernizers and preservationists was highlighted by GE's marketing maxim, '*Automate, emigrate, or evaporate.*' It arose also when an OECD (Organization for Economic Cooperation and Development) report referred to 'the two strategies of the mature industrial countries,' that is, switching to automated methods or abandoning basic industries to LDCs (OECD 1980, p. 83). Productivity growth via robotic processes and other labor-saving innovations (or by abandoning older industries) could be lauded by modernizers, but not by job-oriented preservationists. The latter were more likely to be troubled by the specter of 'jobless growth' (Norman 1980, p. 35) and to turn to a third strategy, protectionism, to maintain jobs.

Perhaps the most fully developed rationale for an industrial policy came from Reich – in the main, a modernizer. Having set forth a well documented indictment of American management with Ira Magaziner in a 1982 book, Reich went on to write *The Next American Frontier,* renowned in part for its appeal to Walter Mondale as a blueprint for the Democratic party presidential campaign of 1984 (Reich 1983). Although Mondale lost, Reich did later go on to become Secretary of Labor in the first Clinton Administration.

What was needed, as spelled out earlier in a 1982 article, were policies to speed the shift of capital and labor into 'high value-added' activities. (In this respect, Reich's program harmonized with Thurow's sunset-sunrise investment policy.) Examples of such policy innovations were employment vouchers, a human-capital tax credit, regional development banks, and, to monitor government influences on capital allocation, a national industrial board.

Reich's larger – and more persuasive – message was that an industrial policy already existed in piecemeal form, through tax, regulatory, and protectionist policies. Accordingly, he contended that the relevant question was not whether to have an industrial policy. Instead, it was whether to monitor, coordinate, and improve upon the de facto industrial policy the US already had.

THE REBUTTAL FROM ECONOMISTS

Economists replied to proposals for industrial policy with telling criticisms on three divergent counts. (1) As a matter of *theory,* the critics questioned the assumption of market failure implicit in calls for government intervention. (2) As a matter of *practice,* they argued that an undesirable bureaucratic layer would be required to administer a targeted program – and that such a program would inevitably revert to protectionism (or, in a left-wing variant, that it would become a captive of big business). (3) As a matter of *evidence,* some economists rejected the notion of a fundamental decline in US trade competitiveness.

(1) The economic arguments against an American industrial policy were persuasive. The national-security case for a program of sectoral intervention was weak, as Branson showed. The microeconomic or market-failure rationale failed also; Krugman's analysis was especially telling.

(2) In an attack on the whole idea of industrial policy as a new task for government, Charles Schultze (chairman of the Council of Economic

Advisors in the Carter Administration) charged that such proposals would needlessly add a new layer of bureaucracy to the federal government (Schultze 1983). From a different perspective, Samuel Bowles, David M. Gordon, and Thomas E. Weisskopf shared Schultze's unease as regards industrial policy in practice. They charged that Rohatyn's plan amounted to a kind of 'corporatism' that would elevate the interests of business over those of consumers, labor, and others (Bowles et al. 1983, Ch. 9).

Reich summarized such misgivings in his comments on Rhode Island's defeated 1984 bond issue for a state industrial policy (1984, p. 32):

> Americans don't like central planning, they don't like complicated plans, and they especially don't trust business-government-and-labor elites to do the planning. These biases are as populist as apple pie, running clear across the political spectrum and rooted deep in our political history.

The political lesson: a US adjustment plan should be fashioned within the existing institutional framework, free from the kind of tripartite administrative apparatus used in Japan and Europe.

(3) Schultze's wide-ranging attack contended that industrial policy proposals assumed that the US economy as a whole was deindustrialized in the 1970s. He rejected the premise outright. And in retrospect he was right, as subsequent chapters will show.

SECOND THOUGHTS

Still, the one-sidedness of the debate may have been deceptive. Economists argued that the US had no industrial problem beyond those of macroeconomic policy. But behind the veil of macroeconomic aggregates was a regional revolution, marked by the fall of the industrial heartland.

The danger in such over-aggregation was that it

> conceals . . . all the drama of the events – the rise and fall of products, technologies, and industries, and the accompanying transformation of the spatial and occupational distribution of the population (Nordhaus and Tobin 1972, p. 2, quoted in Van Duijn 1983, p. 93).

The alternative, Nordhaus and Tobin added in their next sentence, is 'Schumpeter's vision of capitalist development.'

In retrospect, it seems clear that the US faced a critical juncture in its industrial evolution. To get at the nature of this 'maturity crisis,' the next chapter explores the theoretical issue of industry aging. Then Chapter 9 asks whether an entire economy's ability to adapt and to spawn new industries diminishes with affluence and the passage of time.

8. The law of industrial growth

Can we mount a more energetic and successful response to the challenge of newly rising foreign competitors after 1970 than Britain did after 1870? (Abramovitz 1981, p. 10)

In the early 1980s, then, a number of Democrats on the left advocated a US industrial policy to support specific sectors and industries. The Reagan re-election in 1984 ended the debate. Still, many observers came to believe in the inevitability of *Japan as Number One* (Vogel 1979).

THE LAW AND THE PROPHETS

The mounting alarm directed attention to a pair of theoretical questions languishing in history's dustbin: why and how do industries mature and what does industry aging mean for a local, regional, or national economy?

Though long forgotten, industry aging had been explored in the 1930s literature on the retardation thesis, later generalized in a *law of industrial growth* (Alderfer and Michl 1942, pp. 14-17).

To wit: industries mature when major technology gains come to an end, slowing cost reductions, market expansion, and sales growth and leaving older industries vulnerable to the competition of younger rivals with faster productivity growth (see Figure 8.1). Simon Kuznets (1930), Walther Hoffmann (1931), Arthur Burns (1934), Joseph Schumpeter (1939), and Alvin Hansen (1939) thus concluded that *long-term growth entails the eclipse of older by younger industries.*

The second issue, declining industrial competitiveness in the US (and, for that matter, Europe) involved the more recent literature on the *product cycle.* Edgar M. Hoover (1948) and his co-worker, Raymond Vernon (1966), argued that industry maturity makes production increasingly footloose, free to migrate to low-wage, politically receptive locations at home and abroad.

THE VANISHING OF INVESTMENT OPPORTUNITY

These questions were thus initially broached in the 1930s, in a literature temporarily eclipsed by the Keynesian revolution. Ironically, one of Keynes' chief American apostles may have been spurred by the fear that industry aging had triggered macroeconomic stagnation.

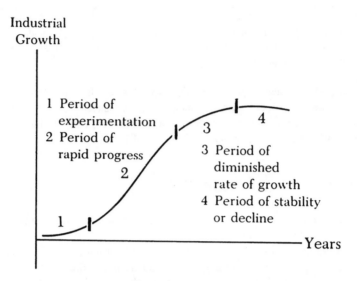

Source: Reproduced from Alderfer and Michl (1942, p. 14).

Figure 8.1 The law of industrial growth

In a famous presidential address to the American Economic Association in December 1938, Alvin Hansen concluded that a decline in investment opportunities had brought an era of secular stagnation. His apocalyptic rhetoric seems oddly familiar:

> The economic order of the western world is undergoing in this generation a structural change no less basic and profound in character than . . . 'the Industrial Revolution.' We are passing . . . over a divide which separates the great era of growth and expansion of the nineteenth century from an era which no man . . . can as yet characterize with clarity or precision. We are moving swiftly out of the order in which those of our generation were brought up, into no one knows what. (1939, p. 1)

As if in reply, Schumpeter rejected any and all inherently economic reasons for the vanishing of investment opportunity (Schumpeter [1942] 1962, ch. 10). In general, he said, the capitalist growth system may be jeopardized by three factors: (1) The rise of big business may result in 'petrified capitalism.' (2) Affluence may erode the legitimacy of capitalism's values and core institutions. (3) Investment opportunities might diminish.

As Schumpeter put it (p. 113), 'The main reasons for holding that opportunities for private enterprise and investment are vanishing are these:'

- the saturation of human wants,
- the slowing of population growth,
- land and resource constraints,
- the waning of technological innovation, and
- a shift in investment projects toward public goods.

Schumpeter rejected each of these possible sources of stagnation, as would most economists today. There is no inherent limit to profit opportunities, he wrote, and thus none to continued private investment, or to continued growth. Further, he rejected the rise of big business as a source of stagnation, saying that in concentrated industries, competition continued, especially via technological innovation.

To Schumpeter, what appeared to be a vanishing of investment opportunity was actually the trough of the 50-55-year Kondratieff cycle, or 'long wave' (as in Chapter 6 above). With a brutal optimism, Schumpeter saw the Great Depression as necessary to purge the economy of outworn practices and to restore efficiency. In the end such Creative Destruction would set the stage for the rise of new industries. New industries would spur the next long upswing, assuring capitalism's unique achievement: the doubling of living standards every 40 years. There were no *economic* limits to growth. (Whether today's global warming issue constitutes an economic limit in Schumpeter's sense is open to debate; he did not see it coming.)

Instead, the limits Schumpeter foresaw were political and cultural. He predicted that the reaction to Creative Destruction itself and a disenchantment with capitalism's core values would eventually usher in a planned regime not unlike socialism. A mature economy would be more regulated and less flexible, so that in the political long run, the growth system would come to an end.

SECULAR STAGNATION, FROM THE SUPPLY SIDE

Hansen shared Schumpeter's belief in long waves, but ardently opposed his *laissez-faire* maxims. In a little-noted passage, he asserted not so much the permanent vanishing of investment opportunity, but its uneven clustering over time. Describing industrial change as occurring by 'gigantic leaps and bounds,' Hansen provided a distinctly Schumpeterian account of the Depression's sources. In particular, he posited a kind of natural law of industry aging:

> [W]hen a revolutionary new industry like the railroad or the automobile, after having in its youth a powerful upward surge of investment activity, reaches maturity and ceases to grow, as all industries finally must, the whole economy must experience a profound stagnation. . . . And when giant new industries have spent their force, it may take a long time before something else of equal magnitude emerges. (1939, pp. 10-11)

This is a far cry from the stagnation thesis that has found its way into textbook footnotes about declining average propensities to consume. Instead, it is an industry-specific vision of economic decline, and as such, it foreshadows the industrial upheaval of the 1970s, and predates references in the industrial-policy debate to 'old-line,' 'basic,' or 'smokestack' industries. So while Hansen is remembered as a pessimistic Keynesian, he might also be linked with Schumpeter in a fear of episodic but protracted retardation from industrial aging.

THE RETARDATION THESIS

Simon Kuznets had dealt with the same problem in 1930 in the course of a more general study of secular movements in production and prices. In a chapter entitled 'Retardation of Industrial Growth,' Kuznets argued that the Industrial Revolution had set off a seemingly unlimited process of economic growth. Individual industries and nations had risen and then been eclipsed.

Among nations, he wrote, 'Great Britain has relinquished the lead . . . overtaken by rapidly developing Germany and the United States.' A concomitant of such national shifts was one from older to younger industries. 'The textile industries which had so spectacular a rise . . . ceded first place to pig iron, then to steel, while in turn the electrical industries assumed the leadership in the '80s and '90s' (1930, pp. 3-4).

To test the hypothesis of retardation in industry growth, Kuznets fitted Gompertz and logistic curves to time-series data for value-added in a large number of industries. He found that most series did indeed conform to the retardation thesis.

Hence the question: 'Why is there an abatement in the growth of old industries?' (p. 5). His answer: a narrowing over time in the scope for technological breakthroughs, cost reductions, and further sales growth. In a searching historical account of the tendency toward the exhaustion of technological breakthroughs in specific industries, Kuznets drew on earlier work by the German economist Julius Wolf.

In 1912, Wolf had posited four 'laws of retardation of progress.' One in particular (tagged 'Wolff's Law' [sic] in Freeman et al. 1982, p. 70), Wolf defined as follows:

> Every technical improvement, by lowering costs and by perfecting the utilization of raw materials and of power, bars the way to further progress. There is less left to improve, and this narrowing of possibilities results in a slackening or complete cessation of technical development.

Kuznets' work and similar findings were generalized in a 1934 NBER (National Bureau of Economic Research) study by Arthur Burns. As Burns put it, 'Following writers on biology and population, some economic statisticians have come in recent years to speak of a "law of growth" in industries and to give this "law" mathematical expression in the form of "growth curves"' (pp. 169-70). By this law, Burns meant only 'that the percentage rates of growth of individual industries tend to decline as their age increases.' In contrast to Hansen, Burns viewed industry aging not as a problem, but only as a normal part of the growth process.

Whereas Kuznets focused more on technology, Burns stressed the rise of new industries as a reason for the decline of old. As Burns put it, 'The introduction of new industries has tended to retard the development of old industries through the channels of competition for production, as well as through the channel of competition for custom [that is, consumer spending]' (p. 134). New industries brought competition for capital, labor, and raw materials, and diverted expenditures away from existing (older) products. Burns' emphasis thus ties in directly with Schumpeter's notion of Creative Destruction: the rise of new industries occurs in part at the expense of older ones.

By the early 1940s, this law of industrial growth had found its way into textbooks on industrial economics. As noted at the outset, one text described the law as the tendency for industries to pass through 'a period of experimentation, a period of rapid growth, a period of diminished growth, and a period of stability or decline' (Alderfer and Michl 1942, p. 14). In Europe, Walther Hoffmann would apply the same law to the British economy, and Fernand Braudel (in discussing examples of its operation in Europe before 1776) referred to the sequence as 'Hoffmann's law' (Hoffman [1931] 1955; Braudel 1982, pp. 344-9).

THE RETARDATION THESIS: SO WHAT?

After 1945, of course, the retardation thesis was soon forgotten in the United States, as the focus of policy concern shifted fairly quickly to inflation. More generally, growing awareness of aggregate demand's role redirected attention away from industry trajectories.

At the same time, the long global upswing in demand dampened any tendency toward growth reduction in mature industries. In a systematic updating of Burns' study, for example, Bela Gold (1964) traced growth patterns in 35 industries over the period 1930-55, and found the S-shaped curve generally irrelevant to industry trajectories. He therefore declared the whole approach useless. But Gold's benchmark years were ill suited to the task of measuring long-term trends. Any tendencies toward S-shaped output curves were swamped by the sustained rapid global expansion that marked the years 1948-73.

The model's value was reaffirmed when Van Duijn updated Burns' and Gold's work and examined patterns covering the century 1873-1973. He found 'an S-shaped growth pattern up to the maturity phase of an industry, with various possible patterns thereafter.' As Figure 8.2 illustrates, and as

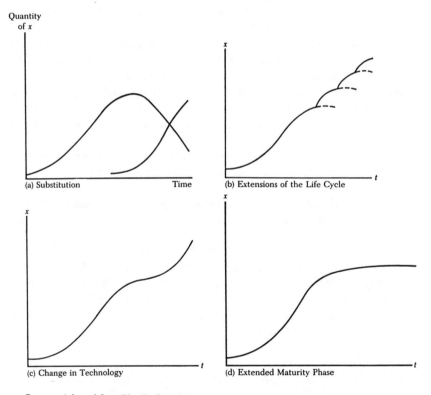

Source: Adapted from Van Duijn (1983, p. 24).

Figure 8.2 Variations in the 'law' of industrial growth

Burns had emphasized in his 1934 study, 'What actually happens to a commodity once it has reached its maturity phase' is thus not determinate, but varies with conditions specific to the industry (Van Duijn 1983, p. 29).

As for the links between the demand and supply sides, Kuznets himself may have summed it up best. Integrating his own earlier work with that of Burns, Kuznets wrote that sustained economic growth requires the spawning of

> new industries whose high rates of growth compensate for the inevitable slowing down in the rate of invention and innovation, and upon the economic effects of each, which retard the rates of growth of the older industries. A high rate of over-all growth in an economy is thus necessarily accompanied by considerable shifting in relative importance among industries, as the old decline and the new increase. (1959, p. 33)

This de facto rebuttal of the preservationist case has been so fully absorbed into the mainstream of economic thought that it is taken for granted. But Kuznets had also posed another question, about industry aging and comparative advantage.

HOW NEW INDUSTRIES DRIVE OUT OLD

Kuznets had pointed out that 'an industry in one country may be retarded by the competition of the same industry in a younger country' (1930, p. 10). How is the competitive position of a region or nation reshaped by the aging of its industries? The obvious answer today is the product cycle.

But as a preface to the product cycle model we are about to consider, there is another and logically antecedent process that also hastens the dispersion of older industries away from initial centers. As Burns had implied in his 1934 book, it is a direct result of the rise of new industries.

Suppose an economy has an average growth rate of labor productivity of 3 percent a year. *Wages will tend to rise at 3 percent, and this will be uniform across industries.* (Workers of equal skill tend to be paid the same no matter in what industry they work.) Then, if productivity growth is not uniform across industries, relative prices must rise in those industries in which productivity growth is laggard (Abramovitz 1985, letter to the author).

The ordinary workings of comparative advantage will then cause the laggard industry to be driven away from the country or region in question. It will gravitate to another country or region where the relation between wages and productivity is more favorable. The kinds of industries that will tend to fit this description are older ones, in which productivity growth has slowed as technical gains are exhausted in accordance with the retardation theory.

In short, as growth in an initial center occurs through the addition of new industries, older industries will tend to be squeezed out, driven to lower-wage sites. Although this may be hard on workers in older industries, the dislocations involved are due directly to growth *per se*. There are thus clear benefits for the country as a whole in that productivity and living standards rise.

All of this logically precedes the product cycle, which is based on standardization of technique – and whose dislocations are not automatically compensated by new growth.

THE PRODUCT CYCLE

To repeat: the question Kuznets posed was how an economy's competitive position is affected by the age of its industries.

A surprisingly complete answer appeared in 1948. Working outside the tradition of the retardation school, Edgar M. Hoover used much of the same language to describe the geography of industry aging (1948, ch. 10):

> The locational histories of individual industries have very often – one may almost say typically – involved an early stage of increasing [spatial] concentration followed by a later stage of re-dispersion. *Ultimately the industry and its main production center 'mature,'* in the sense that the rate of growth of market has slackened off, the fundamental questions of product design have been settled, and the necessary specialized machinery has been devised. It is then that a dispersion phase sets in (p. 175, emphasis added).

The key to this process was labor. A high skill requirement makes for 'a concentrated and rather stable pattern, clustering at points where such a labor supply has gradually developed' (p. 174). Over time, as technical advances typically sever this tie, an industry's processes eventually become routine. Then

> ordinary labor without special training can be used. The normal result is that the industry spreads or moves to other areas, its dispersion from the original centers ... sped by the relatively high wages and inflexible conditions that have become established there by the skilled elite (p. 174).

Nevertheless, the exodus of mature industries is by no means the death knell for the initial production centers. If they can spawn new activities, industry aging can be countered: 'This common association of decentralization with maturity does not by any means imply, however, that industry as a whole will or should progressively decentralize. New industries are continually being born' (p. 175).

This idea of renewal via technological innovation also figured in Raymond Vernon's 1966 landmark essay, 'International Investment and International Trade in the Product Cycle.' Vernon transposed Hoover's argument to the scale of the world economy. Now the US became the initial center, one fated to lose its mature industries to foreign competitors (see Figure 8.3).

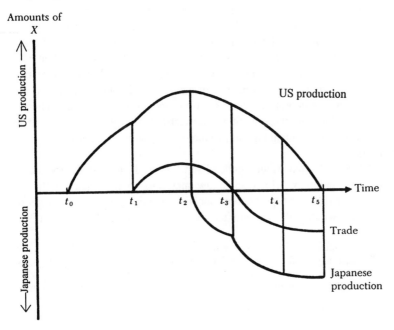

Note: On the vertical axis, Japanese production and export of good X increase with distance below the origin. For example, Japan begins to run a trade surplus in good X at point t_3.
Source: Adapted from Adams (1979, p. 92).

Figure 8.3 Production and trade over the product cycle

Vernon assigned each of three stylized stages of product development a different global location. In stage one, the typical new product would tend to be developed and produced in large American cities, near technical talent and customers. Such initial centers would then export the new product to domestic markets and abroad.

Stage two is precipitated in part by the fear that foreign producers (for example, in Europe) will manage to capture part of their home markets for the product. This fear, Vernon says, spurs US firms to place branches in Europe. They are likely to be aided in this attempt by a progressive re-duction of uncertainty, as least-cost production technologies are found and standardized. Stage two is thus marked by a reduction in US exports of the product abroad.

In stage three, that of maturity, the product can be produced anywhere, and the advantage of low labor costs in LDCs may become paramount. In practice, this will prove most feasible for such footloose activities as textiles, consumer electronics, and other high-value-to-weight items. By this stage, the US tends to have become a net importer of the product.

As a result of Vernon's article, the assignment of standardized or mature products to nations with low-cost labor became a conventional part of trade theory. Trade goods are now typically described as (1) Ricardian, (2) Heckscher-Ohlin, or (3) product-cycle goods. The first are resource tied (wine or oil), the second are mature or standardized commodities, and the third are new goods, not far removed from innovation. Under this scheme, the comparative advantage in some Heckscher-Ohlin goods has shifted to the NICs, while the advantage in product-cycle goods remains in advanced economies.

By 1980, Stephen Magee generalized the product-cycle theory into a product-age theorem, which adds raw materials to the equation. In his words, 'knowledge of production location requires only knowledge of product age, whether it is a manufactured good or a raw material.' That is,

> Young manufactured products are produced in developed countries, while old manufacturing products are produced in developing countries; young raw materials [that is, natural resources] are produced in developing countries, while older [that is, synthetic] raw materials are produced in developed countries. (1980, p. xv)

THE NEW INTERNATIONAL DIVISION OF LABOR

Thus the logic of a new international division of labor, and of a new stage of world development, as industrial capitalism moved south and east. Between 1963 and 1977, the share of world output of manufactures produced by a group of ten NICs increased from 5.4 to about 9 percent. Over this same interval, the share produced by Hong Kong, Singapore, South Korea, and Taiwan tripled, from 0.4 to 1.4 percent (Branson 1981, p. 386).

After 1973, when the growth of manufacturing exports from developed market economies (DME's) was cut from 10 to 5 percent a year, the LDCs as a group continued to increase their exports at 10 percent annually (see

Figure 8.4). The result, said Michael Beenstock, was a world economy in transition:

> The changing balance of world economic power . . . has moved in favour of developing countries. Economic expansion in the Third World has threatened the existing economic structures in the OECD countries, which in turn have been slow to adjust to these new circumstances. The origins of the slowdown are therefore structural, in the sense that market forces have changed and economic restructuring is necessary. (1984, p. 12)

The 'sudden spurt in LDC industrialization' after 1965 created a supply shock in the world market for manufactures (p. 14). Goods prices fell relative to the prices of raw materials. 'The rise in the relative price of raw materials that began toward the end of the 1960s was brought about by supply shocks in the market for manufactures . . . as much as . . . in the market for raw materials' (p. 15).

The result was a 'deindustrialization effect.' Resources were shifted out of OECD manufactures and into other sectors (and to LDCs themselves, via

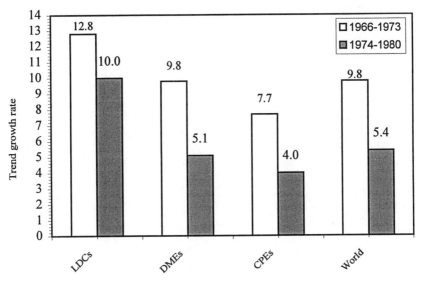

Note: LDCs refers to less-developed countries, DMEs to developed-market economies, and CPEs to centrally-planned economies.

Source: Reproduced from Leechor et al. (1983, p. 10).

Figure 8.4 Trend growth rates of manufacturing exports by group: before and after 1973

capital flows). 'Deindustrialization' in turn created a 'mismatch' problem, the symptom of which was increased unemployment in OECD countries.

Beenstock's definition of deindustrialization did not fit the US record, however. There was no tendency for manufacturing output (in constant-dollar terms) to fall as a share of GDP from, say, 1959 to 1979. Moreover, US manufacturing employment reached an all-time high in 1979. The problem was, the North was losing it almost as fast as the South and West were generating it.

In other words, the US Manufacturing Belt experienced no less pain and dislocation than Europe – and in view of differences in the social safety net, perhaps more. Manufacturing job losses hit black men in declining older cities of the North especially hard. In metropolitan areas losing manufacturing employment, the population share of black men over age 20 with jobs averaged little more than 60 percent in 1980. In Detroit, this 'employment rate' was a stark 52 percent. By contrast, in San Jose, Dallas, and reindustrial Boston, the rate was above 75 percent (US Department of Labor, Bureau of Labor Statistics 1982, Table 13, Table 1).

In short, both sides of the Atlantic had to deal with industrial decline.

9. Maturity and stagnation

No tree grows to the sky. (Kindleberger 1953, p. 375)

Industrial maturity can be described in terms of product aging alone, as in the dictum, 'Regions don't grow old, products do' (Hekman 1979). But a more general approach was the *maturity hypothesis* long advanced by Charles P. Kindleberger (1953, 1961, 1962, 1974, 1978, 1980) in a variation on Schumpeter's older theme.

In early 1973 Kindleberger warned of 'the dynamic failure of the economy to produce new exports to replace those now being eroded by the product cycle.' In a letter to the *New York Times*, he considered whether the origins of this failure might lie in

> a slowing down of American economic vitality and elan – a *climacteric* in the life of the economy and perhaps society, such as Britain experienced after 1870 when it was overtaken by Germany and the United States as we are now being overtaken by Japan (emphasis added).

The laggard US adjustment to the first OPEC (Organization of Petroleum-Exporting Countries) oil price shock of 1973 led other economists to agree. The crowning blow was the second (1979) oil-price shock, which redirected US demand toward smaller, Japanese cars. Japan's triumph and Detroit's humiliation seemed to confirm America's industrial decline.

As Kindleberger implied in the 1973 letter, *the solution to the maturity problem was entrepreneurship*. Given the Law of Industrial Growth (the product cycle), a high-wage economy can counter the dispersal of mature goods and standardized services by creating new ones or by holding on to the design-intensive part of the value-chain. The capacity to spawn new activities will depend on whether existing companies can come up with new products – or, failing that, whether entrepreneurs can start companies from scratch.

This is the entrepreneurial challenge in a nutshell. It is also what has distinguished the US from Japan and the mature economies of Europe, notably France, Germany, and Italy.

The dialogue on maturity came to a head in the early 1980s around the question of industrial policy (Norton 1986). In the course of exploring Kindleberger's diagnosis of economic maturity, this chapter recalls economists' views on three central issues: (1) the British Climacteric, (2) the role of unions as a pivotal variable in a US region's economic culture, and (3) the geographical channels that helped the US transcend the crisis of the mature Manufacturing Belt.

THE SHADOW OF THE BRITISH CLIMACTERIC

The collapse of the Upper Midwest in the late 1970s and early 1980s seemed a fast-history replay of Britain's decline over the past century, a descent some historians trace to a British 'climacteric.' The American equivalent would be 'menopause,' the fading of reproductive capacity.

From the 1870s on, the British economy faced new competition from Germany, the US and other countries. The growth of its older industries suffered, and new industries failed to compensate. By some estimates, its total factor productivity growth came to a dead stop between 1873 and 1913 (see Table 9.1). Britain's decline in the relative per capita output standings of the AICs thus has roots before 1900 (see Table 9.2). Historians trace this malaise to institutional and social features of Britain's landscape.

Table 9.1 The halt in Britain's total factor productivity growth, 1873-1913

Peacetime phase	Growth rates (percent per year)		
	Gross output	Total factor input, with labor quality included	Total factor productivity
1856 - 1873	2.2	1.6	0.6
1873 - 1913	1.8	1.8	0.0
1924 - 1937	2.2	2.0	0.2
1951 - 1972	2.8	1.0	1.8

Source: Matthews et al. (1982, Tables 7.2 and 7.3, pp. 208 and 211).

'All the strategies available to her were blocked off in one way or another,' according to W. Arthur Lewis, by 'ideological traps.'

> She could not lower costs by cutting wages because of the unions, or switch to American-type technology because of the slower pace of British workers. . . . She could not pioneer in developing new commodities because this now required a scientific base which did not accord with her humanistic snobbery. So instead she invested her savings abroad, the economy decelerated, the average level of unemployment increased, and her young people emigrated. (1978b, p. 133)

Table 9.2 Britain's decline in relative per capita output, 1950-1981
(indices of GDP per head, US prices)

Country	1950	1981
United States	156	156
United Kingdom	100	100
Belgium	93	114
Denmark	93	120
Netherlands	90	113
France	85	120
Germany	65	124
Austria	55	112
Italy	48	95
Japan	30	115

Source: Wilfred Beckerman, 'Economic Policy and Performance in Britain Since World War II,' in Harberger (ed.) (1984, Table 1, p. 17).

Some observers saw a parallel between Britain's climacteric, or change of life, and the US and Europe in the 1980s. This maturity hypothesis dovetailed with Schumpeter's prediction of an eventual slowdown in advanced, affluent, inflexible economies. Others, particularly on the left, saw not a climacteric but an epochal 'divide' like the one Alvin Hansen noted in 1938. They regarded the US as poised between an obsolete commitment to a mass-production system, and a new order, yet to emerge.

Kindleberger's Version

In its early stages, Kindleberger's maturity hypothesis was implicitly aggregative in character. It referred neither to the product cycle nor to S-shaped growth for specific industries. Here maturity reflects rising capital-output ratios, or a reduction in the rate of saving, or both. Maturity may thus imply an affluent society in which consumption is enjoyed at the expense of investment.

Figure 9.1 shows an economy-wide S-shaped growth curve, as rendered in the first edition of Kindleberger's international economics text (1953). Kindleberger's thesis was that output growth per capita tends to accelerate in the early stages of growth, then slow down as an economy reaches a stage of economic maturity.

Real income
per capita

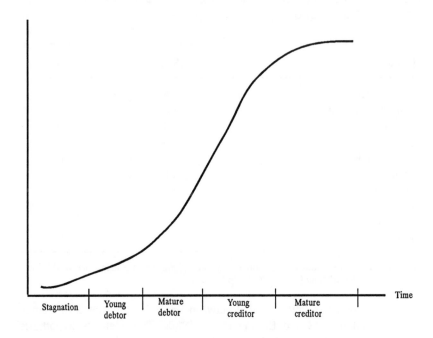

Source: Kindleberger (1953, p. 375).

Figure 9.1 A Gompertz curve of growth applied to development

In this context, consider Kenneth Boulding's life-cycle metaphor for the US economy:

> From about 1880 to 1930 . . . was the period of adolescent growth. The period after 1930 corresponds to young adulthood, when growth shifts away from the physical into the intellectual domain. [Today] . . . we must accept the fact that we are an increasingly mature society. We are not going to expand much in population or in wealth. (1980, p. 7)

This is grim stuff, in that Boulding defined maturity as '*the realization and eventual exhaustion of potential*' (p. 6).

But the question remained whether to take the idea seriously. Indeed, some dismissed the maturity hypothesis as Spenglerian nonsense. Why should maturity matter? In particular, why should maturity reduce an economy's capacity for resilience in the face of exogenous shocks?

Adaptive Capacity

By 1973, as we have seen, Kindleberger had recast the argument in terms of (1) the product cycle and (2) the climacteric. The product cycle dictated a shift to new industries, but some form of socioeconomic fatigue, in his view, eroded adaptive capacity.

As Kindleberger defined it, 'Capacity to transform is capacity to react to change, originating at home or abroad, by adapting the structure of foreign trade to the new situation in an economic fashion' (1962, p. 99). Over time this capacity falls. 'At some stage in the growth process it reaches a peak, and then there seems to be some diminution in it' (1962, p. 102).

Similarly, in 'The Aging Economy' (1978), Kindleberger referred to the urgent 'need to adapt to the diffusion of world technology' (p. 416). In his view, adaptive capacity was threatened in the US by a 'social arterio-sclerosis,' whose symptoms were interest-group politics, anachronistic practices by both labor and management, and a tendency for mature industries to have more political sway than growing ones.

Assar Lindbeck generalized this diagnosis to Europe's AICs in 'Can the Rich Countries Adapt?' (1981) Lindbeck made five points: (1) There was an urgent need for restructuring within Europe's AICs. (2) As a group, the AICs 'showed a reduced ability to carry out this reallocation smoothly' (p. 6). (3) In theory, governments can help via better macroeconomic and microeconomic policies. (4) This seems unlikely, however, 'since political decisions are to a great extent responsible for the lessened allocative efficiency of our economies' (p. 9). (5) As a result, living standards may fall.

Was there an antidote? In his 1978 essay, Kindleberger concluded that the only remedy was a 'sociological equivalent of defeat.' To free an aging economy from obsolete practices and institutions, as Germany and Japan had been purged and modernized after World War II, the treatment needed was shock therapy.

The Intransigence of the Old Regime

Unfortunately, it did take shock therapy to shake the upper Midwest from its regional climacteric. As observers put it in the early 1980s, 'We saw the regions of America reacting quite differently to radically changed economic futures, depending on their particular cultures.' As for adaptive capacity,

> the most resistant to change were the Midwestern states where even in the depression of the '80s many leaders in both management and labor seemed to imagine they could continue their old adversarial ways and regain their lost prosperity without fundamental adjustments. (Peirce and Hagstrom 1983, p. 17)

In *The Nine Nations of North America*, Joel Garreau compared this same 'Foundry' to Britain, but said renewal was occurring anyway, on a continental scale:

> The error, as this continent matures, is in . . . equating the inevitable decline in the Foundry's dominance with an inevitable decline in the world position of the United States or Canada. What's happening in the Foundry today is perhaps comparable to the wrenching realizations Europeans were subjected to . . . not only does the sun not revolve around the earth; the earth does not revolve around London. Yet, somehow, Western civilization survives – even prospers. (1981, p. 65)

Measuring Regional 'Age'

So much brings us back to ground zero: the timing of the beginnings of industrialization. That is, industrial takeoffs (in Manchester in 1844, the North after the Civil War, Texas since 1945, or the Pacific Rim economies today) are presided over by industrialists and their champions. Subsequent political development restores a balance between industrialists and everybody else: labor, farmers, environmentalists, consumers. The more ancient the industrial origins, the more time the political pendulum has in a democracy to swing back to favor other interests and so to generate an anti-business environment or climate.

This was the approach we took in Chapter 3. The touchstone was the share of a Census division's population holding manufacturing jobs in 1909, on the eve of World War I (see Table 3.1). To be more explicit: New England is the oldest US region by this yardstick because 17 percent of its entire population held manufacturing jobs in 1909, at the end of the US heavy industrialization. The Mid-Atlantic division came next with 12 percent, and the East North Central (or Lakes) division next, with 9 percent.

Then the youngest divisions were the West South Central (two percent), Mountain (three percent), and East South Central and West North Central divisions (each between three and four). In between or middle-aged were the partially industrialized Pacific (where the 1849 and later Alaska gold rushes spurred development in California and Washington) and the textile-driven Southeast. Each had between five and six percent of the population holding manufacturing jobs in 1909 (Norton 1981, p. 257).

In the wake of the trade and oil-price shocks of the 1970s, this regional age variable turned out to be a highly accurate 'predictor' of business climates and industrial job growth. The question was, why? An influential answer came from Piore and Sable's 1984 book, *The Second Industrial Divide*, which emphasized management's quest for control of the shop-floor.

DIVIDES: UNIONS OUT OF SYNC

The argument originated in 'American Labor and the Industrial Crisis' (1982). There, Michael Piore linked the crisis for organized labor to unification of the world economy. Piore observed that as mass-produced or standardized goods gravitate to LDCs, US comparative advantage shifts to small-batch or flexible-design production runs. But as US comparative advantage shifted from mature to product-cycle goods, the need for increased flexibility placed unions in a bind.

The problem was that American unions learned to deal with management via the institution of fixed *work-rules,* which originated with the mass-production methods perfected in Henry Ford's assembly line in 1913. Only after 1935 and the Wagner Act were unions granted full bargaining powers, permitting union membership to soar. By then, Frederick Taylor's system of 'scientific management' dominated the organization of the workplace. And it prescribed a rigidly codified division of labor on the shop floor, a system that unions accepted as given and codified in work-rules (Reich 1983, ch. 4).

In other words, what Piore termed the *regulatory system* pivoted on the institutions of mass production, Taylorism, and codified work-rules in older American industries. From this regime in turn stemmed a de facto social contract between management and labor – and a welfare state in which the legitimacy of unions was taken for granted.

By the same token, the new management-union tension was about rigidity: Taylorist work-rules, legacies of the era of standardized mass production. As standardized manufacturing migrated abroad, the need for flexibility required more fluid work arrangements. Thus production-line managers turned militant, while unions fought to retain their shop-floor say.

Regional Alternatives

Piore's argument suggested that the decline of the US North reflected a flight from unions. But in Piore's framework, the redirection of investment was less a flight from high union wages than an attempt to escape rigid work-rules. In other words, managers shifted plants to less unionized sites to regain control of production and introduce new methods.

What made this argument suggestive was that the US displays sharp regional contrasts in the role that unions play. In particular, 'right-to-work' laws (outlawing union shops) are found in 20 states – and every one of them lies outside the Manufacturing Belt (see Figure 9.2). In this light, US regional contrasts provided a bridge between one institutional setting and another.

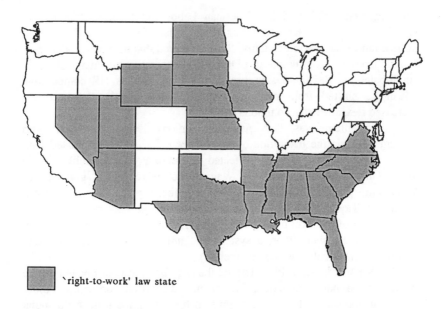

'right-to-work' law state

Source: Bluestone and Harrison (1982, p. 137).

Figure 9.2 Clustering of 'right-to-work' states in the South and West

The Nationwide Decline in Unionization Rates

Unionized workers have been steadily displaced, of course, as production jobs in manufacturing have shifted in make-up and location. For one thing, the decline of the upper Midwest was transparently a blow to blue-collar unions. More generally, production facilities in IT are typically non-union. (See, for example, an account of Intel's success at remaining non-union in Jackson 1997, chapter 16.)

Whatever the impact on work conditions, one result is greater wage flexibility. Another is to give management more control over the shop floor, free from work rules and free to pursue flexible production techniques.

Such changes are but part of the familiar trend toward falling union membership counts, both in absolute terms and as a percentage of the workforce. *Since the mid-1950s the percentage of private payroll employees in unions has fallen from about 36 to about 12.* More recently, in manufacturing the share has gone down from above 30 percent in the early 1980s to about 20 percent in the late 1990s (Duca 1998, Charts 1 and 4). To repeat: by the Millennium only one in five US manufacturing workers belonged to a union.

MARKET- GENERATED ADJUSTMENT: OTHER PATHS

Market-based adjustment, then, worked through the availability of alternative union and tax environments. The other side of the coin was the feedback that pressured states viewed as anti-business to try to improve their images. Then there was another, less obvious dynamic in play as well. In a cumulative cycle, firms adopted flexible production systems in a growth context of import-substitution and city-building.

City-Building

A key to the growth environment of younger regions has been rapid urban development. In this regard, Carol Heim (1984) observed that continentality provided the US with three sources of renewal absent from Britain. In a comparison of the geography of industrial modernization in the two countries, she found American advantages in (1) lower factor costs in the more extensive US periphery, (2) a city-building dynamic in the South and West that generated abundant profit opportunities to entrepreneurs, and (3) a geographical and political diversity that offered ample opportunities for innovation.

The South-West locus of city-building continued unabated in the 1990s. As Table 9.3 shows, from among the nation's 50 largest metropolitan areas in 1998, the 19 with the fastest population growth were all in the South and West. By the same token, a number of large metro areas in the Manufacturing Belt had little or no population growth between 1990 and 1998 (a point made again in Chapter 23).

Profiting from Disequilibrium

By extension, the US could be viewed as deriving a distinctive capacity for structural renewal from its own internal frontier. Both a classical and a more recent conception of the economic frontier are worth noting.

The classical notion of a formative frontier in an American setting is the Turner thesis. Frederick Jackson Turner's famous 1893 essay announced the closing of the literal frontier. The century that followed saw a continuing debate among scholars as whether this or the flow of immigrants to the industrial cities of the Manufacturing Belt was more influential.

Table 9.3 South and West metros grew fastest, 1990-1998,
among the 50 largest areas in 1990

Area	04/01/1990 to 7/1/1998 Percent change	Numeric change	07/01/1998 Estimated population	Revised 04/01/1990 Census population	Rank by 1990 population
1 Las Vegas	55.0	468,900	1,321,546	852,646	34
2 Phoenix	30.9	692,506	2,931,004	2,238,498	14
3 Atlanta	26.6	786,559	3,746,059	2,959,500	11
4 Austin	26.6	232,395	1,106,059	873,664	42
5 Raleigh	25.8	221,388	1,079,873	858,485	45
6 Orlando	22.8	279,725	1,504,569	1,224,844	31
7 Portland (OR) CMSA	19.8	355,580	2,149,056	1,793,476	23
8 West Palm Beach	19.6	169,122	1,032,625	863,503	49
9 Denver CMSA	19.5	385,205	2,365,345	1,980,140	20
10 Dallas CMSA	19.0	765,181	4,802,463	4,037,282	8
11 Charlotte	19.0	220,940	1,383,080	1,162,140	33
12 Salt Lake City	18.2	195,518	1,267,745	1,072,227	36
13 Houston CMSA	18.1	676,550	4,407,579	3,731,029	10
14 Nashville	17.4	171,199	1,156,225	985,026	38
15 San Antonio	16.1	213,589	1,538,338	1,324,749	29
16 Seattle CMSA	15.3	454,061	3,424,361	2,970,300	13
17 Jacksonville	15.2	137,957	1,044,684	906,727	46
18 Miami CMSA	14.5	463,119	3,655,844	3,192,725	12
19 Sacramento CMSA	13.8	204,592	1,685,812	1,481,220	26
20 Minneapolis-St. Paul	11.6	292,458	2,831,234	2,538,776	16
21 San Diego	11.3	282,576	2,780,592	2,498,016	17
22 Greensboro	11.2	117,325	1,167,629	1,050,304	37
23 Washington DC	10.7	451,072	4,673,902	4,222,830	9
24 Grand Rapids	10.7	100,042	1,037,933	937,891	48
25 Indianapolis	10.0	138,703	1,519,194	1,380,491	30
26 Kansas City	9.7	154,151	1,737,025	1,582,874	25
27 Columbus	9.2	124,154	1,469,604	1,345,450	32
28 Tampa	9.1	188,600	2,256,559	2,067,959	22
29 Los Angeles CMSA	8.6	1,249,744	15,781,273	14,531,529	2
30 San Francisco CMSA	8.6	538,522	6,816,047	6,277,525	4

31 Memphis	8.5	86,121	1,093,427	1,007,306	43
32 Oklahoma City	8.4	80,160	1,038,999	958,839	47
33 Cincinnati CMSA	7.2	130,695	1,948,264	1,817,569	24
34 Chicago CMSA	6.9	570,026	8,809,846	8,239,820	3
35 Norfolk	6.7	97,433	1,542,143	1,444,710	28
36 Louisville	5.3	50,255	999,267	949,012	50
37 Detroit CMSA	5.2	270,412	5,457,583	5,187,171	7
38 Baltimore	4.3	101,780	2,483,952	2,382,172	19
39 Boston CMSA	3.3	177,657	5,633,060	5,455,403	6
40 New York CMSA	2.9	558,936	20,124,377	19,565,441	1
41 St. Louis	2.9	71,453	2,563,801	2,492,348	18
42 Milwaukee CMSA	2.4	38,741	1,645,924	1,607,183	27
43 New Orleans	1.9	24,183	1,309,445	1,285,262	35
44 Cleveland CMSA	1.8	52,039	2,911,683	2,859,644	15
45 Rochester	1.8	19,413	1,081,883	1,062,470	44
46 Philadelphia CMSA	1.6	95,329	5,988,348	5,893,019	5
47 Providence	(1.0)	(11,376)	1,122,974	1,134,350	41
48 Hartford	(1.2)	(13,726)	1,143,859	1,157,585	40
49 Pittsburgh	(2.0)	(48,658)	2,346,153	2,394,811	21
50 Buffalo	(3.1)	(26,799)	1,152,641	1,189,340	39
United States	8.7	21,533,354	270,298,524	248,765,170	
Metropolitan	9.1	18,027,782	216,478,090	198,450,308	
Nonmetropolitan	7.0	3,505,572	53,820,434	50,314,862	

Source: US Bureau of the Census, Internet Release of December 17, 1999.

Be that as it may, Turner's language on the internal frontier as a source of change still seems relevant, a century later:

American development has exhibited not merely advance along a single line, but a return to primitive conditions on a continually advancing frontier line, and a new development for that area. This perennial rebirth, this fluidity of American life, this expansion westward with its new opportunities . . . furnish the forces dominating American character. (Turner, in Taylor 1949, pp. 1-2)

In 'The Economics of the Frontier,' Guido di Tella asked why a frontier stage led to subsequent rounds of development in the US and Canada, but not, for example, in Argentina. He introduced the idea of *the frontier as a disequilibrium* state, 'bursting with business opportunities with big profits and economic excitement, evidence of the existence of rent at the frontier' (1982, p. 215). The scramble for rents and quasi-rents generates a powerful stimulus to investment – and to innovative behavior.

More recently, Thurow (1999) lists three varieties of profit-generating disequilibria. The first he terms *socioeconomic*, as when Starbuck's managed to shift tastes from a generic $1 cup of coffee to the $3 boutique version. The second is *developmental* disequilibrium, illustrated by (pre-1997) Hong Kong business people crossing the border into South China and introducing the latest business practices and organization so as to turn a larger profit. The third is *technological*, as with the Internet.

The disequilibrium of interest now is a fourth, *geographical* version. To wit: import-substitution in formerly less industrialized US regions, combined with alternative institutional environments. Whether geographical disequilibria necessarily overlap with developmental ones may be left as an open question.

Import-Substitution as Catch-Up Industrialization

What gives such abstractions bite was a disequilibrium between suppliers and their markets in the US from about 1960 on. Like Britain in 1870 and the northern European economies in 1970, the US North was 'hyperindustrialized' in 1950. The technological changes that weakened the North's industrial role created a profit-generating disequilibrium in the South and especially the West.

Import-substitution was thus a potential avenue open to entrepreneurs in growing markets in the South and West, as goods formerly imported from the North were increasingly produced locally. The loss of the North's traditional export markets was hastened by the filling in, diversification, and catching-up of formerly less developed areas (Wheat 1973; Stevens and Treyz 1983).

For the record, a regression equation reported in Appendix 9A finds the market-as-magnet variable to be one of four major influences on the rate of state manufacturing job growth in the 1970s. The lower a state's job count in manufacturing relative to its population, the faster its job growth during the decade. As the appendix shows, the other influences were right-to-work laws, changes in labor costs, and distance from the core, the four together accounting for 80 percent of the variation.

THE ROLE OF THE ENTREPRENEUR

In turn, import-substitution provided a stimulus to innovation and entrepreneurship on a scale reshaping the national economy as a whole. In this respect, Jane Jacobs (1984) provided a natural complement to di Tella's frontier theory. As she brought out in historical sketches from around the world, the process of import-substitution seldom stops with existing production methods. Instead, it often sets off a local sequence of learning-by-doing and incremental process innovations – the touchstone, in her view, for authentic economic development.

In an earlier work, Jacobs had also taken issue with the Marxian view of class conflict as capitalism's deepest 'contradiction.'

> Marx thought that the principal conflict to be found in . . . industrialized countries, was the deep disparity of interests between owners and employees, but this is a secondary kind of conflict. The primary economic conflict, I think, is between people whose interests are with already-established economic activities and those whose interests are with the emergence of new economic activities. *This is a conflict that can never be put to rest except by economic stagnation.* (1969, pp. 248-9, emphasis added)

In that light, the role of the entrepreneur is to overcome the barriers to innovation that gradually mount as any organization, industry, or society matures. In the United States, the powerful tendency toward stagnation was most concentrated in the long-industrialized Manufacturing Belt, and above all in the Upper Midwest.

By the same token, the climacteric Kindleberger saw for the US turned out to have mainly regional validity. The shock therapy of regional competition ultimately provided an irresistible impetus for economic transformation in the Lakes region – and across the US Manufacturing Belt as a whole.

On the other hand, the residual power of older industries and vested interests can still be seen in something like its full regalia on the other side of the Atlantic Rim.

APPENDIX 9A

As noted in the body of the chapter, four influences accounted for 80 percent of the variation in the 1970-80 rates of state manufacturing job growth. These were market potential (*MKT*), the 1970-80 change in a state's relative labor costs (*DLC*), the presence of a 'right-to-work' (anti-union shop) law (*NON-U*), and a measure of other effects associated with distance from the old industrial core (*PITT*).

Denoting the percentage change in a state's manufacturing job count between 1970 and 1980 as *DJOBS*,

$$DJOBS = -14.1 + 16.6 \, NON\text{-}U - 1.8 \, DLC$$
$$(4.2) \qquad\qquad (3.4)$$

$$+ \, 0.8 \, MKT + 15.4 \, PITT,$$
$$(5.2) \qquad\quad (5.1)$$

$R^2 = 0.80, N = 48,$

where the parenthesized values are *t*-ratios and where

NON-U = 1 in the 20 right-to-work states, 0 elsewhere;
DLC   = the percentage change in a state's relative labor costs;
MKT   = population/manufacturing employment for a state in 1970;
PITT   = distance (1000 m) of a state's largest city from Pittsburgh.

The regression says that 'right-to work' law states had 17 percent faster job growth in manufacturing over the decade. It suggests that a state whose labor costs fell by 1 percent relative to the US average had a growth rate about two points higher than a state in which labor costs matched the US trend. (But the identification problem rules out a causal interpretation here.) As for the market magnet, the latter two variables bear out the idea of decentralized filling-in. Thus the larger the initial ratio of population to manufacturing employment (*MKT*), and the farther the state from the industrial core (*PITT*), the faster the state's manufacturing job growth.

By way of an update, however, Figure 9.3 reveals that the convergence in industrial roles among regions has been far from uniform. In particular, the revival of the auto complex in the Upper Midwest in the 1990s made the region *more* industrially specialized relative to population by the end of the decade. Conversely, Figure 9.4 also shows the lingering under-representation of the Pacific and Southwest divisions, reflecting the broad-based character of their development and the prominence of population-serving services activities in contexts of rapid in-migration.

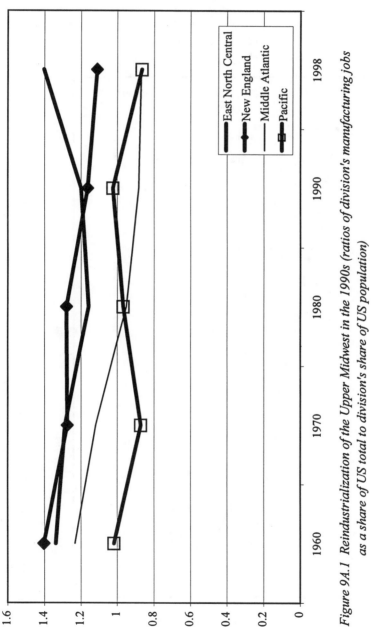

Figure 9A.1 Reindustrialization of the Upper Midwest in the 1990s (ratios of division's manufacturing jobs as a share of US total to division's share of US population)

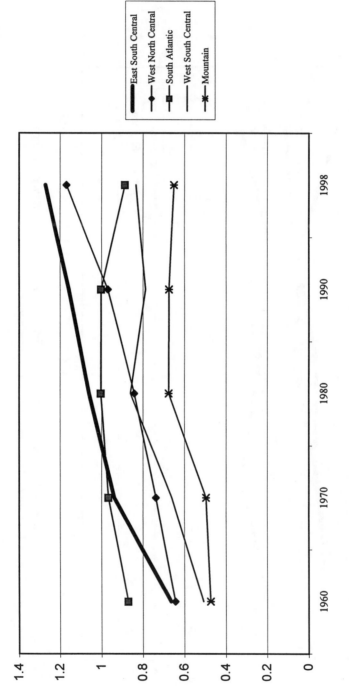

Figure 9A.2 Non-metropolitan industrialization shapes two younger divisions
(ratios: manufacturing job shares to population shares)

10. Eurolandia

America, you have it better than our continent, the old one. (Johann Wolfgang von Goethe 1831, quoted in Augarde, 1991, p. 349)

In the business press, 'Euroland' is shorthand for the adventurous 11-nation zone in Figure 10.1 that now uses the Euro as a common currency. By contrast, 'Eurolandia,' as a chapter title derives from the novel *Islandia*, where everything was designed to suit pre-industrial and hence more humane values (Wright 1942). Somewhere between these two competing images lie the current realities of Europe's mature economies.

Our theme so far in Part II is that after about 1970 the rich nations on both sides of the Atlantic Rim required a kind of shock therapy to shake them loose from their entitlements and calcifications.

In the US the shock therapy in question was in part geographical, as the last chapter illustrated. Lacking such powerful channels of internal spatial revitalization, Europe oldest and largest economies (France, Germany, and Italy: the 'Big Three') have been slower to adapt to the challenge of rising competitors. The result is sometimes termed 'Eurosclerosis.'

At the same time, the UK has now emerged from a century of economic stagnation. As Figure 10.2 shows, the British economy had lower unemployment rates and tax burdens than the Big Three by the late 1990s. In addition, Scandinavia fairly brims with entrepreneurial excitement centering on wireless technologies and the Internet.

Europe therefore offers a parallel experiment in how advanced, affluent economies grapple with the challenge of maturity. What it suggests is that without risk-taking entrepreneurs, even the most advanced economies can settle into a high-unemployment equilibrium for long periods of time.

UNIFICATIONS

Geographically, Europe's history since 1950 can be interpreted as an attempt to become a 'United States of Europe,' a phrase that goes back to the early stages of European unification. The analogy surfaces in the EU's new motto, 'unity in diversity,' an echo of the phrase 'e pluribus unum' on American coins.

As with Canada, the attempt to attain continental efficiency in the American manner often carries the demurrer, 'while avoiding America's excesses.'

81

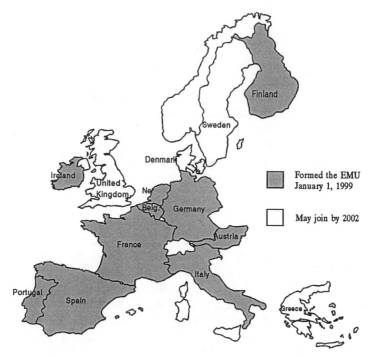

Figure 10.1 European Monetary Union (EMU)--the Euro Zone

Following the creation of the unified internal market in 1992, the European Union (itself the descendant of the European Economic Community or EEC and then the European Community or EC) was christened in November 1993. Thus renamed, the EU had 12 members: the Benelux countries, the Big Three, Denmark, Greece, Ireland, Portugal, Spain, and the UK. Then three 'Nordic' entries – Austria, Finland, and Sweden – came on board in 1995, for a total of 15 EU members.

What is the overlap between the EU and the Euro? Incomplete. Four of the 15 EU members decided to opt out on the Euro when it became the other 11's common currency on January 1, 1999. Technically, then, the Euro Zone has 11 EU nations, but not Denmark, Greece, Sweden, or the UK. These four holdouts retain the option of joining by 2002.

In any case, the divergent paths taken by the UK and the Big Three encompass more than just the single-currency issue.

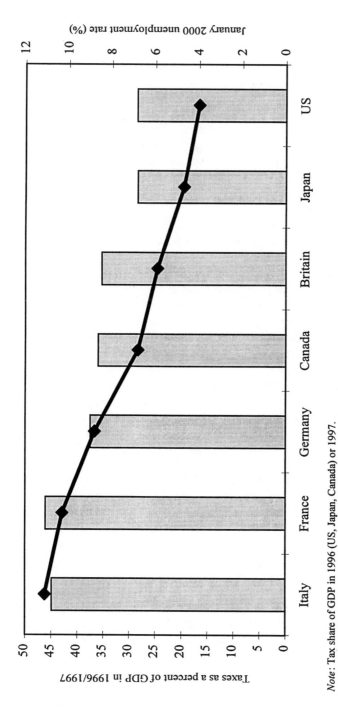

Note: Tax share of GDP in 1996 (US, Japan, Canada) or 1997.
Source: OECD data. Tax shares are from the *Economist*, July 31, 1999, Survey p. 8.

Figure 10.2 Correlation of taxes and unemployment in the G-7 economies

THE BRITISH RESURGENCE

To bring out maturity's role, we can rank Western Europe's economies by age. A workable yardstick comes from W.W. Rostow's timeline for industrial 'take-offs' in *The Stages of Economic Growth* (1960, 1971, p. 38). By this indicator Britain is of course 'oldest,' followed by (2) France, (3) Belgium, (4) the US, (5) Germany, (6) Sweden, and (7) Japan. While not on the list, Italy (in the North, at least) was not far behind.

Maturity: The View from 1990

By the same token, Michael Porter (1990, chapter 10) saw a syndrome of maturity besetting not only the UK and US, but also Switzerland and Germany.

In his view, advanced economies fare best when they function as innovators. With development, the sources of growth may shift from (1) factor endowments (notably natural resources); to (2) investment surges, via import-substitution, or export development in mature industries; to (3) innovation; and, when all else fails (4), accumulated wealth. The innovation phase (where Porter placed Italy, Japan, and Sweden) entails home-grown innovations as well as improvements in borrowed technologies.

In Porter's schema, the end of the line is wealth-driven growth: a stage of decline. 'The problem is that an economy driven by past wealth is not able to maintain its wealth' (p. 556). Worse, 'the range of industries in which competitive advantage can be sustained becomes inadequate to employ the workforce in productive jobs and support a rising standard of living' (p. 559). This unenviable fate Porter assigned in a diagram to Germany, the US, and Switzerland (p. 566).

But the UK – the mother of all wealth-driven economies – Porter classed as being midway through a turnaround sparked by Margaret Thatcher's draconian reforms of the 1980s.

An Anglophone Advantage?

Until the 1980s, in other words, Britain's GDP growth rate trailed the other G-7 economies, so that both its output and living standards had slipped behind France, Germany, and Italy. Under the Thatcher government British performance improved, raising it to the middle of the pack, where it remained in the 1990s – ahead of France and Italy in both decades. (*The Economist,* March 25, 2000, p. 57.)

As we saw at the outset, by the late 1990s the UK had lower unemployment rates than the continent's Big Three. Meantime its GDP had pulled ahead of Italy and about even with France. What counts here is less the UK's absolute performance than its improvement. Some productivity indicators still lag, and the North of England's manufacturing sector continues to struggle, especially when burdened by a high pound. In any case, by 1999 the term 'the economic sick man of Europe' was used to describe Germany, not Britain (Krugman, *Fortune*, July 1999b, p. 32).

As another indicator of the change, the World Economic Forum's competitiveness index ranked the UK number 8 in the world in 1999, up from a rank of 15th in 1996 (see Table 10.1). Meantime France, Belgium,

Table 10.1 The competitiveness of the 'Anglophones,' 1999

Country	Rank 1999	Rank 1996	Change, 1996-1999
Singapore	1	1	–
United States	2	4	2
Hong Kong	3	2	-1
Taiwan	4	9	5
Canada	5	8	3
Switzerland	6	6	–
Luxembourg	7	5	-2
United Kingdom	8	15	7
Netherlands	9	17	8
Ireland	10	26	16
Finland	11	16	5
Australia	12	12	–
New Zealand	13	3	-10
Japan	14	13	-1
Norway	15	7	-8
Malaysia	16	10	-6
Denmark	17	11	-6
Iceland	18	27	9
Sweden	19	21	2
Austria	20	19	-1
Chile	21	18	-3
Korea	22	20	-2
France	23	23	–
Belgium	24	25	1
Germany	25	22	-3

Note: 'Anglophones' or English-speaking nations appear in bold letters.
Source: World Economic Forum 2000.

and Germany ranked far lower, at 23, 24, and 25, with Italy number 35. Though one could debate the fine points of this global competitiveness index, the 1999 ranks do align with another widely noted tendency.

That tendency is the recent success of the English-speaking economies. The UK, number 8, was joined in the upper reaches by top-ranked Singapore (where English is the official *lingua franca),* the US (2), Canada (5), Ireland (10), Australia (12), and New Zealand (13). Whatever the explanation, the English-speaking nations did well during the 1990s – a decade of crisis in so much of the world.

Does all this suggest an Anglo-Saxon conspiracy, a coincidence, or something more routine? Paul Krugman offers four possible reasons for the Anglophones' success. He considers (1) linked business cycles (as between the UK and Australia on the one hand, and the US on the other); (2) the more academic (as opposed to strictly civil-service) ties of the Anglophones' central bankers; (3) English's influence as the global language of business; and (4) the role of the Internet, initially an English-language medium, as somehow a source of advantage *(Fortune,* April 1999, p. 57). He tends to favor (2), the 'Greenspan theory.'

Or Are They Just Hard-Hearted?

An alternative explanation can be inferred from a report on aid to the jobless around the world, compiled by the UN's International Labor Organization, or ILO. The *World Labor Report 2000* finds, not surprisingly, that continental Europe's workers enjoy the highest level of unemployment benefits.

In contrast, the Anglophones are taken to task for cutting back on worker protection, ranking in a lower category than the Big Three:

> The *United States* also trimmed benefits, and has slipped in a ranking of which countries offer the most generous worker protection. . . . *Australia, Canada, Ireland,* Japan, *New Zealand, and Britain* also provide a lower level of benefits than countries in the top tier of the ranking. (Olson 2000, p. C4, emphasis added)

Japan aside, then, the curious correlation of language and economic performance extends also to policies limiting worker protection, or, to take the opposite perspective, encouraging flexibility. The unsettling possibility emerges that something about the faster growth and lower unemployment rates of the English-speaking economies stems from increased flexibility in the labor market – apace with deregulation of formerly protected industries.

THE ELEMENTS OF EUROSCLEROSIS

In short, Belgium and the Big Three continued to struggle with the legacies of economic maturity. This, despite the titanic changes sweeping the continent during the last decade: German re-unification after 1989, Europe 1992's creation of a 12-country unified market, and the bold move in 1999 to the Euro as a common currency.

A list of the malaise's correlates might run as follows:

1. jobless growth;
2. an entrepreneurial gap;
3. labor-market rigidities;
4. the heavy tax burdens required to support extensive social services and income-maintenance plans, partly to support the jobless.

A glance at each of these issues suggests a pattern of perverse interactions.

JOBLESS GROWTH

The US added over 50 million jobs between 1970 and 1998. France, Germany, Italy, and the UK combined added about eight million. The contrast was especially stark for the interval 1990-97, when the US added 11 million jobs while the EU nations had no private-sector job increase at all (Thurow 1999, p. 88). In the late 1990s, job growth returned, but the specter of jobless growth lingered.

In a valuable early essay on Western European responses to the rise of the newly industrializing countries, N. Plessz observed, 'The real question is why . . . "positive" responses have played a lesser role in Western Europe than in North America' (1981, p. 228). As he pointed out,

> while labour-shedding continued, or sometimes accelerated, in the 'declining' industries, *the absorption of labour by 'growth' industries has slowed down dramatically.* In other words, the adjustment mechanism was blocked, at least within the manufacturing sector. (p. 231, emphasis added)

The Erosion of Manufacturing Jobs

As a result, manufacturing employment in Europe's largest economies would ratchet down after 1970 (see Figure 10.3). The sharpest decline, of course, was in the UK, whose count fell from over eight million in 1970 to under five by the late 1990s. In contrast, for both the US and Japan, end-of-century counts found manufacturing employment at the same levels as 30

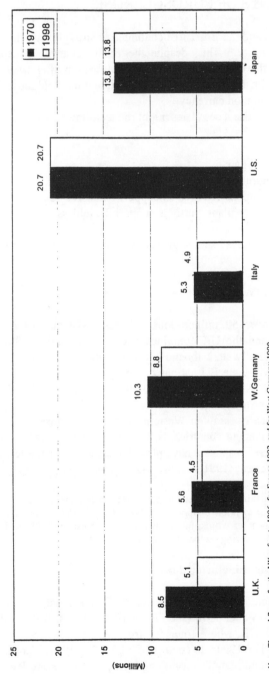

Note: The end figure for the UK refers to 1996, for France 1992, and for West Germany 1990.
Source: US Department of Labor, Bureau of Labor Statistics 1999, Table 6.

Figure 10.3 Europe's big four lost seven million manufacturing jobs after 1970 (in order of percentage decline)

years earlier. The Big Three on the continent had intermediate records, each losing some 20 percent over the three decades (though the data, which stop in the early 1990s for France, for example, understate the losses).

Compounding the problem was slow growth in services jobs. Rapid productivity growth permitted job reductions in manufacturing, but job growth in services activities was missing. The result was the snails-pace increase in total employment in the Big Three

A singular success story was the Netherlands, where employment rose by nearly 50 percent. Aided (as was Ireland) by its role as a base for non-European multinational companies, Holland therefore had labor-market conditions closer to the US or Canada.

Employment Rates

The term 'employment rate' is sometimes used to describe the proportion of the working-age population with jobs. In 1998 and 1999, this indicator ranged near or above 60 percent in the US (where it was 64), Canada, Australia, the Netherlands, Sweden, the UK, and Japan in the late 1990s (US Department of Labor, BLS 2000, Table 5).

By contrast, the employment rate for Germany was only 52 percent. Despite recent job gains, France still had less than half the working-age population employed in 1999. Partly because of an unusually low participation rate for women, the rate for Italy was a modest 42 percent.

The gap widens further for workers under 25, who are most injured by policies on the continent that value existing jobs over job creation. In the US, the sustained expansion drove unemployment rates for this group below 10 percent in 1999. Surprisingly, a similar rate could be found in Germany. Meantime the rate for the UK had fallen to 12.

But in France for workers under 25 the unemployment rate was 26 percent, and in Italy 34 percent. This was the context within which younger French workers could take advantage of the EU's common passport and crossed the channel to find jobs in the UK.

One reason for sluggish job growth and high unemployment has been the puzzling scarcity of entrepreneurs on the continent.

EUROPE'S MISSING ENTREPRENEURS

Thurow (1999 p. 93) makes the point that all of Europe's 25 largest firms in 1998 were already large 30 years earlier. But in the US, newcomers firms accounted for eight of the top 25 in 1998. This contrast points up the comparative absence of entrepreneurs in Europe. A further result, as

Thurow (1999, p. 85) points out, is Europe's lag in the world's growth industries:

> Europe saves and invests a lot, it is well educated, and it has a strong technological base. But nowhere is it a leader in creating the new man-made brainpower industries. . . . In 1998 the production arm of its last indigenous computer manufacturer, Siemens Nixdorf, was sold to Acer of Taiwan. . . . The entrepreneurs that should exist aren't there.

A Ten-Country Comparison

Some of the reasons for the gap can be seen in a 1999 study of ten countries. The Global Entrepreneurship Monitor (GEM) project was a cooperative endeavor between Babson College in the US and the London Business School, together with their correspondents in the eight other nations. The project included surveys of 10,000 adults and 300 interviews of experts in the ten countries.

The GEM study rated three economies – the US, Canada, and Israel – as highly entrepreneurial, as measured both by attitudes and by the rate of new-business starts and expansions. Two – Italy and the UK – placed in the middle of the list.

Trailing were Denmark, Finland, France, Germany, and Japan. While the inclusion of Finland might seem surprising in light of recent reports of an entrepreneurial upsurge there, a great deal of Finnish activity derives from a single firm, Nokia – a conglomerate that used its core competencies to focus solely on telecom in the 1990s.

To measure entrepreneurship, the GEM study tabulated new-business formation of any kind, including expansions within existing businesses. Entrepreneurship, then, was 'Any attempt at new business or new venture creation, such as self-employment, a new business organization, or the expansion of an existing business, by an individual, a team of individuals, or an established business' (Reynolds et al. 1999, p. 3).

The project sought (1) to measure differences in this variable among countries, (2) to link it to contrasts in economic growth, and (3) to find out why countries differ in their entrepreneurial performance. While the intricacies of the methods and interpretations could be debated, it would be hard to dispute the general characterizations of the US as the most entrepreneurial of the ten nations. Some of the US attributes are as follows:

- 'At any point in time, 8.5 percent of the US adult population is starting new businesses – the highest start-up rate among the GEM countries' (Reynolds et al., p. 32).

- Women in the US are ten times more likely to start new businesses than women in Finland or France (at the bottom of this ranking).
- At least 5 percent of the US population is investing in a new business or prospective start-up of their own or to assist someone else.

The explanations offered from the surveys and interviews to account for this US proclivity to finance and start new firms are familiar. Americans value independence and are alert to entrepreneurial opportunities. The prominence of entrepreneurs in the culture provides role models. Higher education in general and business-related courses in particular are widely available.

By contrast, Germany ranks toward the bottom of the list – but is viewed as something of an up-and-comer among the five nations ranked low on the scale:

- Germany's start-up rate is below average, but higher than the other four (Denmark, Finland, France and Japan).
- Attitudes toward starting a new business are becoming more positive.
- The rate which Germans invest in new businesses approaches the US.

Still, popular attitudes shun the risks of starting a new business. Both individual wealth and bankruptcy (that is, failure) are looked down upon. In contrast to what experts perceived, only 15 percent of the general public in Germany saw much in the way of entrepreneurial opportunities in the nation. In addition, the infrastructure was regarded as weak, notably for venture capital (Reynolds et al., pp. 37-8).

Hurdles

Another recent account highlights the (east) German entrepreneur Stephan Schambach's creation, Intershop, one of the world's three largest online shopping software producers – but views it as the exception that proves the rule. In this view, 'Europe suffers from a dearth of "technopreneurs," because it does too little to encourage and too much to discourage them' (Valencia 2000, p. 17).

Among nations, the exception is Sweden, 'the continent's hottest market for Internet start-ups, by some measures hotter than America' (p. 18).

Elsewhere on the continent, however, the barriers entrepreneurs face remain formidable (p. 18). They include (1) regulatory hurdles facing start-ups, (2) an imbalance between risk and reward, (3) a lack of university ties to companies, and (4) despite some recent reforms, still daunting labor-market rigidities.

LABOR-MARKET RIGIDITIES

Krugman likens French jobs to rent-controlled apartments in New York City: 'Those who provide them are subject to detailed regulation by a government that is very solicitous of their occupants' ('Unmitigated Gauls,' June 5 1997, *Slate*). The outcomes are also similar: extreme difficulty in dislodging existing tenants (or firing people), a restriction of the supply, and severe obstacles facing newcomers trying to get housing (or a job). The effect has been to maintain higher real wages for jobholders, while forcing younger workers to live off the state or migrate.

Such tendencies have begun to ebb in recent years, yielding to more flexible practices and increased job creation. But the legacy was still visible in unemployment rates that averaged 10 percent for France, Germany, and Italy at the Millennium.

German Reunification: What Went Wrong?

No one champions 'the dole': government subsidies and benefits high enough to dampen efforts to get a job. Less obvious, perhaps, is the damage done by the centralized governmental structures of the European welfare states. When combined with national wage agreements, for example, high and uniform jobless benefits can freeze dislocated workers in place.

An example was the reunification of Germany after 1989, when pay scales were made uniform across the country. In the name of fairness, the policy had the perverse effect of discouraging investment in the East. Since productivity levels were far lower there, uniform pay scales meant that employers in the East would be paying the same wages as in the West, but for less efficient workers (that is, at higher unit labor costs).[1] Outside investment therefore largely stayed away.

As a result, Germany's East has come to resemble the North of England in the 1980s: a region on the dole, with much less investment from outside than a more market-based wage system would have encouraged.

TAXES, GOVERNMENT, AND CULTURE

The Big Three's extensive social programs and generous unemployment benefits carry a high tax cost. To be sure, part of the tax bill reflected continental Europe's distinctive values, including preferences for extensive public services and public support for art and culture on a scale unknown in the US. Nevertheless, as unemployment rates have risen, so have associated public costs. In France and Italy taxes as a share of GDP rose perceptibly between 1980 and 1997, reaching shares of about 45 percent (see Figure 10.4).

This was the background to Figure 10.2, which showed that among the G-7 economies, the Big Three had both the highest tax shares and the highest unemployment rates in the late 1990s. Such was the context for current German and French tax-cuts.

Even as these and other aggressive measures are being launched to scale back government's role, the cultural resistance to market forces took on renewed intensity.

Red Tape?

As a spate of recent books on globalization point out, the cultural resistance to market forces is about more than just unions or labor practices (Barber 1995, Friedman 1999, Micklethwait and Wooldridge 2000). It is also about preserving national identities and resisting 'Americanization.'

One form of resistance operates through regulation, as imposed not only by governments but also by trade associations. In Italy, for example, the proprietor of a Roman hair salon has violated an ordinance by keeping his business open at night during the full moon, when some Italians believe hair grows back thickest and fastest.

A competitor complains, 'If I close at 7 p.m. and a rival across the street stays open until 11 p.m. I'll be forced to stay open, too. . . . W]e are a traditional country. We don't need these changes at all.' An economist comments, 'In Italy, competition is seen as harmful, and it makes you work too hard. We have a humane and pleasant way of life, and we have a hard time adapting to inevitable change.'

Another retailer, who supports more flexible rules about hours, stops short at allowing stores to hold sales at other than the two months allowed each year, February and mid-summer. 'You are depreciating the art of commerce, reducing the transaction to just the price' (Stanley 2000, p. 10).

The moral of the story is that the seemingly stultifying Italian regulations of small and family business are accepted by many businesses themselves as a welcome restraint on competition.

For them, Internet commerce would seem to be an accident waiting to happen. On the other hand, Italy's countless admirers in the rest of the world will readily understand the Italian desire to maintain a unique and authentic culture in the face of an approaching 'global mall.'

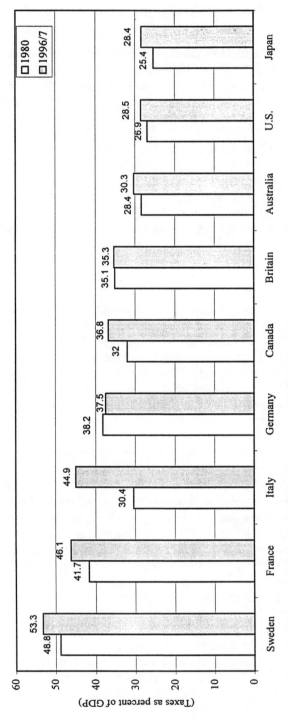

Note: 1980 is for West Germany. End figures for the US, Japan, and Canada are for 1996, others 1997.

Source: OECD data in the *Economist*, July 31, 1999, Survey p. 8.

Figure 10.4 Taxes as a share of GDP range highest on the continent

Some American economists also applaud the Big Three's labor practices as cultural expressions of distinctive national values. In 'Single-Peaked Capitalism: The Relation between Economic Institutions and Outcomes,' Richard B. Freeman thus contends that the distinct economic cultures of Europe, Japan, and the US may be appropriate to each, rather than converging toward the American reliance on market forces (Freeman 2000).

THE NEW LABOR PARADIGM

Be that as it may, a clear alternative is the increase in flexibility – and in insecurity – that has emerged in the US as a correlate of the New Economy. John Duca of the Federal Reserve Bank of Dallas notes in 'The New Labor Paradigm' (1998) that 'the new rules of work and pay' in the US have become more market-sensitive. The new rules of work can be seen in the decline of private-sector unionization and in the growing numbers of temporary and part-time workers.

The new rules of pay include fewer long-term wage contracts, fewer indexation clauses tying wage adjustments to inflation, and much more profit-sharing, especially in competitive sectors such as trade-sensitive manufacturing and the deregulated transportation industries.

The consequences for American workers are (1) increased variability in pay and jobs; (2) greater reliance on portable pension mechanisms such as independent retirement accounts (IRAs); (3) the need for workers to maintain their skills for long-run employability, not necessarily with the same employer; and (4) a sharp increase in profit-sharing, a form of incentive-based compensation that is eclipsing fixed bonuses.

Does all this constitute a loss of ground for the US workforce? Not, writes Duca in 1998, when you compare its results to the alternatives in continental Europe and East Asia. The result of job-protection measures in the Big Three has been jobless growth. The result in Korea and Japan is that needed adjustments are delayed, grow more urgent, and require larger and more painful layoffs when reality finally takes hold.

The net effect for American workers is increased uncertainty in the short run, combined with increased employability in the long run, given the high rate of net job creation. In Duca's view, the same combination of short-run uncertainty and long-run employability can now also be seen in the UK.

Greenspan's Law

Duca's analysis thus complements the last chapter's account of the unbuffered intensity of the *ad hoc*, decentralized US system of adjustment.

The results are by now familiar: flexible labor markets, high rates of job creation and job destruction, limited loyalties as between companies and workers, and the shift from welfare entitlements to work requirements for the poor.

What softens these blows, in Duca's interpretation, is the New Economy's success as a job-generation machine. In practice virtually anyone who wanted to work in the US at the Millennium could find a job. Moreover, and despite the early 1990s stereotype, the second half of the decade saw rapid and broad-based gains in higher-paying managerial and professional positions (Zandi 1999).

We return, then, to the link between the two outcomes – that is, economic flexibility and job creation. As Alan Greenspan commented in January 2000: *'The greater the ability to fire people, the greater the willingness to hire people'* (Televised testimony before a Senate committee January 26, 2000).

Meantime, Duca writes, on the continent, instead of moving toward a more flexible labor regime, the Big Three are hoping the Euro will provide an 'elixir' to get them out of the high unemployment trap (Duca 1998).

WILL THE ECB STIFLE THE BOOM?

In the summer of 2000, unemployment rates in France, Germany and Italy still averaged about 10 percent. In the interests of defending a Euro that has plunged more than 20 percent against the dollar since its introduction in 1999, the European Central Bank (ECB) in Frankfurt had raised interest rates for the sixth time in a year. The reasoning advanced by ECB head Wim Duisenberg of the Netherlands was that the weak Euro threatened to raise inflation by raising the prices of imports.

This move threatened to choke off what appeared to be a boom in the making. After a decade of macroeconomic stagnation, the expansion seemed finally to have arrived. Indeed, the boom rested in part on the falling Euro itself, which made Zone exports cheap to the rest of the world.

Beyond such transitory influences, some analysts continued to predict a period of rapid GDP growth and falling unemployment – reflecting the benefits of a variety of structural reforms. In outline:

- Falling labor costs, in part in response to high unemployment, have meant that 'the euro zone countries may now be following the Anglo Saxon lead in pricing workers into employment' (Sam Brittan, 'A Brighter Prospect for Europe,' *Financial Times,* May 11, 2000).
- France and Germany were imposing major tax reforms.

- Virtually every Euro-zone nation has eliminated large central government deficits that, as in the US in the early 1990s, had in some cases reached 3 percent or more of GDP.
- Smaller northern economies are currently leapfrogging the US in wireless technology, which may redefine the IT pecking order.
- If realized, a replay of the US New-Economy scenario would cut costs by 5 percent for businesses generally and raise productivity growth by a percentage point toward recent US rates of about 2.5 percent (PriceWaterHouseCoopers, May 2000).
- As to corporate governance, the British telecommunication company Vodafone's takeover of Germany's Mannesman in early-2000 symbolized an increase in management accountability to shareholders. The message seemed to be that EU managers would have to increase profitability or face hostile takeovers.

Such straws in the wind appear to add up to a more entrepreneurial Europe, in which even such intangibles as the migration of professionals across national boundaries to live and work may diminish cultural inhibitions and unlock creative energies.

In any case, the ambivalence of the Big Three toward unbridled market forces stems in part from the messiness of the American model. This aversion may seem more plausible, once we take a closer look at the rearrangement of US manufacturing in the 1970s and 1980s.

NOTES

1. Germany's policy of wage uniformity had a curious precedent in the politics of theUS minimum wage law, enacted half a century earlier. In the New Deal climate of the late 1930s, a minimum-wage law sounded like a good idea. But the regional politics of the legislation had a devious logic. Fearing erosion of manufacturing jobs to the Southeast (especially in textiles, which had been shifting out of New England from about 1890 on), congressional forces from the North pushed for a uniform national standard. They saw that if the South, with its lower productivities, had the same wage floor as the North, employers would have less reason to move south.

    Northern interests prevailed. The minimum wage was introduced as a nationally uniform rate, shoring up the industrial base of the high-wage states of the Manufacturing Belt. But this was far from the end of the story. Dampening the low-wage industrialization of the South had another effect. After World War II, as black workers were displaced in growing numbers from southern farms, there were fewer new factory jobs available in the South. The upshot was that more blacks and whites alike joined the large-scale migration to northern factories in the late 1940s, a decade after the nationwide minimum wage took effect.

11. New-wave industrialization

> Unfortunately, those who gained these new construction jobs [in the US cities of the 1850s] were usually not those who had been driven off their farms. (Fogel 2000, p. 55-6)

The drive for improved productivity in the 1970s and 1980s destroyed millions of manufacturing jobs, but it created as many as it destroyed (see Figures 11.1 and 11.2). In a telling and convenient statistical oddity, *the job count for US manufacturing was 19.7 million in 1990, the same as it had been 20 years earlier, in 1970.*

This chapter draws two lessons from the record of manufacturing job changes in the US between 1970 and 1990. The first is diagnostic. We consider a regional explanation for the resilience of US manufacturing employment.

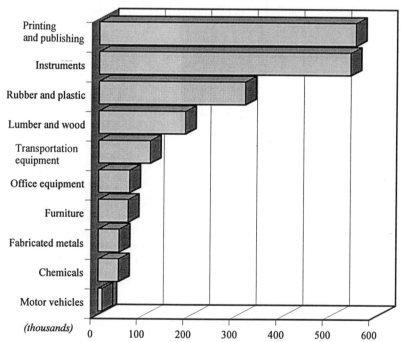

Source: US Department of Commerce, Bureau of Economic Analysis machine-readable SA25 data.

Figure 11.1 1.9 million jobs added by job-gaining sectors in US manufacturing, 1970-1990, just offset

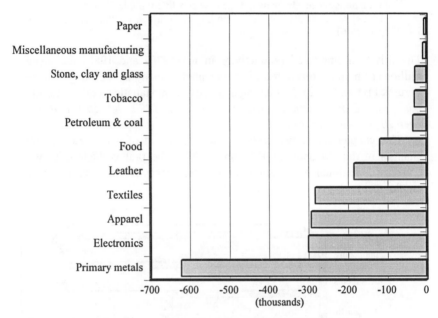

Figure 11.2 1.9 million jobs lost in declining sectors, 1970-1990

The second, more subjective lesson is that Creative Destruction is a realistic label for the harshness of what happened across American regions. The new manufacturing employment sprang up in new places, far from the cities and regions that lost jobs. The adjustment process by which the Manufacturing Belt reached a new equilibrium required workers to leave the region in search of jobs elsewhere (Blanchard and Katz 1992).

SOMETHING LOST, SOMETHING GAINED

Regionally, 2.4 million manufacturing jobs were lost by the Manufacturing Belt (the North) from 1970 to 1990. And the same number, 2.4 million, were gained by the South and West. Was the regional balancing-act only a sterile redistribution of the same jobs from one address to another? Or did the leveling-up of jobs from more to less industrial regions also spark a transformation of the US industrial base?

To structure the issue, we can pose the question as a stylized experiment. The null hypothesis (H_o) is that 'the North's losses were the periphery's gain.'

This rhetorical formulation was sometimes heard back in the Sunbelt-Snowbelt confrontation, the 'Second War between the States' of the 1970s. It implied a hand-me-down or product-cycle scattering of mature jobs, bid away from the high-cost North by job-hungry, union-busting states in the South and West. For that matter, the variables tested in Chapter 9 could be interpreted in these terms.

The alternative hypothesis (H_a) is that *the South and West's gains were mainly in jobs new to the economy as a whole.* If this proves a more accurate reading – and it does – the implication is that the industrialization of younger regions around new industries upgraded the US manufacturing base.

THREE TRANSFORMATIONS

Beneath the surface stability of the count for US manufacturing employ-ment from 1970 to 1990 were three major crosscurrents of rapid turnover and change. The first (and mildest) found non-production jobs replacing production jobs. The second was sectoral, between job-adding and job-losing activities. The third, as already noted, was geographical, between regions of the nation that lost jobs and those that gained them.

(1) Non-Production Jobs Replaced Production Jobs, 1970-1990

Figure 11.3, compiled from a different, Bureau of Labor Statistics (BLS) data series, shows the levels of both total and production employment, 1950-90. As before, it finds total manufacturing employment in 1990 at about the same level as in 1970 (by this BLS series, just over 19 million). But it also shows that production employment was down one million in 1990 relative to 1970. For context, over the 40 years, 1950-90, the level of production employment in the US ranged from a low of 12.1 million in 1961 to a high of 15.1 million in 1979.

As an aside, office or administrative jobs (of the kind eliminated in droves by re-engineering in the early 1990s) grew by a million or more each decade between the 1950s and the 1970s. That is, production jobs increased by 1.7 million, 1950-80, but office and supervisory jobs grew by twice as much, 3.4 million jobs.

Figure 11.4 shows one reason for the slight decline in production workers after 1970, that is, a doubling of manufacturing productivity per

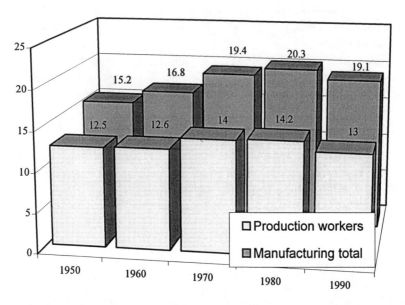

Sources: 1950-80 data from the US Bureau of Labor Statistics, *Handbook of Labor Statistics*
August 1989, pp. 290, 292; 1990 data from US Bureau of Labor Statistics, *Employment and
Earnings*, August 1992, p. 12

*Figure 11.3 Deindustrialization? US manufacturing employment held steady,
              1970-1990, while production employment was down one million*

worker. Output doubled and employment remained about the same over the
20-year period, 1970-90. That implies an average compound productivity
growth of some 3.5 percent a year.

The slowdown in US productivity growth and in living standards after
1973 thus emanated from sectors other than manufacturing. The
manufacturing sector as a whole rebounded from the 1970s (when job
growth surged and productivity lagged) to come back strongly in the 1980s.

(2) Expanding Sectors Made Up for Declining Sectors.

As noted at the outset, Figures 11.1 and 11.2 portray the numerical balance
as between 'winners' and 'losers' among industry groups. From among the
21 two-digit SIC (Standard Industrial Classification) categories covering the
manufacturing sector, the number of jobs gained in the sectors adding jobs
(1,934,600) just offset the number lost in job-losing sectors (1,887,000).

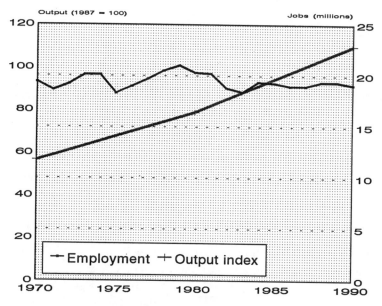

Note: Index value rose from 56.4 in 1970 to 109.9 in 1990.
Source: Statistical Abstract (1992, Table 1252).

Figure 11.4 Manufacturing output doubled, 1970-1990, while manufacturing employment remained unchanged

What sectors had the largest numerical gains? Figure 11.1 shows that printing and instruments each had over 500,000 new jobs.

Printing-and-publishing benefited from some measure of insulation from international competition by virtue of the kind of face-to-face interaction among suppliers and customers that makes it more like a service activity than most manufacturing lines. In contrast, other job-adding groups such as instruments, transportation equipment, office equipment (the two-digit category that included computers), and chemicals are high-tech, export-oriented sectors.

As Figure 11.2 reveals, mature industries dominated the US sectors losing employment. Steel (included in 'primary metals') plummeted by 600,000 jobs. The ancient trio of leather, textiles, and apparel together lost about one million. Thus three-quarters of the nearly two million jobs lost in shrinking sectors came from the activities that were among the hallmarks of the nation's nineteenth-century industrialization.

Other job-losing two-digit categories had diverse stories. Consumer electronics had notorious trade vulnerability *vis-à-vis* Japan. Tobacco processing had the Surgeon General's Report to contend with. Food processing and petroleum and coal products had other stories, the first having to do with mechanization and leveraged buyouts, the second with cycles in commodity prices.

But the conclusion remains clear. Industry maturity explains much of the employment losses in the manufacturing sector over the period of accelerated trade competition, 1970-90.

(3) Gains in the South and West Offset Losses in the North

Where precisely did the new two million jobs spring up? Half the states had job gains in manufacturing in each of the three decades, 1960-90. As Figure 11.5 shows, this included most of the states in the South and West, along with Wisconsin. The net effect found 1970-90 gains in virtually every state in the South and West – and in two-thirds (34) of the states in all.

Where were job losses concentrated? The Mid-Atlantic and East North Central states (save only Wisconsin), along with Connecticut, Rhode Island, West Virginia, and Maryland: these 11 contiguous states lost manufacturing jobs in fair weather and foul, in the bi-coastal eighties as well as in the Sunbelt seventies. In short: the Manufacturing Belt, outside New England.

NEW INDUSTRIES THRIVED IN YOUNGER REGIONS

Were the South and West's gains at the expense of the North, or were their increases new to the economy as a whole? The answer can be gleaned from the sector-by-sector performance of each of the two mega-regions.

We can begin with the North. Perhaps most striking are the losses the North incurred in the six sectors that *added jobs nationwide* (see Figure 11.6). Office equipment, including computers (down 300,000), transportation equipment (partly aircraft), and chemicals: these three were major export sectors in which the North as a whole failed to add employment. On the other hand, the Manufacturing Belt did gain jobs over the 20-year period in four of the ten US growth sectors.[1]

As for the sectors that shrank nationwide, the Manufacturing Belt had losses in all 11 categories, typically sharper than the total US losses (see Figure 11.7). Another hard-hit sector, paced perhaps by the absence of population growth, was food-processing, whose losses exceeded those even for textiles or apparel.

In contrast, the South and West added jobs in every US job-gaining sector, usually by more than the total US gain (see Figure 11.8). In a number of expanding sectors nationally, the balance was struck by losses in

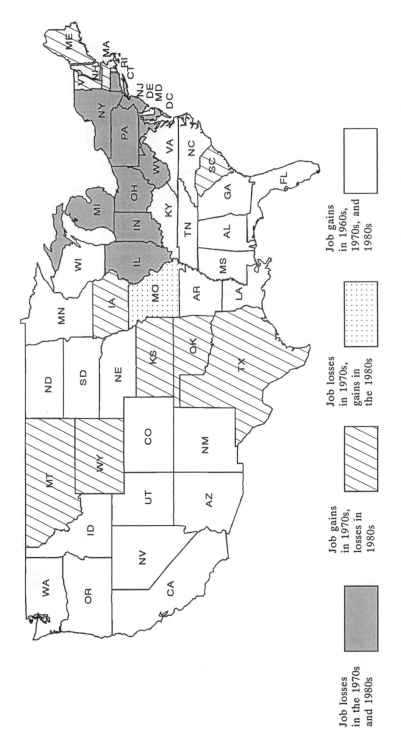

Figure 11.5 Deindustrialization? Half the states added manufacturing jobs every decade, 1960-1990

Job losses
in the 1970s and 1980s

Job gains
in 1970s,
losses in
1980s

Job losses
in 1970s,
gains in
the 1980s

Job gains
in 1960s,
1970s, and
1980s

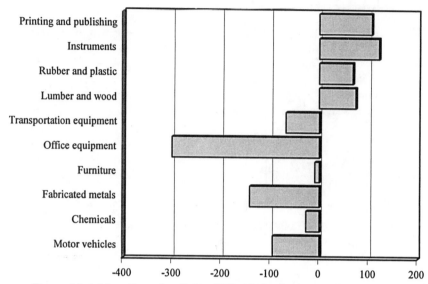

*Figure 11.6 Manufacturing Belt: 1970-1990 job changes (000) in
manufacturing sectors that added jobs nationwide*

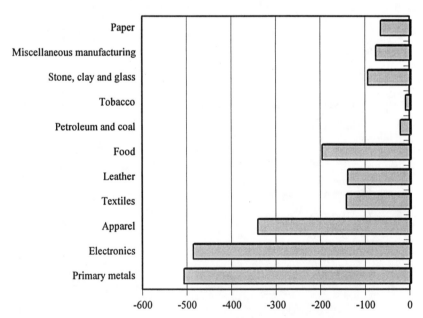

*Figure 11.7 Manufacturing Belt: 1970-1990 job changes (000) in
manufacturing sectors that lost jobs nationwide*

the North, as outweighed by larger gains elsewhere. Such was the pattern for transportation equipment (including aircraft, the key export item), office equipment, chemicals, and motor vehicles as well as the less glamorous fabricated metals and furniture.

An example of the regional dynamic at work to redistribute manufacturing south and west is motor vehicles, which defied expectation and added jobs nationwide over the interval. One reason: principally Japanese 'trans-plants' were sited largely in the mid-South, infrequently in the North. Their impact on job growth was thus to shift jobs away from Detroit.

The stereotypical (null-hypothesis) pattern of the North's losses registering as gains in the South and West showed up in only three sectors (see Figure 11.9). These were paper products, miscellaneous manufacturing (including jewelry), and stone-clay-and-glass. Each had gains above 50,000 jobs in the South and West, which nearly matched the number lost in the North. By contrast, in a few sectors (food, apparel, and electronics-except-computers), gains in the South and West were swamped by much larger losses in the North, a pattern at odds with the null hypothesis.[2]

GAINS . . .

Figure 11.10 focuses the issue. It shows that some 90 percent (2.1 million) of the 2.4 million jobs lost by the North were jobs in sectors that lost jobs economy-wide. Nor did the North register gains in the nation's expanding sectors, where declines equaled 270,000 jobs.

As to the South and West, 2.2 million of its 2.4 million gain were in the sectors that added jobs nationwide. Less than 200,000 of the net gains outside the North came in industries that were losing jobs in the US as a whole. In only three sectors (paper, miscellaneous, and stone-clay-and-glass) do we find evidence supporting the null hypothesis, 'the North's loss was the periphery's gain.'

The upshot is that for the younger economies of the South and West, manufacturing jobs were 'created,' not 'stolen' from the mature North. With minor exceptions like paper products or stone-clay-glass, job growth in the South and West was new to the economy. Putting it the other way around, *most of the jobs lost in the North were lost by the economy as a whole.* And nearly all the new manufacturing jobs added in growing sectors sprang up in the South and West.

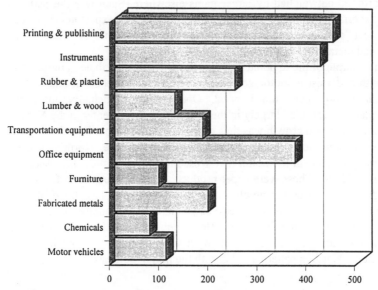

Figure 11.8 The South and West: 1970-1990 job changes (000) in manufacturing sectors that gained jobs nationwide

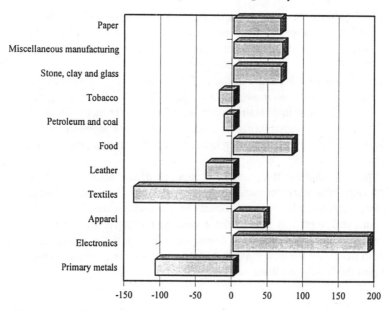

Figure 11.9 The South and West: 1970-1990 job changes (000) in manufacturing sectors that lost jobs nationwide

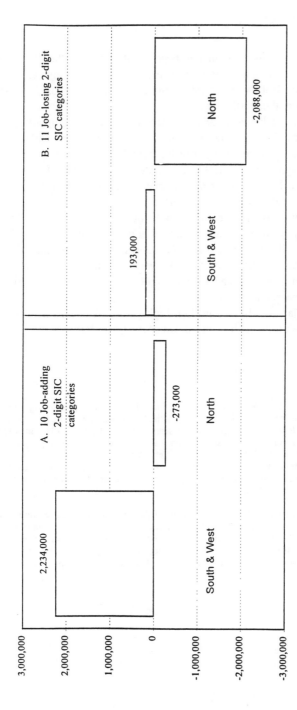

Figure 11.10 South and West gains were almost all in US job-adding sectors: the North lost manufacturing jobs even in US job-adding sectors

. . . AND LOSSES

The emphasis in this account has been on the success the US industrial system had in maintaining aggregate manufacturing employment over the period 1970-90. But the down side is the 2.4 million jobs lost in job-losing industries and in the North as a region.

Calls in the 1970s and 1980s for protectionism by companies, unions, and politicians in the now resurgent Rust Belt were understandable responses to the geographically driven renewal of the industrial system. The issues arose again in the 1990s in connection with NAFTA (the North American Free Trade Agreement), as manufacturing employment declined in the US and rose in Mexico and Canada.

Looking back, both the pain of job dislocation and the value of renewal – if necessary, in new regions – can be understood in theory as Creative Destruction. Still, that was of little interest to the people injured by economic change. Their ranks would swell in the early 1990s as the transformation would spread to white-collar managers and technicians in Fortune 500 companies.

In particular, nearly two million high-paid defense workers would be stripped of their jobs by the wind-down of the Cold War.

NOTES

1. The example of SIC 37, office equipment, including computer production, points up the limits of our methods. Our charts show only the before-and-after totals for 1970 and 1990. Within this interval, New England had descended to the depths in 1975, then rebounded apace with the minicomputer surge along Route 128 that generated thousands of new manufacturing jobs by 1984, then collapsed yet again when the mini-makers failed to get on board the PC train. Where does any of this show up in our charts? Only in aggregate, Belt-wide losses of 300,000 lost jobs in SIC 37, a category in which computer employment was itself only one component.

2. An anomaly is textiles. This is an old industry that had long since gone South, but which now suffered job losses in the South as a result of intense foreign competition, which accelerated in the high-dollar early 1980s. Textiles is thus frequently cited as an example to be avoided in the annals of economic development: a cheap-labor industry, which can therefore be out-competed by East Asian plants of whatever ownership.

12. End game: downsizing defense

> Every gun that is made, every warship launched, every rocket fired signifies, in the final sense, a theft from those who hunger and are not fed, those who are cold and are not clothed. This world in arms is not spending money alone. It is spending the sweat of its laborers, the genius of its scientists, the hopes of its children. (President Eisenhower in a speech in Washington, DC, 16 April 1953, near the end of the Korean War, cited in Augarde 1991, p. 73)

The Cold-War economy can be dated from 1939 to 1989 (Chapter 6). Over that 50-year span military priorities justified (1) a fiscal policy marked by routine federal budget deficits and (2) implicit technology and industrial policies of the kind that spawned the Interstate Highway System, the space program, and ARPAnet.

By the same token, the end of the Cold War after 1989 rekindled the stagnationist suspicions both Marxists and also many Keynesians had long entertained about American capitalism. And Japan was in the passing lane.

To that extent, defense conversion provided a test case as to how well firms, regions, and the US economy could adapt to exogenous shocks.

And shock it was. Defense spending in the US as a share of GDP fell from 6.4 to 3.9 percent from 1987 to 1995. In those same years US defense employment plummeted from 3.9 to 2.1 million, a loss of nearly two million high-paying jobs (Grant 1997, p. 5).

This chapter tells how defense conversion happened in practice. But we should begin by noting both global and historical contexts.

DEFENSE CONVERSION AS INDUSTRIAL EVOLUTION

A good definition of defense conversion appeared in the 1996 annual report of the Bonn International Center for Conversion (BICC). Comparing the US experience to that of other nations, the BICC team (led by Project Director Michael Brzoska) got at the core economic meaning of conversion, that is, resource reallocation:

> Disarmament and conversion are now occurring, not only in the former cold war alliances but also in countries throughout the world, on a large scale. Between the mid-1980s and the mid-1990s disarmament took place at an exceptional pace; the rate is comparable only to the drawdown after such major conflicts as World Wars I and II. With the consequent reduced use of military resources, *conversion – the civilian reuse of these resources –* has been transformed from a largely utopian project into a combination of practical problem and potential opportunity. (BICC 1996, on-line summary, p. 1, emphasis added)

Everywhere, observes BICC, the resource reallocation occurred on a massive scale. Global defense-industry employment peaked at nearly 18 million workers in 1987 and had fallen to below 11 million by 1995. Over the period 1987-94 trade in major conventional weapons was cut in half from over $46 billion to below $22 billion (both in constant 1990 dollars). Thus the US conversion experience was but one (and perhaps not the most wrenching) among many around the world.

Defense-conversion can be viewed as part of the larger panorama of US industrial history. Like earlier episodes it entailed the freeing up of economic resources from declining to growing activities. As the last few chapters have emphasized, the pain and progress of such transitions (out of textiles and then steel, and from the farm to the city) are a pervasive theme in American development. In other words, the US experience of demilitarization was part of a time-honored pattern – *out with the old, in with the new.*

As with more market-based US phase-outs, the story unfolded on a continental scale. Just as the upper Midwest bore the brunt of Japan's competitive challenges in cars and steel, defense cuts hit hardest in the most defense-dependent states.

California, Connecticut, Massachusetts, and New York absorbed hammer blows that turned the mild national recession of 1990-91 into regionalized five-year stagnations (see Figure 12.1). By 1997, however, both California and the Northeast had fully adapted and resumed job growth apace with the national average. At the Millennium, *the most striking thing about differences in regional job growth was their absence.* For the first time in decades, in other words, employment growth in every region approximated the US rate.

But just what did happen to wean individual state economies from defense dependency? In particular, did big defense firms learn how to compete in the civilian market?

As a caveat, to pose the question in these stark terms is to lose sight of the dual orientation of Boeing, GE, and similar companies that have traditionally served both military and civilian markets.

Still, for more specialized defense companies the issue was fairly clear. Could firms used to producing on a cost-plus basis for a largely captive market leave it behind for the hurly-burly of competition? The challenge, conceptually, was new-product development.

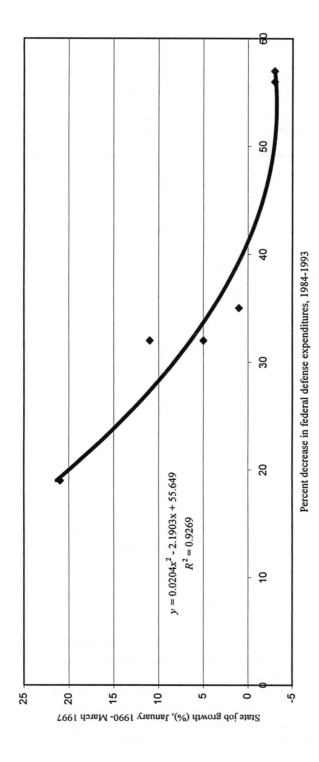

$y = 0.0204x^2 - 2.1903x + 55.649$

$R^2 = 0.9269$

Percent decrease in federal defense expenditures, 1984-1993

State job growth (%), January 1990- March 1997

Source: Based on data from Hansen 1997 (p. 122).

Figure 12.1 Defense cutbacks and state job growth in the 1990s (descending: Texas, Missouri, California, Massachusetts, New York, Connecticut)

THEORY: HOW DIVERSIFIED FIRMS MOVE FORWARD

A similar question arises routinely in the civilian sector within conglomerate or multi-product companies (see Figure 12.2). It can be illustrated

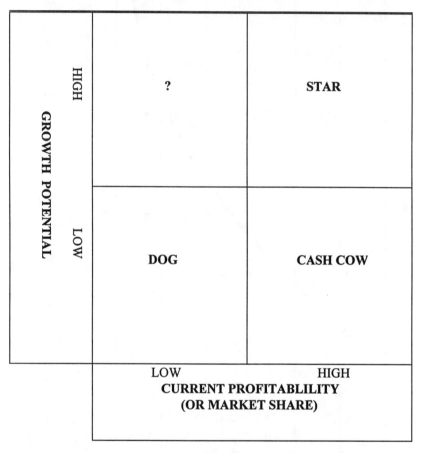

Figure 12.2 The product-portfolio approach to strategic planning

with the Boston Consulting Group's (BCG) product-portfolio matrix, which
arrays products according to two criteria: current profitability (or, in a variant,
market share) and growth outlook.

Products that rank high on both counts are 'stars,' low on both are
'dogs.'   Products low on profitability but high on growth are 'question
marks,' in that the question arises whether to invest in the new product
heavily enough to reap the future gain.   One source of funds for such

investment is the 'cash cow,' typically a mature product throwing off profits and requiring little investment but offering limited growth potential.

Then four strategies that can be pursued are (1) *build* the question mark by investing in it, (2) *hold* cash cows and stars, (3) *harvest* all but the stars by ceasing investment in them and milking them for cash, and then (4) *divest* dogs and cash cows (O'Brien 1996, p. 173).

Reference to the BCG model brings up a profound change in attitudes about the need to move from stagnant to growing activities. Some 20 years ago Barry Bluestone and Bennett Harrison decried such logic as leading to *The Deindustrialization of America*. But in a dramatic reversal of his similar views (as given in Chapter 7), Lester Thurow has more recently declared, 'The American system was built to open up the new and close down the old. That is what it does best' (1999, p. 54).

GE: THE STANDARD – AND THE EXCEPTION

When Jack Welch as Chief Executive Officer (CEO) of GE decided in the early 1980s to strip the company of 'non-performing' product lines, his thinking paralleled that depicted in Figure 12.2. His ruthless and prescient decision rule was to jettison any product lines from among the 350 at GE that could not realistically compete as the number one or two products in their respective industries (Slater 1999).

To the dismay of workers and communities GE shut down dogs and harvested cash cows in a strategy devoted only to the creation and support of stars, cutting the GE workforce from 412,000 to 229,000. Plants that may have been making respectable profits were nevertheless shut down as part of the shift to faster-growing services.

For GE, then, unloading some of its defense lines and moving on was no great challenge. By 1999, 41 percent of GE's total profits of $10.7 billion came from GE Capital, a financing agency, and another hefty chunk from NBC, a television network (Murray 2000). The result has been to elevate GE's market capitalization to second (behind only Microsoft) at the end of 1999.

As Thurow observes, the strategy has made GE the great exception to the rule among mature US companies, the only one of the 12 largest US corporations in 1900 still around in 2000 (Thurow 1999, p. 24). Nor was GE a model that more specialized defense companies like Raytheon managed to emulate.

REGIONAL ADJUSTMENT: THREE PATHS

Generalizing from product-portfolio analysis, three broad channels of conversion (or structural modernization) are open to any region. Within a region's existing firms (for example, defense contractors), existing products can be produced more efficiently with new processes, or shopped to new markets (for example, abroad). Or such firms can 'convert,' meaning develop new products for civilian markets. Finally, the region's new or small firms can innovate and expand to fill the void left by downsized defense firms.

Putting it differently:

1. Established firms can do the same thing as before, only better ('trying harder'), to claim a larger slice of a shrinking pie, or to find new markets abroad.
2. Established firms can convert to new products.
3. New firms can do new things.

Figure 12.3 portrays these channels in a diagram. The conversion or upgrading processes can be traced down from the national level to the regional. For the nation as a whole the conversion can take place as an adjustment from a declining to a growing region, as profiled in Chapter 11.

Figure 12.3 Channels of structural adaptation

Here our focus is on adjustment with a given region. We can label the channels (1), (2), or (3) in the diagram, to match the possibilities just described.

(1) Trying Harder in the Midwest . . .

A good civilian example of the first channel is the Midwest comeback in the 1990s. The explanation is the resurgence of agriculture and of a reinvigorated US auto complex, spearheaded by the traditional (post-makeover – and, for Chrysler, post-takeover) Big Three. As with half the nation's regions, the Upper Midwest experienced minimal dislocations from defense cutbacks after 1989 because the region was less defense-dependent during the Cold War. In part for this reason, the erstwhile Rust Belt matched the US average in job growth between 1990 and 1997, adding nearly 3 million jobs (see Chapter 3).

At first glance, the story of the Midwest comeback is 'the more things change, the more they stay the same.' Yet that would be too simple. In particular, while the region in 1996 had four more auto plants (31) than it had had in 1979, the increase came about as 13 new plants more than offset the nine plants that closed (Testa et al. 1997).

In this Darwinian adaptation the technologies and organization of the work flow in the new plants bear little resemblance to what had gone before. The region's watchword in the 1990s was *lean manufacturing*. In other words, the comeback took place only after a transformation over the past generation, as marked in part by the adoption of Japanese techniques and practices.

. . . and Abroad

'Trying harder' was also one of the responses by defense companies to federal cutbacks over the past decade. The defense-sector equivalent of the Midwest comeback is the quest for new export markets. The historical pattern finds the US trying harder to export its weapons after a hot war or military buildup, as in the Reagan years (Mirmirani and Li 1997). With the Cold War's end, US arms exports expanded during the 1990s, a practice official policy endorsed as job-saving. For better or worse, US defense firms had striking success in the arms bazaar. In a world arms market that was cut in half between 1987 and 1995, US companies claimed some 70 percent of world arms exports by mid-decade.

By 1995, American firms thus dominated the list of the world's top 20 defense companies. As Table 12.1 shows, Lockheed in California, Boeing in Washington, and Raytheon in Massachusetts each had more than $10 billion in defense revenues. That placed them at numbers 1-3 in the top 20 list, where they were joined by eight other US firms.

Table 12.1 US defense firms led the global list in 1995

	Company	Country or HQ state	1995 Defense revenues ($bn)
1	**Lockheed Martin**	**Maryland**	19.4
2	**Boeing/McDonnell Douglas**	**Washington**	17.9
3	**Raytheon/Hughes/TI**	**Massachusetts**	11.7
4	British Aerospace	Britain	6.5
5	**Northrop Grumman**	**California**	5.7
6	Thomson	France	4.7
7	Aerospatiale/Dassault	France	4.2
8	GEC	Britain	4.1
9	**United Technologies**	**Connecticut**	3.7
10	Lagardere Groupe	France	3.3
11	Daimler-Benz Aerospace	Germany	3.3
12	Direction des Constructions Navales	France	3.1
13	**General Dynamics**	**Virginia**	2.9
14	Finmeccanica	Italy	2.6
15	**Litton Industries**	**California**	2.4
16	Mitsubishi Heavy Industries	Japan	2.2
17	**General Electric**	**New York**	2.2
18	**Tenneco**	**Connecticut**	1.8
19	**TRW**	**Ohio**	1.7
20	**ITT Industries**	**New York**	1.6

Note: State headquarters locations have been added by author.
Source: Defense News, as reported in the *Economist* (June 14, 1997, p. 4).

(2) Did Defense Firms Convert?

In the second channel of regional conversion, existing firms can shift to new product and service lines. Despite many such attempts and much publicity, there is scant evidence of defense firms changing their spots. On the whole, *conversion did not happen for large defense firms.*

As Anthony J. Marolda (1997, p. 32) has written, in 'Commercialization of Defense Technology: The Key Success Factors':

> After many years of working with defense companies of all sizes, and conducting two national surveys of the defense industry on the subject of

commercialization and conversion, we concluded that is not possible for a company of significant size that is primarily in the defense business to convert to primarily nondefense businesses.

At the same time, what may be possible even for large defense companies is gradually to diversify into commercial product lines that draw upon the companies' core competencies. In the 1997 study, Marolda drew on the two national surveys he conducted to define the 'key success factors' (p. 43). These included

1. a technology base that lends itself to commercial applications,
2. strong support by top management,
3. an overseeing task force representing diverse viewpoints,
4. adequate resources to deliver on the entire chain of commercialization.

By this more modest standard, Marolda found that one in four defense firms had managed by 1991 to spawn successful commercial products from defense technologies. While an update might find a higher proportion, Marolda's point remains convincing. 'Conversion' in any economically interesting sense does not typically happen within firms.

(3) Place Conversion via New Firms

The third and critical conversion channel is *the birth or attraction of new firms and the expansion of firms in other sectors*. A vivid illustration of the shift from defense to commercial activities can be found in Charleston, South Carolina. After the closing of a naval base and shipyard there in 1993 (that is, after the city had survived the first couple of rounds of cutbacks), Charleston lost 8,000 civilian jobs. It has since gained 6,000 new ones from the 40 companies that have moved to Charleston to take advantage of base-conversion inducements local officials put together in response to the crisis (Shenon 1997).

START-UPS AND INNOVATION IN THE COLD WAR

For that matter, even during the height of the Cold-War era, new firms had played a decisive role.

Initially the priorities of the Cold War economy seemed well served by the corporate R&D lab. In practice if not formally, what emerged was a de facto US industrial policy in which Pentagon research contracts had civilian spillover effects that led to new products and processes.

That this apparent synergy was only partial and temporary is clear from a recent history of twentieth-century US innovation. According to Mowery and Rosenberg, 'In some key technologies, such as aircraft, semiconductors, and computers, defense-related R&D investments during the 1950s generated important technological "spillovers" from military to civilian applications' (Mowery and Rosenberg 1998, p. 34).

In microelectronics and jet engines, they observed, performance requirements remained 'generic' for both military and civilian uses, and spillovers from military to civilian uses continued to occur in the 1960s. A notable exception was software, a field in which few spillovers from military to civilian applications occurred.

For a variety of reasons, small firms added energy to the mechanism by which Pentagon spillovers helped spark new industries:

> In industries that effectively did not exist before 1940, such as computers and biotechnology, major innovations were commercialized largely through the efforts of new firms. These postwar US industries differ from their counterparts in Japan and most Western European economies. . . . The significant technological contributions made by large firms in semiconductors, for example, were not matched by their role in commercializing these technologies. . . . *start-up firms have been far more active in commercializing new technologies in the United States than in other industrial economies.* . . . (Mowery and Rosenberg 1998, p. 41, emphasis added)

The authors attribute the greater prominence of start-ups in the US to four factors (pp. 42-3), which I summarize as follows:

1. A pattern of military procurement that especially in the 1950s and 1960s contributed to the formation of high-tech start-ups.
2. The restrictive US antitrust climate, which lowered entry barriers to smaller firms, mandating licensing of technical information by such established firms as IBM and AT&T.
3. The number and diversity of research centers in universities and government as well as industry – any of which might see an employee leave to capitalize on a discovery.
4. Venture capital, as invented by American Research and Development (ARD) in Boston in 1945.

On all four counts the US Cold War system of innovation proved more stimulating and supportive of new and young firms than the environments of Japan or Europe. And the last two – the abundance of research centers and the sophistication of venture capita – would outlive the Cold War as incubating influences.

THE GUNBELT THESIS

Some observers linked the geography of city and regional growth to the pattern of Cold War R&D, procurement, and military-base expenditures. An early journalistic account was that of Kirkpatrick Sale, in *Power Shift* (1975). Similarly, in *Cities and the Wealth of Nations*, Jane Jacobs observed, 'In the meantime, the Sun Belt cities of the South and West have been rising, and this would be all to the good, except that in large part their economic bases consist of military production . . .'   (1984, p. 179).

Such ad hoc theorizing was superseded in 1991 by a full-blown treatise, *The Rise of the Gunbelt: The Military Remapping of Industrial America* (Markusen et al. 1991). Referring to the creation of the military-industrial complex in the 1950s, the authors comment, 'Its geographical manifestation was the meteoric rise and sustained dominance of the gunbelt – the stretch from New England down the Atlantic Seaboard, across the central states, and into the lower Mountain and Pacific regions' (p. 25). The region they saw left out was the industrial Midwest, 'a fact that proved a significant element in its decline after 1970' (p. 25).

The Transition, as in Seattle

Whatever its merits, the limitations of the gunbelt thesis can be seen in chapter 7 of the book, 'Seattle: Aerospace Company City' (Markusen et al. 1991). The phrase 'company city' updates the traditional term, 'company town,' to describe the Seattle economy's dependence on Boeing. In retrospect, at least, it is striking to read an account of Seattle published in 1991 that makes no mention whatsoever of Microsoft. (Neither Bill Gates nor Microsoft appears in the book's index.)

Ironically, then, the gunbelt thesis underscores the shift in the US economy's wellsprings of growth and innovation with the end of the Cold War. Either Microsoft at the beginning of the 1990s was too minor a player to mention in an account of Seattle's economy, or it represented an anomaly not easily covered by the thesis.

ENTREPRENEURIAL IMPACTS: THREE CASE STUDIES

For a closer look at the third channel of conversion, the expansion of new and small businesses, we turn now to case studies on Virginia, Texas, and California. Together they bear out Marolda's conclusion. The hardest-hit states adapted to the new order not via adjustments by established firms, but through the rise of smaller businesses in high-growth civilian sectors of the economy.

Northern Virginia's Privatized Prosperity

We can begin by noting a surprising 'backwash effect' that followed from defense cutbacks: a recentralization in the National Capital area of some administrative functions. Re-centralization happened as much in Virginia as in Washington, DC, itself. The state was already home not only to the Newport News shipbuilding complex in the Hampton Roads-Norfolk region of tidewater Virginia but also to the Pentagon, across the Potomac from Washington. The local geography of the recentralized activity has been largely suburban, in Northern Virginia (Haynes et al. 1997).

Often work formerly done within federal agencies was outsourced to private contractors (including some former government employees), partly to convey the impression of tight control over federal government employment growth. It appears that some of this seemingly cosmetic privatization may have indeed triggered increased competition and an entrepreneurial boom in Fairfax County, Virginia.

The entrepreneurial stimulus to the National Capital region was redoubled by the rapid ascent in the 1990s of America On-Line and MCI to the commanding heights of the world's Internet and telecommunications sectors. Each is headquartered in Northern Virginia. The result has been to catapult the region to a newfound prominence in the nation's IT landscape. By late 1999, in fact, some observers were declaring it to be part of an elite trinity, matched in the US only by Silicon Valley and Route 128.

Texas: From Defense Electronics to PCs

The key to Texas's successful conversion has been the continuing and rapid transformation of Texas from a resource-dependent to an information-based economy (Hansen 1997). Texas's high-tech prowess used to be symbolized by the semiconductor firm Texas Instruments. Today it is summed up by the state's primacy in PCs. The world's top two PC companies are Dell (Round Rock, in the Austin area) and Compaq (Houston). Unlike Texas Instruments, neither traces its expansion to military spending. Instead, each originated with classic (and civilian) entrepreneurial types, Rod Canion (who did, to be sure, leave TI to found Compaq) and Michael Dell, who started Dell out of his college dorm room.

Between the private sector's rapid job growth and the coordinated planning efforts of the state and local governments, dislocated defense workers faced good odds for reconnecting with the growing economy.

But was Texas's conversion success typical of experiences elsewhere in the nation? The answer seems to be yes. Studies by the Congressional Budget Office showed that from 97 bases closed (out of 495 total operating in 1988), relatively few communities or regions suffered much from the closings (Shenon 1997). This finding, Shenon observes, was also reported by a Rand Corporation study of California, a state that registered nearly two-thirds of all lost jobs from US base closings.

As that statistic suggests, California's conversion experience was a story unto itself.

California: The Paths from Aerospace to Infotainment

In 'California's Recovery and the Restructuring of the Defense Industries,' Luis Suarez-Villa (1997) analysed the state's surprisingly strong mid-decade rebound from the doldrums of the early 1990s. How important was conversion by defense firms in fostering that recovery? He concludes that it was not a factor. 'Rather, California's recovery was a product of the upswing in the national economy, which boosted demand for many of the state's products, and of *the rise of many small and medium-sized firms in a few. . . very dynamic sectors . . .*' (p. 90, emphasis added). The growth industries included commercial high technology, wholesale trade, the film industry, and producer services.

Suarez-Villa noted three paths open to California's defense contractors as the decade opened: downsizing, mergers with other defense firms, and diversification into commercial activities. Downsizing (as illustrated by job cuts of about 50 percent each by such giants as McDonnell Douglas, TRW, and Lockheed Martin) was all but universal as a response. Also common was the merger route, as taken by Lockheed and General Dynamics (Space Division), Lockheed and Martin Marietta, and Northrop and Grumman.

The level at which 'conversion' occurred in California was therefore less within defense firms than via *the market-based recycling of technical talent from defense companies to more entrepreneurial firms*. This process is symbolized by California's striking share (25 percent) of all the nation's firms that doubled in size between 1989 and 1994.

The conclusion? Conversion occurred not within firms but through the rise of new enterprises and the expansion of existing non-defense sectors. In other words, what may look like conversion at the level of the firm was typically some constructed mix of downsizing, mergers, and acquisitions.

Instead, conversion occurred as workers were released from downsized defense firms and re-employed in expanding civilian activities. Figure 12.4 provides a vivid illustration of such conversion, as it happened in the real world. The figure shows that between 1988 and 1997 entertainment employment in Los Angeles County ultimately expanded by enough to offset losses in the area's defense sector. More specifically, some high-skilled workers released from defense activities wound up finding high-paid jobs in the entertainment sector (Pollack 1997).

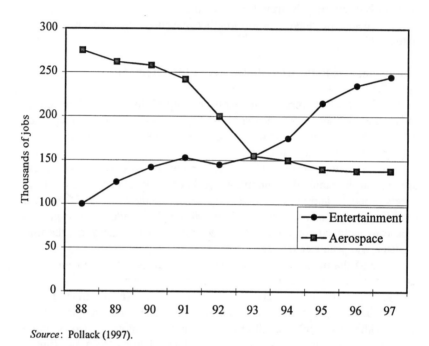

Source: Pollack (1997).

Figure 12.4 Conversion: from aerospace to entertainment employment in Los Angeles County

CONCLUSION

In sum, one reason for the US resurgence during the 1990s was the nation's success in moving beyond its entrenched military-industrial complex to more bountiful orchards. In the difficult and anxiety-ridden first half of the 1990s, the US economy completed a painful but effective escape from the Cold-War economy.

   Two lessons to be learned from the experience are (1) the resilience and dynamism of the US economy and (2) the inability of specialized defense companies to convert to civilian markets. If we were to generalize: *changing an entrenched corporate culture is nearly impossible, but newcomer firms can help drive an economy forward to new sources of growth.*

Part III of this book will portray the regional revolution in American computing. In that separate domain, the story will turn out to parallel the events summarized in this chapter. When something radically new begged to be done after the invention of the microprocessor in 1971, established firms failed to meet the challenge.

But first, it will prove useful to explore more fully the reasons for the malady. Accordingly, the next chapter concludes Part II with a look at classical and more recent theories of innovation and entrepreneurship.

13. Destroying the old order

> In the mature enterprise . . . power has passed, inevitably and irrevocably, from
> the individual to the group. That is because only the group has the information
> that decision requires. (Galbraith 1967, 1985, p. 104)

To summarize Part II: The US and Western Europe experienced crises of
economic maturity from the late 1960s on, as Japan would, in a different
key, in the 1990s. Solutions were much easier to identify than to carry out.
The product cycle in a unifying world economy meant that the advanced,
affluent economies had to spawn new activities and reorganize the old.

Two things had to happen. First, established corporations needed to shift
from dying to expanding product lines and from existing to improved
production processes. Second, young and start-up companies had to try out
new ideas.

Both established and newcomer firms had to innovate. Why was that so
hard? One reason is that most successful companies are deeply afraid to do
anything really new. Another is that entrepreneurship is a scarce resource.

These are two deceptively simple propositions. To lay the groundwork
for Part III, this chapter sketches what economists have had to say about
them. The discussion unfolds in three steps:

(1) Why do established leaders within an industry falter when a radically
    new technology arrives?
(2) What do corporate research-and-development (R&D) labs do – and
    why does that sometimes fall short?
(3) In light of the first two questions, who is 'the entrepreneur'?

We can begin by considering the inability of established US electronics
companies to adapt to the coming of the transistor in the 1950s.

THE TRANSISTOR: A PARABLE

The transistor was invented at Bell Labs in 1947. It provided an on-off
electronic switch that made vacuum tubes obsolete as electronic
components. In *Innovation: The Attacker's Advantage*, Richard Foster
traced the responses to this earthshaking invention by the companies that
led in the production of vacuum tubes in 1955 (see Table 13.1, based on
Foster 1986, p. 133).

Table 13.1 Replacement of vacuum tube leaders by semiconductor firms

Rank	Vacuum tube leaders 1955	Transistor leaders 1955	Semiconductor leaders 1982
1	RCA	Hughes	Motorola
2	Sylvania	Transitron	TI
3	GE	Philco	NEC
4	Raytheon	Sylvania	Hitachi
5	Westinghouse	TI	National
6	Amperex	GE	Toshiba
7	National Video	RCA	Intel
8	Rawland	Westinghouse	Philips
9	Eimac	Motorola	Fujitsu
10	Lansdale	Clevite	Fairchild

Source: Foster 1986, p. 133.

Of the ten leading vacuum tube companies, only two (RCA and Amperex, a division of North American Philips) made the transition to survive as producers of transistors and later integrated circuits. Foster perceived three kinds of errors on the part of the eight leaders in 1955 who failed to survive the transition.

• Four of the firms failed to pursue the new technology (the transistor) at all.
• Three other firms bet on the wrong technology (germanium rather than silicon).
• One, Westinghouse, proved culturally unable to straddle the old and new technologies simultaneously – to 'cannibalize' their product lines and move on.

In contrast, newcomer firms had no such reluctance to invest in and commit to the new and superior technology. While some challengers might fail, a clean slate and a clear commitment conferred a sufficient advantage that some newcomer would prevail. The speed of the transition in this and comparable cases was rapid. A typical decline in market share by the initial leaders averaged one full percentage point per month.

Foster concludes, 'Whenever technological discontinuities occur, companies' fortunes change dramatically. *The leaders in the current technology rarely survive to become the leaders in the new technology*' (p. 115, emphasis added).

For the record, Table 13.2 brings the story up to date by reporting global market shares for semiconductors in the year 1999. What it shows relative to the 1982 ranks is a reversal between two US firms, Illinois's Motorola and Intel, the new global leader. Here, then, is a first glimpse of the regional realignment that would maintain a US lead within the world's semiconductor industry – a story to be told in Chapter 16.

Table 13.2 Top ten semiconductor firms in 1982 and 1999

Rank	Top ten semiconductor companies (bold: dropouts) 1982	(bold: new firms) 1999	Global mkt. share 1999	Worldwide 1999 revenue (billions of $)
1	Motorola	Intel	15.9	26.8
2	TI	NEC(J)	5.5	9.2
3	NEC(J)	Toshiba(J)	4.5	7.6
4	**Hitachi(J)**	**Samsung(K)**	4.2	7.1
5	**National**	TI	4.2	7.1
6	Toshiba(J)	Motorola	3.8	6.4
7	Intel	Hitachi(J)	3.3	5.6
8	Philips(N)	**Infineon(G)**	3.1	5.2
9	Fujitsu(J)	**STMicro(F)**	3.0	5.1
10	**Fairchild**	Philips(N)	3.0	5.1
		Others	49.5	83.4
		Total 1999	100.0	168.6

Note: Initials appear for Japan, Netherlands, Korea, Germany, and France.
Source: Foster (1986, p. 133) and Dataquest, March 27, 2000.

Disruptive Technologies

More recently, Clayton Christensen describes *The Innovator's Dilemma* as the inability of well managed mature firms to compete in new markets served by what he terms *disruptive* technologies (Christensen 1997).

In contrast to *sustaining* innovations, which established firms can generate through their own R&D or absorb smoothly from outside, disruptive technologies overturn the established order. In outline: At first it does not make sense for the technology strategists in established firms to squander resources on a penny-ante game – but then the stakes rise, the market shifts, and the newcomers take over.

The irony is that in the face of a disruptive technology good management can contribute to failure. The reason lies in the way new technologies relate to the 'value network,' a reflection of the product's specific 'architecture' (p. 32). Does the new technology provide managers in the existing organizational structure, with existing incentives, a way to increase profit margins on existing products?

The answer for a disruptive technology is no. In particular, the more closely the leader listens to its most-valued existing customers, the less alert it will be to the threat brewing on the margins of its market. Newcomers will start by selling a bare-bones product to the low end of the market, then improve the package over time while still charging a lower price. At some point the over-served established market will start to turn to the minimalist newcomer, and all bets are off for the leaders.

So much suggests how entrepreneurial invasions can take place. The disruptive technology will be left to down-market firms, seemingly providing a product different from and inferior to that of the mainstream firm. Within its home value network, the initially inferior technology improves in performance and in its range of possible uses. When the time comes, the jump to adjacent applications or industries becomes feasible. The invasion begins.

This is the scenario Christensen finds played out in a wide variety of sectors. Not only Sears and steel, but disk drives, Route 128's mini-computer complex, even Apple's failure in the 1980s to develop a competitive laptop. But such references get us ahead of the main story, to be told in Part III of this book.

The lesson at this point is simply that all the R&D in the world may not make up for corporate myopia in the face of a disruptive innovation.

THE TECHNO-STRUCTURE RUNS DRY

That lesson emerges also from the failure of well-funded, fully staffed research arms of companies like RCA, AT&T, and Xerox to translate their technological prowess into successful products in the 1970s and 1980s.

For perspective on that R&D crisis, we can return now to first principles.

Schumpeter's Hypothesis

The story told in this book relies on Schumpeter's model of the entrepreneur. In 1942, Schumpeter recalled the bygone days of the heroic entrepreneur in no uncertain terms:

[T]he function of entrepreneurs is to reform or revolutionize the pattern of production by exploiting an invention or, more generally, an untried technological possibility. . . . Railroad construction, in its earlier states, electrical power production before the First World War, steam and steel, the motorcar . . . [T]he entrepreneurial function . . . does not consist in either inventing anything or otherwise creating the conditions which the enterprise exploits. It consists in getting things done. (p. 132, emphasis added)

But in the next line, Schumpeter declared the role of the individual entrepreneur to be fading, as 'innovation itself is being reduced to routine' in the corporate R&D lab. 'Technological progress is increasingly becoming the business of trained specialists . . .' (p. 132). So much was consistent with what came to be known in the field of industrial organization as 'the Schumpeterian hypothesis.'

Schumpeter himself softened the proposition in his 1947 essay, 'The Creative Response in Economic History,' where he posed the matter as a question needing further research.

It would be more accurate, in other words, to link the idea of the large corporation as the main source of innovation with Schumpeter's student, Alfred Dupont Chandler, and his colleague, John Kenneth Galbraith.

Chandler: Institutionalizing Creativity?

Chandler applied Schumpeter's framework to US industrial evolution and concluded that the R&D lab was the culmination of the story. In a milestone essay, 'The Beginnings of "Big Business" in American Industry,' Chandler treated nineteenth-century changes in demography and technology as the precipitants for US industrial evolution (Chandler 1959). The driving force was the entrepreneur's creative response, as in Schumpeter's 1947 article ('The Creative Response in Economic History').

In a coherent and impressive chronicle, Chandler divided the period from 1815 to 1959 into five stages, each defined by a different set of technological and demographic opportunities (see Table 13.3). Each set of opportunities triggered creative responses by entrepreneurs or (in the first stage, farmers), in the form of innovations (or migrations). The changes thus achieved in each stage would in turn redefine the opportunity set available to the next.

The last of the five stages begins in 1920, with the coming of the industrial research laboratory. From Chandler's vantage point in 1959, the R&D lab appeared to be the end of the evolutionary sequence of stages, precisely because innovation had become institutionalized. All this seemed to make the industrial research lab in the large corporation, in effect, the end of industrial history.

Table 13.3 Chandler's stages of US industrial evolution

---

1.   *1815-1850: The expansion of the farm population inland*
      Arable land inland from the Eastern seaboard allows production of
      the food and raw materials needed to fuel Europe's industrial
      revolution, industrialization begins in New England.

2.   *1850-1880: The building of the railroads*
      The railroads were built initially to connect inland farmers with port
      cities. The Golden Spike (1869), linked western resources to eastern
      industrialists, whose management model was the railroad enterprise.

3.   *1880-1903: The growth of the national and urban market*
      Given railroads and new communications technology, the North was
      a newly integrated and rapidly growing market and spurred the rise
      of the large corporation, the 'big business' in Chandler's title.

4.   *1903-1920: Electricity and the internal combustion engine*
      The two breakthroughs in energy conservation technology provided
      the main spur to innovation and development in this era, a transition
      from Edison's pioneering research laboratories to the fifth stage.

5.   *1920-?: Institutionalized corporate research and development*
      The industrial research laboratory within the large corporation. The
      harnessing of science, Chandler concluded, laid the basis for an
      endless stream of new profit opportunities.

Source: Chandler 1959.

Galbraith: The Death of the Entrepreneur (1967)

It was Schumpeter's colleague, John Kenneth Galbraith, who was the most
vigorous proponent of the hypothesis. Galbraith's view, as developed in
The New Industrial State (1967), was that only what he called the *techno-
structure* of the mature corporation could handle the intricacies of scientific
and technical information:

> In the entrepreneurial enterprise power rests with those who make decisions. In
> the mature enterprise this power has passed, inevitably and irrevocably, from the
> individual to the group. That is because only the group has the information that
> decision requires. (p. 104)

To understand Galbraith's declaration, it helps to recall GE's motto in that era, 'Progress Is Our Most Important Product.' This, from the company that launched the first formal US corporate R&D lab in the year 1900 (Buderi 2000, Chapter 3). As the phrase suggests, the symbol of innovation in the middle of the twentieth century was the white-coated scientist or technician in a corporate R&D lab, at GE or Dupont or the Massachusetts Institute of Technology (MIT), perhaps working on something for the Pentagon.

Moreover, at first glance, a recent timeline of twentieth-century innovations seems to confirm the shift from the classical nineteenth-century entrepreneur to the corporate R&D lab. Table 13.4 lists major twentieth-century innovations. (It is adapted from a longer list compiled by the new Tech Museum of Innovation in San Jose and the San Jose *Mercury News*.)

Any such 'greatest hits' list will have a certain arbitrary quality in both the selections and the dates, as this one does. Still, such entries as the triode vacuum tube (1906), bakelite (1908), cellophane (1912), and later nylon (1934) and teflon (1938) seem to point up the role of organized, science-based research in the generation of new products.

Creative Soloists

Yet, as a closer look at some of these very products would reveal, appearances can be deceiving.

Even at the height of the corporate era, in other words, the individual had by no means disappeared from the picture. In their landmark 1958 study, *The Sources of Invention* (as updated in 1969), Jewkes et al. interpreted the origins of 70 major twentieth-century discoveries:

> *More than one-half of the cases can be ranked as individual invention* in the sense that much of the pioneering work was carried through by men who were working on their own behalf without the backing of research institutions and usually with limited resources and assistance, or, where the inventors were employed in institutions, these institutions were, as in the case of universities, of such a kind that the individuals were autonomous, free to follow their own ideas without hindrance. (p. 73, emphasis added)

Table 13.4 Major innovations, 1900-1969

Year	Innovation
1900	Radio voice transmission
1901	Motorcycle
1904	Subway system (New York City)
1906	Triode vacuum tube
1908	Bakelite (synthetic plastic)
1910	Synthetic rubber
1911	Air conditioner
1912	Cellophane
1913	Henry Ford's assembly line
1915	Transcontinental telephone
1918	Mechanized warfare
1919	Dial telephone
1926	Electric phonograph
1927	Lindbergh's solo trans-Atlantic flight
1928	Penicillin
1929	Foam rubber
1934	Nylon
1935	Radar for aircraft detection
1936	Fluorescent light
1937	Jet engine
1938	Teflon
1939	Television broadcast
1941	Aerosol spray can
1942	Xerox photocopy
1944	Aiken's electromechanical computer
1945	Atomic bomb, Tupperware (commercial polyethylene)
1946	ENICA (Electronic numeral integrator and computer)
1947	Transistor (Bell Labs)
1948	Microwave oven
1949	Gyrator washing machine (Maytag)
1950	Cable TV
1951	Direct long-distance dialing, Electronic digital computer, UNIVAC 1
1952	Jet airliner
1953	Sony's pocket transistor radio, IBM's 701 computer
1954	Photoelectric cell, Silicon transistors
1955	Polio vaccine

Table 13.4 Major innovations (continued)

Year	Innovation
1956	FORTRAN computer programming language, Transatlantic cable telephone service, Nuclear power generator
1957	Sputnik satellites, US satellite Explorer I
1959	Commercial transistorized computers, Xerox commercial copier, Integrated circuit (Texas Instruments)
1961	DNA molecule decoded, Soviet cosmonaut orbits Earth, Shepard's US space flight
1963	Tape cassette, Artificial heart
1967	Human heart transplant
1968	Intelsat 3A communication satellite
1969	Armstrong walks on moon, Unix operating system, Videocassette tape

Sources: San Jose Tech Museum of Innovation and the San Jose *Mercury News*.

Going on the attack, Jewkes et al. cite a morsel of Galbraithian overstatement: 'A benign Providence . . . has made the modern industry of a few large firms an almost perfect instrument for inducing technical change . . . .' They then dismiss Galbraith's contention in surprisingly personal terms:

> Since then nearly all the systematic evidence has run counter to any such doctrine. Yet, so far as we are aware, Professor Galbraith has said nothing in defence, or in modification, of his views. In his latest book, *The New Industrial State*, he merely repeats his unfounded assertions and dogmatically dismisses anyone who presumes to differ from him. (p. 227)

Galbraith's proposition may not have been true then, but at least it aligned with and reinforced a widely held popular stereotype.

Today the whole idea rings false. Events have made clear both the fallibility of the managerial corporation and the power of individuals (often, to be sure, in networks) to gather strategic data and make decisions quickly.

What happened, then, after 1967, to discredit the techno-structure?

The Decline of the Corporate R&D Lab

Despite the images Chandler and Galbraith put forth of a reliable stream of inventions that would be turned into innovations, by the mid-1980s Foster would recall an awkward dance between the research lab and product development after 1945.

Until 1960 the fashion was 'the lab in the woods.' World War II breakthroughs like radar and synthetic rubber made 'good science' prestigious, despite its remoteness from the production end (Foster 1986, p. 54). Then, following Theodore Levitt's influential 1960 article, 'Marketing Myopia,' priorities flipped, making R&D an adjunct to the needs of marketers. The limit of that approach was that it failed to pursue a company's specific core competencies or skill-based sources of competitive advantage. In turn, 'By the end of the 1960s, it was not fashionable to be "pro-technology." R&D budgets were slashed. Ph.D.'s drove taxi cabs, and companies started to look for new opportunities through diversification. The conglomerate era had arrived' (Foster, p. 56).

Foster's account appeared in 1986, a watershed year. Though he was not in a position to recognize the meanings of some of the changes then going on, it was clear that the typical Fortune 500 R&D lab had lost its way. From the vantage point of the mid-1980s, in other words, it appeared that the 'attacker's advantage' Foster studied was shifting to Japanese firms.

Among other things, large Japanese companies began to dominate the ranks of the top patenting organizations by the mid-1980s, a decade when US patent registrations remained flat. This seemed an ominous sign. From one, myopic point of view, registering patents is what R&D labs are all about. In this partial and incomplete view of the problem, Japan's great electronics companies seemed poised to do the same thing to the US computer sector they had done to automobiles and consumer electronics.

The Chasm between Invention and Innovation

Whatever they measure, however, patents do not measure innovation. Formally, the US Patent Office grants patents when it accepts applications to register new ideas. These could be for new business practices, new hardware or industrial processes, or for a chemical formula to be used by pharmaceuticals companies. The patent then confers monopoly rights to the holder, normally for a period of 20 years. In practice, patents are widely licensed or exchanged among companies.

By contrast, *innovation is the commercialization of invention.* The invention, which may or may not get patented, is the initial idea. The innovation is the process of putting the idea into practice for a profit.[1]

A much-cited example of the chasm between discovery and commercialization was Xerox's Palo Alto Research Center (PARC). Xerox never did commercialize PARC's dazzling series of PC breakthroughs, because they did not improve Xerox's position in the copier market. RCA's unexploited VCR and flat-screen technologies, coupled with its failed video-disk system in the early 1980s, constitute another legendary fumble. Similarly, when the new technology of packet-switching became available for use on ARPAnet after 1969, both AT&T and IBM ignored it in favor of more traditional, analog methods of data transmission.

As a recent account by Robert Buderi puts it, the problem was the '*corporate Ivory Tower*,' a lingering legacy of the 1950s and 1960s:

> As the 1980s opened, a plethora of big labs found themselves overly fat, awash in multiple priorities, lethargic or outright apathetic in transferring technology, and poorly attuned to what customers wanted. In the face of determined and amazingly nimble competitors who attacked the giants at their Achilles' heels, many American companies were primed to get their clocks cleaned. . . . [T]hroughout the 1980s . . . *market share was lost not only to the Japanese but to daring start-ups such as Apple, Compaq, 3Com, Cisco Systems, and Microsoft*, who became mighty powers in their own right. (Buderi 2000, p. 110, emphasis added)

THE ENTREPRENEUR AND THE US RESURGENCE

As it happens, each of the 'daring start-ups' Buderi mentions originated in one of three western states: California, Texas, and Washington (see Table 13.5). The theme of Part III of this book is that it would take such start-up and younger firms from the South and especially the West to reassert US technological leadership in the world economy.

For now, and to clear the decks, we need to consider two more preliminary issues. One is a definition of entrepreneurship that is flexible enough to include corporate managers. The second is the scarcity of entrepreneurs – as it presents itself culturally and geographically.

Innovation and Entrepreneurship

In this book the touchstone for entrepreneurship is Schumpeter's criterion: innovation. In practical terms, that means the number of entrepreneurs is far smaller than the number of small-business owners. A franchised Mail Boxes, Etc., or video store does not qualify. The point of such a restrictive view of the entrepreneur is that for Schumpeter, the role of the entrepreneur is to change the world, in some small or large way.

*Table 13.5 Major innovations, 1971-1998 (IT innovations: **bold**)*

1971	**Microprocessor (Intel)**
1972	Medical CAT scan
1973	MRI medical imaging
1975	**Altair, first personal computer**
	Bill Gates, Paul Allen found Microsoft
1976	Concorde supersonic airliner
	Steve Wozniak, Steve Jobs start Apple Computer
1978	Test-tube baby
1980	Portable VCR camera
1981	Reusable space shuttle
	IBM personal computer
1983	**GUI (graphic user interface)**
1984	Genetic fingerprinting (DNA identification)
	Apple's Macintosh
1985	**Microsoft operating system for IBM PC**
1987	**Supercomputer**
1990	Hubble space telescope
1992	**Internet public access**
1993	**Intel's Pentium microprocessor**
	Quark discovered
1994	**Personal digital assistant (PDA)**
	Netscape Web browser
1995	**Microsoft Windows 95 operating system**
	DVD standardized
1997	Dolly the sheep is cloned
1998	FDA approves Viagra

Sources: San Jose Tech Museum of Innovation/Mercury Center and the San Jose
    Mercury News Staff.

An appendix to the chapter compares this and other views of the entrepreneur. Also considered is a corollary to Schumpeter's definition, the concept of Creative Destruction, as given new relevance by a school I term the 'ecologists,' as represented by Christensen and Levinthal.

As to whether mature corporations can behave entrepreneurially, the venerable Harvard Business School (HBS) believes so. Described in the press as the School's current mantra, their definition of entrepreneurship is *'the pursuit of opportunities beyond means that are currently available'*[2] (Leonhardt 2000, p. 3:1).

The undeniable beauty of this formulation is that it smacks of a solution to Schumpeter's question: Can a large, bureaucratic organization foster individual risk-taking?

Not that there is any contradiction between the HBS mantra and Schumpeter's classical definition. As distinct from the traditional manager, the entrepreneur is a person who tries out a new idea. The implied HBS promise is that creative, energetic managers within large, mature corporations can become entrepreneurial. How? By going beyond the resources available to find new ways to do things. Putting it another way, this is the challenge the School is posing to its students.

What Do Corporate R&D Labs Do?

In this same spirit, suppose we accept the view of the latter-day corporate R&D lab as a born-again resource, freed by the shocks of the late-1980s and early 1990s from its ivory-tower legacy. Of the $150 billion spent each year in the US for private research and development, 90 percent is in any case devoted to 'the D,' product development. Of the 10 percent remaining, nearly all is now used in carefully controlled applied research programs.

What, then, do R&D labs do? Today as in the past, they generate patents. But that, as we have seen, is a different mission from innovation.

On balance, it seems fair to say that the primary purpose is not typically to come up with radical breakthroughs. The obvious exceptions are the pharmaceuticals and perhaps more generally the biotech companies: one big discovery can put them in clover for a generation. In other industries, the typical R&D arm's function might be described as *keeping the company abreast of current strategic information generated anywhere in the world.*

Rebel Angels

Helping a mature company ride the wave of change is a far different thing from blazing new trails. The question remains: Why does it often take new companies to blaze the trails? And why does all that happen in some places more readily than others?

The answers may lie in the notion of a region or nation's *economic culture*, the value set, incentive system, and organizational context that inspire or thwart potential entrepreneurs. As a matter of economic history, the question is open to endless exploration, as suggested most recently in Peter Hall's *Cities in Civilization* (1998), a study of artistic and industrial creativity in specific cities through the ages.

Looking for a common denominator among history's most creative cities, Hall zeroes in on the role of

[A] group of creative people who feel themselves to some important degree outsiders: they both belong and they do not belong, and they have an ambiguous relationship to the seats of authority and power. They may feel that way *because they are young, or because they are provincial or even foreign, or because they do not belong to the established order* of power and prestige; not seldom, most or all of these things. (p. 286, emphasis added)

Similarly, in the England of the early Industrial Revolution, the entrepreneurial class was famously outside the established Church of England. The men in question were not scientists but darkly driven Calvinists who believed in the virtue of hard work and accumulation, devoid of display. This was the group of righteous non-conformists Max Weber profiled in *The Protestant Ethic and the Spirit of Capitalism* (1905). E. Digby Baltzell applied Weber's logic to New England's Calvinists in *Puritan Boston and Quaker Philadelphia* (1979). Boston emerges from the comparison as a center of energy, dynamism, and creativity. The common thread is redemption through work, where wealth is not a path to conspicuous consumption but the end in itself: a sign of salvation.

According to S. Gordon Redding in our own day, another group of outsiders, the Overseas Chinese, embody almost identical values. In *The Spirit of Chinese Capitalism* (1993), Redding attributes the entrepreneurial energy of the Overseas Chinese to their 'spirit,' or value-set (acquisitiveness, patriarchy, thrift, privacy) and to an enclaved, networked existence as ethnic islands amid larger, often hostile host populations.

Privileged Outsiders: The PC Revolutionaries

In this context it seems natural to wonder about the origins of the creators of the PC and Internet revolutions. In the regional realignment of the US computer industry in the 1970s and 1980s, geographical outsiders who became entrepreneurial insurgents included not only immigrants as symbolized by Intel's Andrew Grove, but 'provincials' like Steve Jobs and Steve Wosniak, Bill Gates and Paul Allen, Craig McCaw, Steve Case, Michael Dell, and more recently Jeff Bezos. (We omit another trail-blazer, Britain's Tim Berners-Lee, solely on the basis of his not-for-profit motives and setting.)

As a type, they can be stylized as white male upper-middle class 20-somethings from the West: California, Hawaii, Texas, and Washington. As with the agents of change in Hall's great cities, they could be viewed as at once insiders and outsiders. They tended to have mainstream or privileged ethnic and social backgrounds, but to hail from the provinces, places far from the origins and corporate power of American computing.[3]

Such observations barely scratch the surface, of course. But they lead us to new questions: Why did the PC revolutionaries all come from the western part of the US? And why did they have so few counterparts in Europe and Japan?

Cultures of Constraint

Places dominated by large organizations may lack the breathing room, financial sources, and intellectual fresh air needed for entrepreneurs to flourish. Earlier chapters, for example, have suggested that the industrial legacies of the Upper Midwest, France, and Germany have retarded the move to new wellsprings of growth.

A classic exploration of this issue in the US was Benjamin Chinitz's 'Contrasts in Agglomeration: New York and Pittsburgh' (1961). Chinitz suggested that a region's industrial mix and in particular the relative importance of smaller firms shape its entrepreneurial environment. Noting New York City's greater adaptive capacity, he hypothesized, 'You do not breed as many entrepreneurs per capita in families allied with steel as you do in families allied with apparel' (p. 95).

Steel and apparel represented Pittsburgh and New York, the one a company town and the other more diversified. In this view, the corporate dominance found in a Pittsburgh or a Detroit narrowed the aspirations of high-school and college graduates and tended to monopolize the region's financial resources so as to limit the financing of start-ups.

How Industries Produce Regions

This same point has been made for regions writ large. In their 1989 book, Storper and Walker title a chapter, 'How Industries Produce Regions.' In other words, a view that stops with the question of how regions produce industries takes in only half the picture. In their view a region's pattern of historical industrialization creates a characteristic class structure and political environment, not to mention the hopes and aspirations of the young.

More specifically, Douglas Booth used Dun and Bradstreet data on new business incorporations to measure regional innovative capacity (Booth 1986). He concluded that the Midwest was much less innovative than New England. Why? Talented high-school and college graduates in the Midwest traditionally aspired to safe, highly paid management jobs with the region's Fortune 500 companies. By contrast, in New England fewer safe havens dotted the horizon, so that energetic talent was more likely to take risks, a tendency encouraged by the region's tradition of venture capital.

THE ARGUMENT

Such studies are only partial glimpses of an elusive and evolving picture. The purpose of Part III of this book is to spell out the nuances of the geography of IT innovation in a more complete narrative recollection. One theme is that the US resurgence in the world economy has flowed in part from its ability to encourage new businesses.

A convenient capsule summary of the larger scenario can be found in a recent analysis of the disk-drive industry. A 1999 article, 'Arrested Development: The Experience of European Hard Disk Drive Firms in Comparison with US and Japanese Firms,' examined the responses of large and small hard-disk-drive (HDD) firms in each setting to technological shifts between 1973 and 1996. The abstract summarizes the results:

> Leading incumbent US HDD firms were frequently forced out of the market. Leading Japanese incumbent firms in the same industry were not displaced by these changes. *US startup firms thrived under these technological shifts, displacing US incumbent firms.* Japanese startups did poorly. European firms encountered the worst of both worlds: its incumbent firms were frequently displaced by technological changes, as were US firms; while startup firms (with one exception) performed as poorly as those in Japan. (Chesbrough 1999, p. 287, emphasis added)

In the US IT sector as a whole, the role of the entrepreneur has been to accelerate the pace of technological change. As often as not, that results in the overthrow of established firms.

The function entrepreneurs serve, in a larger sense, is therefore to counteract the powerful tendencies toward stagnation that afflict advanced affluent economies. In the face of the entitlement that time and affluence seem to encourage, *the destruction of the old order* may be necessary for an economy to advance over time to new and more promising sources of growth.

By the same token, the discussion in the appendix to this chapter on approaches to entrepreneurship concludes with a new theory of Creative Destruction.

NOTES

1. In case the difference is not clear, consider the odd case whereby British Telecom is considering pressing a claim that in 1980 it had applied for and in 1989 received a patent for a process closely resembling if not identical to the hyperlink. This realization occurred by accident only in the year 2000, when someone stumbled upon an old patent record (Bray 2000, p. D1). If such a patent exists and proves valid, the question arises – what happened? A certain rough justice might be served, in that hyperlinks were first joined to the Internet

by an Englishman, Tim Berners-Lee, in a project at CERN, the European particle physics consortium in Switzerland, by 1990 (Berners-Lee 1999).

The idea was never put into practice by British Telecom, who seem not to have known what to do with it. If not, they had plenty of company during the 1980s in the numerous US managerial corporations who also came up with ideas they could not translate into successful products or services.

2. The HBS definition would seem to derive not only from the School's Michael Porter but also from the West-Coast writer, Fernando Flores. In *Understanding Computers and Cognition* (1984), Flores and Winograd put forth the idea of the creative conversation within an organization. Rather than a check-list or menu of options to help a CEO make decisions, the notion here is of an exploration among all the informed participants in the process to discover possibilities that in today's management jargon would be termed 'outside the box,' unconstrained by the prevailing assumptions.

3. Perhaps a comparable regional phenomenon in literary terms would be the pronounced tendency for the American Nobel-Prize winners in literature for work done in the first half of the twentieth century to hail from the Midwest or South. Although Eugene O'Neill grew up in New York, Hemingway was from Illinois, and Sinclair Lewis and (though he did not win a Nobel Prize) F. Scott Fitzgerald came from Minnesota. William Faulkner, of course, stayed in his home state of Mississippi. John Steinbeck (the fifth American winner of the Prize) hailed from and wrote about California.

APPENDIX 13A: THE ENTREPRENEUR: SEVEN KEYS

The touchstone for entrepreneurship by any reckoning, writes Mark Casson, is *judgment*, the ability to size up uncertain circumstances and determine a plan for action. As he puts it, judgment is 'a capacity for making a successful decision when no obviously correct model is available or when relevant data is unreliable or incomplete'[1] (Casson 1993, p. 633).

However, the entrepreneur disappeared from the mid-twentieth-century stage on two counts – as a casualty of the corporate techno-structure and, in economic theory, as an actor who had lost a role. First, Schumpeter's entrepreneur was declared obsolete by Galbraith, who said, 'only the group has the information that decision requires' (Galbraith 1967, p. 104).

Second, and also as a matter of information, economic theory disposed of the entrepreneur as well. When the simplifying assumption of perfect information came into general use in economics, largely to pave the way for mathematical models, economic doctrine dispensed with judgment as a requirement for starting or running firms. *Managers managed.* To that extent the word 'entrepreneur' disappeared from the vocabulary of twentieth-century economics (Casson, p. 631).

The discipline has relaxed that assumption in the past few decades. Increasing attention has gone to how markets operate under imperfect information. Accordingly, room has been created again for judgment – and for entrepreneurship as a fourth factor of production, along with land, labor, and capital.

In the meantime, of course, entrepreneurship has become a staple of business-school curricula everywhere. If anything, such treatments offer an embarrassment of riches and a multiplicity of meanings. For example, do all the 600,000-800,000 businesses started in the US each year result from the actions of entrepreneurs? Is entrepreneurship synonymous with small business? In the body of the chapter, and following Schumpeter, the answer given is no: instead, the touchstone is innovation.

But there are other views of the entrepreneur, including updates of Schumpeter. To provide a fuller account of the matter, we can compare past and current conceptual approaches to the question, Who is the entrepreneur?

(1) Cantillon (1697-1734): Risk

The origin of the word goes back to Cantillon, nearly 300 years ago. To quote Casson once more,

> The term *entrepreneur*, which most people recognize as meaning someone who organizes and assumes the risk of a business in return for profits, appears to have been introduced by Richard Cantillon (1697-1734), an Irish economist of

French descent. The term came into much wider use after John Stuart Mill popularized it in his 1848 classic, *Principles of Political Economy*, but then all but disappeared from the economics literature by the end of the nineteenth century. (p. 631)

According to Cantillon, the entrepreneur was the actor in the production process who managed *risk*. The entrepreneur employs workers, pays them for their labors, and in the process insures their efforts against market fluctuations in the price of the output. To that extent the entrepreneur bears the risk of losses from a fall in product prices. The profit that may accrue to the entrepreneur is the reward.

(2) Knight (1885-1972): Uncertainty

A decade after Schumpeter's dissertation was published in German, Frank Knight's dissertation appeared in 1921 in book form as *Risk, Uncertainty, and Profit*.

Knight's contribution was to distinguish between risk, which could be calculated in the actuarial sense and insured against, and *uncertainty* – arising from contingencies whose probabilities could not be estimated. Risks might stem from seasonal variations in weather, seemingly subject to measurable frequency distributions compiled from past years. Uncertainty, by contrast, is an inevitable characteristic of trying to predict consumer responses to a new product, or to guard against sudden shifts in taste.

Extending Cantillon's theory, Knight pointed out that the entrepreneur could cover risks in the sense of insuring against them. Not so with uncertainty. Profit thus becomes the reward for bearing uncertainty, and differences in the long-term profit rates of different industries can be read as measures of their varying degrees of uncertainty.

(3) The Austrians: Arbitrage

Then there are the Austrians, which in this context does not include the Austrian-born Schumpeter. To such members of the Austrian School as Friedrich Hayek and Israel Kirzner, the entrepreneur is the person who buys low and sells high. The entrepreneur plays a pivotal role in the Austrian vision of the price system as an information-gathering mechanism, too complex to be run by command-and-control bureaucrats. That role is to discover the prices of inputs or finished goods and services, then decide whether to deal.

Though pivotal in the Austrian price-system, this figure holds less interest for our purposes. The Austrian entrepreneur is an arbitrager who gathers the relevant price data, discerns whether profits can be made from the difference between the prices that have to be paid and those that can be obtained, then decides whether to make a deal. In this sense, real-estate developers and perhaps even stock-brokers qualify as entrepreneurs.

(4) Bhide (2000): Incrementalism

A business-school professor and the son of an Indian entrepreneur, Amar V. Bhide has worked with students over the years to compile hundreds of case studies of successful start-up firms. In *The Origin and Evolution of New Businesses* Bhide draws on such case studies and on *Inc. Magazine*'s database and concludes that risk plays at best a minor role in the typical start-up sequence for the subset of firms that would then grow rapidly (Bhide 2000; Gendron 2000).

Instead, in the typical case someone already working for a successful firm attains an insight as to how an incremental improvement could be made, at little risk, in an established market. The entrepreneur is thus an experienced player in an established game, but someone who has found a way to provide some *slight improvement* in the production, sale, and delivery of the product.

In turn, the successful entrepreneurial venture will tend to have a number of other characteristics as well:

- The product or service is likely to be a *'medium-ticket' item* (costing $500 to a few thousand dollars).
- It may well be s*old directly by the entrepreneur* in a personal (if not always face-to-face) transaction.
- Finally, the needs and preferences of the typical customers tend to be ambiguous (not standardized) so *selling is subject to the personal influence of the entrepreneur*.
- With little by way of capital or formal procedures, the entrepreneur then jumps into the game with a start-up, improvises as needed, and, in a key to the start-up's success, *out-hustles* the competition.

This ad-hoc, improvisational, adaptive style helps the elite start-up maneuver the rapids and learn quickly in the beginning. At some point in the life-cycle of the young firm, however, the transition to rapid growth and increased size requires a role reversal, a shift *from spontaneity, intuition, and hustle to strategy, planning, and coordination.* Absent this sort of radical makeover, the promising start-up will be unable to break out of the pack or to manage rapid growth and reach great size.

Wal-Mart and Microsoft are examples Bhide cites of firms that made the transition. At this crucial inflection point, all bets are off. The very informality and improvisational style that helped get the start-up off the ground must now be scrapped in favor of orderly management. What sets the biggest winners apart, in Bhide's view, is the discipline and capacity for such a change. Not surprisingly, that tends to mean a change away from the start-up's first-round employees to a much different cast of characters.

(5) Gilder (1981): Faith

George Gilder's visionary 1981 work, *Wealth and Poverty,* invokes three characteristics: generosity, selflessness, and faith. A contrast can be drawn between his approach and the subsequent rationalist, menu-driven model of entrepreneurial behavior put forth by Peter Drucker (1985) or William Baumol (1993). (See Spinosa, Flores, and Dreyfus 1997, chapter 3.) For Gilder, once the idea possesses the entrepreneur, that sets the course of action. Nothing can be right until that single idea is brought to fruition.

Gilder's entrepreneur, as exemplified in Henry Ford, is a humble and dedicated adventurer. This is a person possessed by a vision of a different world, obsessed by the aim of endowing the world with new possibilities.

Gilder's role in resurrecting the entrepreneur as a heroic figure is sometimes overlooked because his message came packaged with an attack on welfare. Yet it remains perhaps the most fully realized version of the non-rationalist model of the entrepreneur. His is a vision that emphasizes a mystery of personality in the entrepreneurial spirit that can never be completely dissected and codified for business-school how-to manuals. As with Schumpeter, the entrepreneur is history's hero.

(6) Schumpeter (1883-1950): Innovation

Schumpeter rejected the neoclassical theory of the competitive firm. As we have seen, Schumpeter made the entrepreneur the *primum mobile,* the engine of change that for Marx before him had flowed from class conflict. The entrepreneur for Schumpeter is the person who innovates, turning a discovery into a new product or process. When such innovation occurs on a large scale, the result is Creative Destruction.

A biological metaphor lies at the core of Schumpeter's concept of long waves, as described above (in Chapter 6). In addition to technological innovations in the steel industry, in energy conversion, and in transportation,

> The opening up of new markets, foreign or domestic, and the organizational developments from the craft shop to such concerns as U.S. Steel illustrate the same *process of industrial mutation – if I may use that biological term –* that incessantly revolutionizes the economic structure from within, incessantly

destroying the old one, incessantly creating a new one. This process of Creative Destruction is the essential fact about capitalism (p. 83, emphasis added).

One criticism of Schumpeter's theory of the entrepreneur is that it is said to refer mainly to epochal breakthroughs, accomplished by heroic figures. As Casson writes, 'His analysis left little room for the much more common but no less important "low-level" entrepreneurship carried on by small firms' (p. 632).

While this criticism may be true of the examples Schumpeter emphasized, however, his actual definition did include small-scale innovations. 'It need not be the Bessemer steel or the explosion motor. It can be the Dearfoot sausage' (Schumpeter 1947, p. 151).

Another criticism focuses on Creative Destruction. Writers such as Rosenberg (1982) and Bhide (2000) reject the idea, saying that the history of technology is full of overlaps and coexistences of the old the new. Without doubt, such examples abound.

This book, by contrast, cites examples of Creative Destruction. One pattern is geographical (as in Chapter 11). Another is 'ecological,' in the sense developed by Christensen and Levinthal.

(7) The Ecologists: Invasions

An ecological view of the entrepreneur is a blend of Bhide's incrementalism with a sense of invasion and conquest consistent with Creative Destruction.

A key link between this school and Schumpeter is the use of biological metaphors. In a nutshell: To explain evolution, (1) Darwin advocated *natural selection* (giraffes with long necks being better adapted to reach the leaves on higher branches), (2) Mendel introduced the science of genetics, which was interpreted later to highlight the role of *mutations*, whereas an influential school of contemporary biologists highlight (3) *speciation*.

As summarized by Levinthal in a 1998 article (p. 218):

> The modern perspective, introduced by Gould and Eldredge . . . hinges not on a single mutational event but on speciation – the separation of reproductive activity. The initial speciation event is minor in the sense that the form does not differ substantially from its predecessor. However, as a result of a separate reproductive process driven by genetic drift and a possibly distinct selection environment, the speciation event may trigger a divergent evolutionary path.

As Levinthal writes of speciation, 'These ideas are applied here to provide insight into the pace and nature of technological change.' His analogy: 'As in the process of punctuation in the biological context, the critical factor is often a speciation event, the application of existing technological know-how to a new domain of application' (p. 218).

In turn, the application of the metaphor can reveal something about human agency, the role of entrepreneurs in advancing the pace of technological change. '*The process of "creative destruction" occurs when the technology that emerges from the speciation event is successfully able to invade other niches . . .*' (Levinthal, p. 218, emphasis added).

The case he explores is the development of wireless communication technology. His conclusion, consistent with the speciation theme, is that the great events in the twentieth-century history of wireless were not dramatic technical breakthroughs but rather applications of existing techniques to new commercial domains.

In this light, the entrepreneur takes on a distinctive function, modified from earlier conceptions. Neither the titanic figure of the nineteenth century, nor the lab-coated Dow Chemical scientist, Levinthal's invader is an opportunist. The opportunity lies in applying known technologies, with modifications as needed, to compete with conventional methods in established industries.

The moment of truth lies not in the discovery itself (the invention), nor in the development of a first product or process (an innovation). Instead it occurs as an insight leading to the adaptation of an existing technology to new activities. It is as if the nineteenth-century swashbuckler and the twentieth-century corporate scientist were merged in the figure of an *arbitraging engineer*. All the same, the image of ecological invasion restores the entrepreneur's classical role as the agent of Creative Destruction.

Why should established leaders fail to defend themselves against attacks by newcomers? With this question we return to the main narrative, and to Part III. Suffice it to say here that when the challenge is ignored, '*the disruptive technology can then invade . . . knocking out the established technology and its established practitioners, with stunning speed*' (Christensen 1997, p. 41, emphasis added).

NOTE

1. A related variable here is *trust*, an entrepreneur's willingness to delegate decision-making power to a subordinate or steward who is then empowered to take action in the face of the unknown. Whether owners can or should trust managers in this regard is a subject of debate. The answer, according to Casson, will depend in good part on whether managers or stewards have an objective function (a goal) as powerful and disciplining as the owner's profit motive.

PART III

The Revolution

Roadmap:

The origins of the New Economy can be traced back to 1971, when Intel invented the microprocessor but IBM and the Route 128 companies failed to exploit it. That task fell to newcomers, entrepreneurs from such western states as California, Texas, Utah, and Washington.

Part III recounts this regional revolution in American computing, highlighting the roles of both geeks and freaks and the immigrant Andrew Grove, who rescued Intel and the US semiconductor industry with one decision in 1985.

Chapters 14-18 are all of a piece, an account of how the regional revolution powered the US resurgence in IT.

Chapter 19 is a postscript with a different focus, the dispersal of IT employment away from the Northeast and from California in the years 1986-1996. As a more specialized technical inquiry, it can be readily skipped without loss of continuity.

14. The coming Japanese conquest
15. The rise of the Wild-West companies
16. Sea change
17. The US comeback, 1989-1994
18. The Internet decade
19. Postscript: state IT roles

14. The coming Japanese conquest

> [T]he Japanese have now embarked on 'take-lead' strategies they hope will ensure that Japan will inevitably become the undisputed No. 1 in computers. This is a matter of great concern because it is difficult to find an example of any American or European industry that has successfully fought back . . . where the Japanese have decided to go for leadership. (Forester 1993, p. 86)

Radical advances in technology can dislodge established regions or nations from the top ranks of wealth and power. As Simon Kuznets observed, Britain lost its lead to Germany and the US when the key sectors in the world economy shifted from steam power and textiles to electricity and chemicals (Chapter 8).

Something similar happened *within the US* when the microprocessor was invented at Intel in 1971. The outcome of that basic breakthrough would be to strike down the established IT giants of the American Northeast, in favor of younger companies in such western states as California, Texas, and Washington.

In the PC era the younger firms in the West revolutionized world computing and in so doing won back a leadership role that was rapidly shifting to Japan. Two quick comparisons help put this idea in perspective:

- The decade after 1987, the period of the unexpected US resurgence *vis-à-vis* Japan, saw a reversal in the market valuations of America's leading IT firms (see Table 14.1). The West's Intel and Microsoft leapfrogged the Northeast's IBM and DEC (Digital Equipment Corporation) (Norris 1997).
- More generally, by a recent ranking nine of the world's top ten IT firms are American, and eight are from the three western states.

The next few chapters link the American comeback in information technology in the 1990s to the regional realignment that marked the PC era. To that end, we need to recall how different the world looked a decade ago.

THE COMING CONQUEST (CA. 1989)

In 1989, Japan gave every indication of pulling away from its technological competitors. The Rising Sun seemed to herald not only a national victory but also an affirmation of the Ministry of International Trade and Industry's (MITI's) strategic intervention and of industrial policy generally. A glance

153

at several specific IT sectors shows how comprehensive a victory was
expected.

Table 14.1   Reversal of fortunes: US computer giants, 1987-1997
(Largest US corporations, ranked by market capitalization in billions $)

	12 May 1997			31 August 1987		
Value $bn	Company	Rank	Value $bn	Company	Rank	Rank 1997
201	GE	1	102	**IBM**	**1**	9
165	Coca-Cola	2	71	Exxon	2	3
148	Exxon	3	57	GE	3	1
142	**Microsoft**	**4**	36	ATT	4	21
125	**Intel**	**5**	30	DuPont	5	15
112	Merck	6	29	GM	6	33
103	Ph. Morris	7	29	Ford	7	32
90	P. & G.	8	28	Ph. Morris	8	7
86	**IBM**	**9**	28	Merck	9	6
83	J. & J.	10	25	**DEC**	**10**	324

Source: Norris (1997).

Note: Computer companies in bold.

Semiconductors

Japan had caught the US in its output of semiconductors by 1986, and by
1988 and 1989 it was supplying over 50 percent of the world market.
Despite a partial captive market (for example, IBM producing its own chips
for its own computers), 'merchant' memory chips for sale in the open
market had been largely taken over by Japan.

That left mainly microprocessors for the US – but even this creative side
of semiconductor chips was being bought up by Japanese firms. According
to MIT's (the university, not the Japanese ministry) *Made in America*,
'Without some dramatic realignment of the American merchant industry, its
decline is likely not only to continue but to accelerate' (Dertouzos et al.
1989, p. 261).

Computers

The shift from desktop microcomputers to portables seemed to signal a shift toward Japanese leadership. The flat screens in laptop and palmtop computers had liquid-crystal-diode (LCD) displays, a Japanese strength. (This was also another example of a US discovery – at RCA in 1963 – which only the Japanese had seen fit to commercialize, for use on digital watch faces and video games.)

Hence the evolution of the industry toward laptops was thought to help Japan. Charles H. Ferguson thus wrote, 'Some say: "Japan will make the commodities and the US will profit from design, software, and marketing." This is fantasy' (1990, p. 66). His prescription: US government-industry consortia along Japanese lines.

Software

Even in software, the Fifth Generation project (artificial intelligence, or AI) Japan initiated in 1982 was still being touted as a locomotive coming through the tunnel. This was the accepted outlook despite Japan's language and other handicaps in software. If MITI could make it happen in VCRs, the prevailing view then intoned, why not software too?

HDTV

In 1989 lobbyists for a US high-definition television (HDTV) effort to counter Japan's were making major inroads within the Executive Branch of the federal government. They converted Robert Mosbacher, the Secretary of Commerce, and Craig Fields of the Pentagon's Defense Advanced Research Projects Agency, DARPA (now ARPA), to the view that the US was hopelessly behind Japan and could only catch up in this 'critical' (that is, to national security) technology with help from the government. While not central to IT, HDTV was nonetheless feared in the US as an advanced technology that would permanently guarantee Japan's supremacy across consumer electronics and home entertainment generally.

ANTICLIMAX

But a funny thing happened on the way to Japan's inexorable conquest. The effort fell apart on all fronts: chips, boxes, software, television – and even telecommunications. You name it: if it required creativity and a rapid response, Japan lost the race. They lost it, as a rule, to US companies headquartered in the western states, in an arc from Texas to Seattle.

Who were these companies? Why did they spring up in the western half of the US? How did they defeat Japan's bid for leadership in IT, the world's premier growth sector?

15. The rise of the Wild-West companies

End of an era. The Texans have taken over. (Vellante 1998 following Compaq's purchase of DEC)

One way to answer these questions is to list a series of examples in which old-style companies in the Northeast ('managerial corporations') bungled opportunities to innovate. In the vacuum, younger and more creative firms ('entrepreneurial firms') took advantage of the culturally wide-open spaces of the West to move the industrial system to its next stage of development.

This chapter tells the story of the regional realignment in terms of six cases, or episodes. Each is intended to point up the regional dimension to the difference in firm behavior. Figure 15.1 notes a few pivotal locations.

1. FAIRCHILD SPAWNS INTEL (1968)

In contrast to mainframes and minicomputers, personal computers are blown up from thumbnail-sized microprocessors. Silicon Valley started with transistors, moved on to memory and logic (or microprocessor) chips, and evolved into a complex producing the whole IT spectrum. Its origins as a semiconductor center would later give the Valley a decisive advantage over Route 128.

In this sense, it can be said that Silicon Valley is 'a place that was invented one afternoon in 1957 when Bob Noyce and seven other engineers quit en masse from Shockley Semiconductor' to found Fairchild Semiconductor. This was a division of the established Syosset, New York firm, Fairchild Camera and Instrument (Cringely 1993, p. 36). The path leads from New Jersey's Bell Labs to a moment in 1968 when Noyce and crew would again leave, this time from Fairchild.

Background: The Origins of Silicon Valley

A key technological moment in the Valley's development was William Shockley's arrival in 1955 from Bell Labs (now Lucent). Shockley had been a co-inventor of the transistor in 1947 for Bell Labs, which would later garner him a Nobel Prize. (An honor he would later sully by using it to propound racist views.) In 1955 Shockley returned from New Jersey to his home state to start a transistor company in Mountain View, near Stanford.

He called it Shockley *Semiconductor* because the transistor could be switched on or off to register a 0 or 1 in binary code, depending on whether

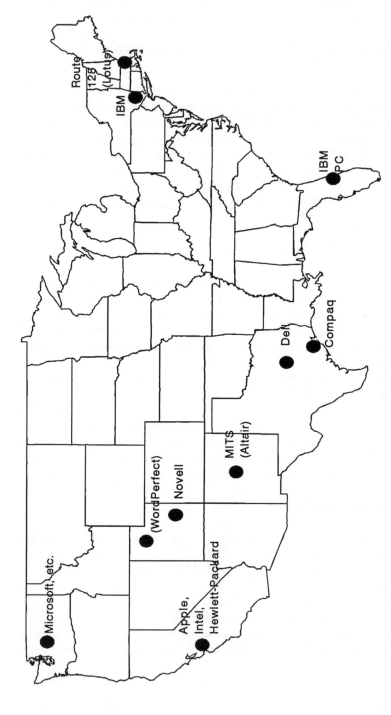

Figure 15.1 US computing's westward evolution

it was in a conductive or non-conductive mode. This 'semiconductor' property is present in the minerals germanium and silicon. Years later, in 1971, a newsletter writer named Don C. Hoefler accordingly coined the term, 'Silicon Valley' (Rogers and Larsen 1984, pp. 25-6).

Shockley moved west to Mountain View in part because it was his home ground and his mother still lived there. But business logic also favored the move. Two key components were already in place to create a seedbed for new enterprises. One was the Stanford Industrial Park launched in 1951 and followed in 1954 by the Stanford Research Park. The impetus was not economic development but the desire to make money from real estate the university owned yet (by the terms of Leland Stanford's gift) could not sell.

The second keystone was Hewlett-Packard, started by the two Stanford students on the eve of World War II to manufacture electronic oscillators, under the guidance of an electrical engineering professor studying negative feedback, Fred Terman. The two components had come together in 1954 when H-P took a lease in the Stanford Research Park and served as the anchor for subsequent tenants (Rogers and Larsen, ch. 2).

The Traitorous Eight

Shockley had barely started his semiconductor company when it foundered on a legendary spin-off, which would eventually beget Intel. Fairchild's Traitorous Eight, (as Shockley saw them) share credit with Texas Instruments (TI) for inventing integrated circuits (ICs). Germanium ICs were designed by Jack Kilby at TI in Dallas, but he lacked a method of layering transistors on a flat surface. Jean Hoerni, one of the Fairchild Eight, came up with a 'planar' technique to embed rather than stack component layers.

Noyce carried the idea through to create complete circuit maps on a single silicon slice, clearing the way for photolithography (or 'burning' the circuits into the slice) and thus for batch production. TI and Fairchild both announced the breakthrough in 1959. ICs came into production within two years, for use by the US government at $100 apiece to miniaturize the future Apollo moon rocket's onboard computer (Palfreman and Swade 1991, pp. 87-91). Table 15.1 lists this and other major IT advances.

Intel

A decade later, Noyce, Moore, and the newcomer Andrew Grove jumped ship again to found Intel, a more egalitarian company than Fairchild's eastern owners would permit. As a minister's son from Iowa, Noyce did without dress codes, reserved parking places, closed offices, executive

Table 15.1 Major IT innovations, 1971-1995

1971	Microprocessor (Intel)
1975	Altair, first personal computer Bill Gates, Paul Allen found Microsoft
1976	Steve Wozniak, Steve Jobs start Apple Computer
1981	IBM personal computer
1983	GUI (graphic user interface)
1984	Apple's Macintosh
1985	Microsoft operating system for IBM PC
1987	Supercomputer
1992	Internet public access
1993	Intel's Pentium microprocessor
1994	Personal digital assistant (PDA) Netscape Web browser
1995	Microsoft Windows 95 operating system

Sources: San Jose Tech Museum of Innovation/Mercury Center and the San Jose
        Mercury News Staff.

dining rooms, and the other status trappings of more hierarchical and
bureaucratic mature US corporations. The remote control thus foundered on
the divergent philosophies of Syosset and Silicon Valley:

> *Noyce couldn't get Fairchild's eastern owners to accept the idea that stock*
> *options should be a part of compensation for all employees, not just for*
> *management.* He wanted to tie everyone, from janitors to bosses, into the overall
> success of the company. . . . This management style still sets the standard for
> every computer, software, and semiconductor company in the Valley today. . . .
> Every CEO still wants to think that the place is being run the way Bob Noyce
> would have run it. (Cringely, p. 39, emphasis added)

2. XEROX FAILS TO MARKET PARC'S DISCOVERIES

Noyce's brush with the Northeast's resistance to change was repeated at
Xerox PARC, this time over bringing new products to market. In 1970, the
New York copier firm, Xerox, founded Palo Alto Research Center (PARC)

as a flat organization of some 50 creative researchers whose mission was to create 'the architecture of information.'

As PARC'S web site puts it, they responded 'by inventing personal distributed computing, graphical user interfaces, the first commercial mouse, bit-mapped displays, Ethernet, client/server architecture, object-oriented programming, laser printing and many of the basic protocols of the Internet.' Preoccupied with copiers, however, the New York-based Xerox failed to bring any of these potentially breakthrough technologies to market. That remained for such western firms as Hewlett-Packard, Apple, and Utah's Novell.

3. IBM AND DEC IGNORE THE COMPUTER-ON-A-CHIP

Noyce and his colleagues had formed Intel in 1968, as a spin-off (like its competitor National Semiconductor and some 50 other companies) from Fairchild. Intel made its mark on the world in November 1971 when it announced a triple breakthrough: the microprocessor, dynamic random access memory (DRAM), and erasable programmable memory (EPROM) for software (Gilder 1989, p. 101). Here was the package to make personal computers a reality.

But the big computer companies of the Northeast were not interested: 'IBM and DEC . . . decided there was no market. *They could not imagine why anyone would need or want a small computer; if people wanted to use a computer, they could hook into . . . time-sharing systems*' (Palfreman and Swade, p. 108, emphasis added). The microprocessor languished, scorned by the mainframe and minicomputer establishments – and not pushed by Intel – for another three years.

Adolescent Energy

What would it take to bring the new firepower into play? The answer came with the now legendary January 1975 issue of *Popular Electronics*, whose cover showed the MITS Altair kit for a home-made microcomputer based on an Intel 8080 processor chip. Inspired, Steve Wosniak devised the Apple I to impress the hobbyists at the Homebrew Computer Club in Palo Alto. When Steve Jobs entered the picture the result was the Apple II, which found a ready market.

Wosniak's hardware breakthrough was matched on the software side by the 19-year-old Seattleite, Bill Gates. Using a DEC PDP 10 minicomputer at Harvard to emulate the MITS Altair, Gates and his high-school friend from Seattle, Honeywell programmer Paul Allen, devised a modified version of Dartmouth's mainframe BASIC programming language. Moving from the Boston area to New Mexico to be near the MITS facility, they formed Microsoft to market MITS BASIC, their microcomputer version of the mainframe programming language. Over the next five years, Microsoft would then develop, market, and license other languages for microcomputers, reaching $2.5 million in sales and 25 employees by the end of 1979.

In other words, the four seminal figures in the PC industry after 1975 (when IBM in New York and DEC in Massachusetts saw no future in it) were barely 21 on average and hailed from the San Francisco Bay area and Seattle.

Microsoft (and Compaq in Houston, Dell in Austin, Texas Instruments in Dallas, and WordPerfect and for a time Novell in Utah) are reminders that the technological transformation of American computing ranged from Texas to Seattle. If Silicon Valley was the West's capital, it sometimes followed the lead of the provinces.

4. PC ROOTS: BOCA, SILICON VALLEY, SEATTLE

The next episode was played out not in the West at all, but in Florida. Yet the theme remains the same: new territory as a spur to innovation.

Microsoft's initial takeoff following the New Mexico start-up brought the company to IBM's attention. In the mid-1970s, IBM had in fact introduced an expensive PC-like machine that drew little response from its corporate customers and was quickly abandoned. By 1980, as microcomputer sales by Apple, Radio Shack, Atari and Commodore generated over $1 billion, IBM decided to try again.

This time IBM's development team was placed far from Armonk, New York, headquarters in Boca Raton, Florida, with a one-year project deadline. The crash-program deadline, unprecedented at IBM, forced the PC project chief, Bill Lowe, to design a machine built from other people's components – another radical departure for the company.

Enter Microsoft. Lowe's plan was initially just to buy Microsoft BASIC, a standard feature of existing microcomputers, and to run it over a CP/M operating system from Gary Kildall's Digital Research of Pacific Grove, California (next door to Monterey). But when negotiations with Kildall misfired because he did not show up for the meeting in Pacific Grove, Lowe turned to Microsoft for the operating system as well. Gates replied that IBM should use a 16-bit microprocessor, the new Intel 8088 chip. But since Gates had no operating system for a 16-bit processor, Microsoft now had to come up with one.

Gates' solution was to spend about $50,000 to buy an existing 8088 operating system, QDOS ('Quick and Dirty Operating System') from Tim Paterson's Seattle Computer Products and to rename it MS-DOS. In August 1981 the IBM PC appeared on schedule, featuring an 8088 Intel chip, MS-DOS (called 'PC-DOS' by IBM), and Microsoft BASIC, with available Microsoft versions of FORTRAN, COBOL, and PASCAL.

The package was thus equal parts hardware from Boca Raton and Silicon Valley's Intel and system software from Seattle. The creative points of origin were far removed from Armonk, New York.

Such was the beginning of the IBM-Microsoft collaboration that ended in 1990 with a complete reversal of fortunes, symbolized by IBM's plummeting employment, from 395,000 in 1984 to 243,000 in 1994. Microsoft's standard-setting strategy succeeded to the point where its stock-market value, like Intel's, surpassed IBM's by 1993. Not the least ironic aspect of the reversal is that IBM unloaded stock in Microsoft and Intel that, if retained, would have been worth $18 billion by the mid-1990s.

5. ROUTE 128'S EPIDEMIC OF MANAGEMENT FAILURE

In the meantime, it wasn't just IBM who took a tumble in the 1980s. Something comparable was also happening along Boston's Route 128, where the big four minicomputer companies (Digital, Wang, Data General, and Prime) had entered the 1980s as giant-killers, Davids to IBM's Goliath. The reindustrialization of New England from the early 1970s to the mid-1980s had been an inspiring story.

Unfortunately, it did not last. After about 1985 the two outwardly similar high-tech clusters, Boston's Route 128 and California's Silicon Valley, moved in opposite directions. Along Route 128, the 'Massachusetts Miracle' (as touted by defeated presidential candidate Michael Dukakis) collapsed in a heap, wiping out tens of thousands of jobs across New England. But Silicon Valley kept on adding employment, despite California's high taxes and housing prices.

A little-noted reason for this eclipse was management failure along Route 128. All the major players in the New England complex saw the handwriting on the wall in the early 1980s. The future of computing was the PC, not minicomputers, let alone mainframes. Yet not one of the successful and profitable companies had the boldness to cannibalize their profitable minicomputer lines to shift to a PC strategy.

What could account for this collective failure of nerve? Technologically, Route 128's minicomputers were actually mainframe computers shrunk down, not microprocessors blown up, like the PC. For that reason it was much harder for the Route 128 companies to introduce new and uncertain personal computers. Putting it differently, the economies of scope favoring Silicon Valley's microprocessor-based complex were missing along Route 128. Facing the technology barrier, managers along Route 128 stayed too long with cash-cow, proprietary (or closed) systems in minicomputers.

The long-term outcome would be a default IT role for Route 128 as a software and now Internet specialist, a role MIT's presence more or less guarantees. But the immediate result was for hardware production to move west, to Silicon Valley and then to Texas.

6. HOW TEXAS BECAME THE PC STATE

As we saw in Table 14.1, Route 128's leader had fallen in capitalization from America's tenth largest corporation in 1987 to number 324 in 1997, just before its acquisition by Houston's Compaq.

Today Texas has the two leading PC producers in the world, Compaq and Dell. The reasons go back to oil exploration.

Texas Instruments

Compaq's provenance traces a fairly precise lineage of industrial evolution. In the 1930s engineers with a new instrumentation technology for seismographic oil exploration came from the Northeast to Dallas to found a company called Geophysical Services. In 1951, the original firm gave way to Texas Instruments. The technologies TI employed led naturally to semiconductor research and in 1959 to the co-discovery of the integrated circuit by Jack Kilby, a TI engineer. Military and space contracts from the federal government spurred the company's ascent to one of the top semiconductor manufacturers in the US by the 1970s.

Compaq

In 1982 four TI engineers from the company's Houston facility broke away to form a spin-off. Their leader was Rod Canion, and the company was Compaq. The breakaway team patiently reverse-engineered the then new IBM PC, so that it could legally invent its own BIOS (or interface) chip to emulate the PC for 100-percent software compatibility. Their success created Compaq's breakthrough as the legitimate king of the PC clone-makers. Compaq rose from its inception to Fortune 500 status in only four years – a record Dell would itself later break. Of course, that was not the end of the story: Canion would later be fired when Compaq stumbled.

What is the meaning of the TI-Compaq story? The link between resource endowments and innovative capacity. Historically, the development of technological strength in an American region can typically be traced to the region's resource base (Perloff and Wingo, 1961). A given resource endowment either generates or fails to spark a related set of resource-processing activities that in turn encourage the development of new skills and technologies (Norton and Rees 1979). The 60-year path from oil exploration to Compaq's world leadership in PC production displays just this logic.

Dell

In contrast, Dell's meteoric rise in the 1990s has no such precisely traceable lineage. Instead, Michael Dell's strategy has been to devise a new distribution system to 'mass-customize' the PC to order and to get the product delivered in a matter of days through the mail. The whole thing took root in Dell's college dorm room in Austin, seemingly nurtured by an economic culture that favored innovation and entrepreneurship. His creation would eventually become the chief rival to Houston's Compaq.

WIDE OPEN SPACES

This chapter has recounted six episodes that reveal the role of 'wide open spaces' in the PC revolution:

1. Intel began with a break from Fairchild Semiconductor in part because Fairchild's East-Coast parent imposed too much hierarchy.
2. Another New York company, Xerox, proved unable to commercialize PARC's dazzling stream of inventions.
3. Neither IBM nor the Route 128 minicomputer firms knew what to do with Intel's microprocessor after its invention in 1971.
4. When it finally managed to create a PC, IBM did it only through a crash program in Florida, far from a jealous corporate headquarters.
5. Even after the IBM PC, Route 128 remained in denial and faded.
6. Entrepreneurs in Texas established the new center of the global computer industry, one in a spin-off, the other from a dorm room.

16. Sea change

[I]ntel is the personal creation of its chief executive, Andy Grove. (Jackson 1997, p. 10)

The story so far: Intel's invention of the microprocessor in 1971 set the stage for the PC – which the Northeast's computer firms then failed to develop. That task was left to newcomers, notably adolescent or 20-ish prodigies from California and Washington State. After several failures, IBM finally managed to emulate Apple's success, but only by moving the PC project's design far from Big Blue's headquarters, to Boca Raton in Florida, and only by using components from Intel and Microsoft.

By the mid-1980s, as Japan moved into the IT passing lane, IBM summoned its PC management back to its Armonk headquarters, where the PC was smothered – partly by 'analysis paralysis,' partly by jealous competition from IBM's mainframe managers. Meantime, and thanks to Compaq's early success at reverse-engineering, the initial outsourcing to Intel and Microsoft meant that clones using the same components were now taking away larger and larger shares of the PC market. IBM was about to fall, and the great Japanese electronics firms were ready.

PRIDE AND PARANOIA AT INTEL

Moreover, Japan had by the mid-1980s seemingly wrested the semi-conductor lead from US producers. In particular, Intel, itself the inventor of the DRAM memory chip, lost money in 1983 and 1984 in the face of heightened Japanese competition in that sector.

What happened next is the stuff of legend. For continuity, we pick up the thread from the early days of the company.

No R&D Lab, No MBA's

In 1968 Robert Noyce and Gordon Moore were the last two of the Traitorous Eight still working at Fairchild Semiconductor. As they had a decade earlier, Noyce and Moore obtained financial backing from venture capitalist Arthur Rock. They formed Intel and promptly hired Andrew Grove (who had worked under Moore in R&D at Fairchild) as the new Director of Operations.

At Intel they did without a separate R&D lab. All three men had Ph.D.'s: Noyce from MIT, Moore from the California Institute of Technology, and Grove from Berkeley. Thus armed, they saw no reason for a separate R&D unit within the company. Nor would one be created until 1995, when Intel's global supremacy was established. (Incidentally, Microsoft also did without an R&D lab until 1991 – by which time Windows 3.0 was already up and running. (See Buderi 2000, chapter 10.)

Instead, Moore ran R&D functions personally. Noyce, himself the co-inventor of the integrated circuit (IC) in 1959, handled the public side. And as 'Director Ops' Grove took charge of everything connected with production.

Were these three legendary figures entrepreneurs, managers, or a mutational hybrid? Already renowned and successful, Noyce and Moore were motivated, as Moore said, by the prospect of getting back to the excitement of doing a start-up (Jackson 1997, p. 20). And excitement there was.

Within the first two years Intel came up with the three big innovations that put the company on the map. Two, EPROM and DRAM, advanced the infant technology of memory chips. The third was a new use for semiconductors: the microprocessor (or, as it would come to be known later, the computer on a chip). The company thus originated with a flurry of major innovations. Moore and Noyce had returned to the promised land.

At the same time, however, Grove came up with the slogan, '*Intel delivers.*' His point was that the company was not merely an innovator, but could also be counted on as a supplier. Whereas Moore and Noyce had returned to the entrepreneurial quest, Grove saw himself as a master of the art of management.

The Outsider

Born Jewish as Andras Grof in 1936 in Hungary, Grove spent World War II in hiding from the Nazis (Jackson, p. 31). In 1956, after the unsuccessful rebellion against Hungary's Soviet-backed government, Grove emigrated to New York City. Three years later he graduated first in his class at City College with a degree in chemical engineering. He then enrolled at Berkeley, where the weather suited him better, and after another three years earned a Ph.D. in physics. In 1963 he joined Moore's R&D operation at Fairchild, while lecturing in physics at Berkeley – and eventually writing a book on semiconductor properties.

Grove's biographical sketch at the end of *High Output Management* (1983, 1985, p. 237) describes its author as a man of several parts. 'As a scientist, Grove participated in bringing about major breakthroughs in the technology of semiconductors. As an entrepreneur, he helped found Intel Corporation, which he now serves as president.' As the title suggests, however, the book addressed neither science nor entrepreneurship but management.

In the 15 years from its inception, Intel had gone from the two founders and Grove to 20,000 employees. By 1983 some 40 percent worked directly in production, attended by another 15 percent to service the machinery and improve the design of the process. Another 25 percent handled the paperwork present in any large company. The remaining 4,000 worked on product development, sales, and service (Grove 1983, p. xi).

Cooking

As Director Ops, it had been Grove's task from the start to keep the growing company competitive in a tumultuous industry. This he did through a tightly formulated control system. This he explained in the book in terms of what it takes to deliver breakfast in a short-order restaurant – a job he had held in college.

One principle is batch production; it costs too much to produce something on-demand, customer by customer. Another is that the task in either setting has three components: *process, assembly, and tests.* A third is that in each sequence (breakfast or micro chips) the operation will hinge on a specific step, such as preparing the eggs, a time-sensitive procedure.

Grove proposes the breakfast analogy as a template not just for moving chips through the manufacturing sequence, but for every activity within the company. A first step is quantification: attaching a numerical measure to each component's output, so that output (rather than just activity) can be tracked and compared to goals. This, he says, has been done at Intel for janitorial services (number of square feet cleaned), personnel (number of new hires), and so on.

What, then, is the role of the individual manager, especially the middle-manager? In outline:

1. Each function, encompassing all 20,000 employees (in 1983) can be understood and represented in terms of output-oriented or *quantified goals.* The common unit is the team.
2. The goal of the manager should be to *leverage* his or her impact by choosing only the specific daily activities that maximize the output of all relevant teams under the manager's influence.
3. Then, in accordance with 'the sports analogy,' motivate each employee to reach *peak performance* with task-relevant feedback. And as noted in

the last chapter, the system of rewards operated throughout the company, not just among managers.

Grove advanced this theory of management as a general approach within all manner of organizations, including government bureaucracies. To that extent, in this 1983 manifesto Grove considered himself to have come up with an approach as general as Frederick Taylor's 'scientific management' in the early days of the twentieth century.

And yet this sort of closed-system perspective came up short in the crisis then brewing. Despite the system of 'constructive confrontation' Grove had instituted to air issues and controversies, Intel had succumbed to the corporate myopia that prevented the company from recognizing a sudden change in the business environment.

What was also needed, it turned out, was the capacity to view a problem through an outsider's eyes.

PARADIGM SHOCK

'There is at least one point in the history of any company when you have to change dramatically to rise to the next performance level. Miss the moment and you start to decline' (Grove 1993, p. 58). At Intel the moment came in 1985 (see Figure 16.1). The problem? By the early 1980s Japanese memory-chip firms had caught up with Intel and other US companies.

In *Only the Paranoid Survive*, Grove writes that '10X' changes can come from any of a half dozen places in a business's environment (Grove 1996, p. 30). Such 'order of magnitude' changes are unlikely to be recognized at first yet may threaten a company's survival. As we saw in Chapter 13, Christensen (1997) has termed a specific version of the recognition problem *The Innovator's Dilemma*.

The recognition issue has also been described as a problem of paradigm-shock in Steven Covey's anecdote of the proud captain of a mighty vessel signaling a smaller boat to give way on a dark night at sea. The answer the captain receives: 'I am the light-house keeper' (Covey 1989, p. 33).

Grove (1996, p. 89) recalls the comparable moment of recognition in a conversation with then Chairman and CEO Gordon Moore in mid-1985:

> [I] turned back to Gordon and I asked, 'If we got kicked out and the board brought in a new CEO, what do you think he would do?' Gordon answered without hesitation, 'He would get us out of memories.' I stared at him, numb, and said, 'Why shouldn't you and I walk out the door, come back and do it ourselves?'

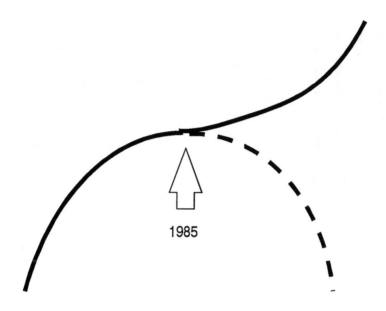

Source: Grove (1993, p.57).

*Figure 16.1 Grove's transformation curve for Intel in 1985: aban-
doning DRAM's to Japan, embracing microprocessors*

The company surrendered memory chips to Japan and turned solely to
microprocessors (at the time, 286's).

THE BREAK-UP OF THE OLD COMPUTER INDUSTRY

What happened between Intel's company-saving decision and 1990 Grove
describes as 'The breakup of the old computer industry. . . [which] gave
Intel its chance and made the mass-produced computer possible' (1993, p.
57).

The change can be described in terms of Grove's sketch of vertically
integrated companies vs. new horizontal tiers differentiated by component.
As Figure 16.2 shows, the old system had self-contained, relatively closed
and proprietary systems *á la* Route 128 and IBM. 'These vertically
integrated companies would compete against [each other] . . . and buyers

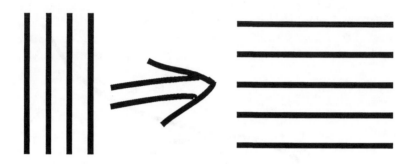

Source: Grove (1993, p. 57).

*Figure 16.2   Grove on how IT firms compete: horizontally, via open
architectures*

had to commit to the whole package of one manufacturer or another (Grove
1983, p. 57).

Open Systems

By contrast, the new, horizontal model of competition was based on open
(that is, published) technical standards and full compatibility between every
component-maker's products and every other's. In Figure 16.2, for
example, each horizontal line represents a product axis along which
companies in a particular segment of the market (systems software,
monitors, printers, software applications, etc.) compete.

The products from each segment must be fully compatible with those on
every other horizontal tier – or customers will not buy them. This new
system Grove termed 'industrial democracy,' in the sense that 'It resists
central guidance. Nobody can tell anyone else what to do' (p. 57). In
contrast to the old regime, choices abound and competition drives prices
down.

Consumers also benefited from an accelerated pace of technological
change. In a demonstration of the 'Arrow effect,' IBM had notoriously
restricted the pace of technological change with a view to maximizing its
profits over time. Its mainframe installations were known for 'golden
screwdriver' techniques, in which a demand for more performance (at
higher rental rates) would prompt a visit from an IBM technician who
would insert a few lines of code into existing software and unlock new
power in the machine (Carroll 1993, p. 217). Similar restrictions of
hardware potential marked IBM's missteps with its PC-AT in the mid-
1980s.

The new rules forced the pace of technological change and translated lab potential into product. Grove's analogy is skis. '*Any ski boot works with any binding. Any binding fits any ski. That permits innovation to take place independently in boots, bindings, and skis*' (1993, p. 57, emphasis added).

STANDARD-SETTING

But who would make the profits required for high levels of sustained R&D? Charles Morris and Charles Ferguson contend that the key to profitability is to control the standards, protocols, and formats by which the different parts of an information system are linked. Put the other way around, we find a (perhaps belated) recognition that Japan is only human.

> Scale, friendly government policies, world-class manufacturing prowess, a strong position in desk-top markets, excellent software, top design and innovative skills – none of these, it seems, is sufficient, either by itself or in combination with each other, to ensure competitive success in this field (Morris and Ferguson 1993, p. 87).

Instead, the key in their view was *proprietary control over a dominant open system*.

Examples were Microsoft in system software, Novell in network software, Sun in network hardware and software, Adobe and Hewlett-Packard in printer protocols, and Intel in microprocessors. These Wild-West companies managed to make the codes and standards for their products established as industry norms. Then the proprietary, company-specific control of the open system gave the company in question an edge in the race to pump out new products.

As Grove observes, 'A leading-edge product requires leading-edge manufacturing capability, and you can't buy it' (Grove 1993, pp. 57-8). It requires massive investment, which requires massive profits, which come from competition via standard-setting.

That is the puzzle the successful Wild-West firms solved in the late 1980s. In turn, their ability to handle the pace of innovation given by Moore's Law while still maintaining continuity of standards created shock waves worldwide. It gave the US a second wind as the race with Japan carried into the 1990s.

17. The US comeback, 1989-1994

Japan has almost no equivalents to the independent start-ups that have come to dominate many market segments in the United States, including PCs, disk drives, and packaged software. (Dedrick and Kraemer 1998, p. 92)

In *Only the Paranoid Survive*, Andrew Grove sums up the 'new rules of the horizontal industry' around three points, which add up to a strategy for reaping 'increasing returns.' (1) Specialize according to your strength, while also maximizing compatibilities, so that, in effect, the skis, bindings, and poles are completely interchangeable. (2) Be a 'first mover,' embracing the opportunity given by a change in markets or technology. (3) Price for volume, not on the basis of costs, then do everything possible to bring down unit costs through economies of scale (Grove 1996, 1999, pp. 51-2).

While there are numerous books about 'the' New Rules, this summary gets to the heart of the increasing-returns logic linked to Brian Arthur of the Santa Fe Institute. As he put it in a reprinted 1990 article, 'Increasing-returns mechanisms do not merely tilt competitive balances among nations; they can also cause economies – even such successful ones as those of the United States and Japan – to become locked into inferior paths' (Arthur 1994, p. 10).

This ominous passage seemed to sound a warning to the US when it originally appeared in the *Scientific American* in February 1990 (pp. 92-9). But a decade later the meaning has been reversed. Something about the technology trajectories and industry structures of Japan in the 1980s caused that nation's great electronics companies to miss out on the PC revolution.

Since there was little or no breathing room for entrepreneurial start-ups, Japan as a nation thus fell far behind in the global IT race during the 1990s.

LINKAGES AND REVERSALS

In each of the four sectors sketched in Chapter 14, then, what actually happened was the opposite of what most people had expected in 1989.

Semiconductors

In 1985 Grove and Moore made the momentous decision to re-focus Intel around microprocessors, abandoning memory chips to the Japanese. Figure 17.1 shows Japan taking the lead in that year, pulling far ahead by 1989,

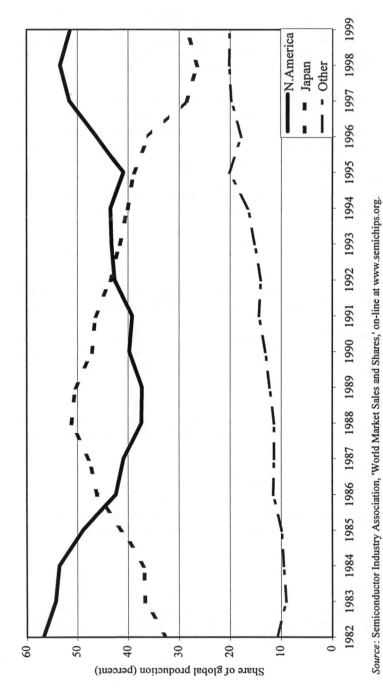

Source: Semiconductor Industry Association, 'World Market Sales and Shares,' on-line at www.semichips.org.

Figure 17.1 The US resurgence in global market shares for chips in the 1990s

then being overtaken by 1993. From 1995 on, the US share of total semiconductor sales surged, reaching 50 percent again by 1999.

Japan's share, in the meantime, fell to about 30 percent. The US excelled in the high-markup microprocessor end of the chip spectrum. In addition, Korea mounted a successful low-end challenge in commoditized memory-chips, as in earlier drives in steel and shipbuilding. By the same token, the increase in global shares by other producers to about 20 percent reflects the growing presence of both Korea and Taiwan.

Computers

Computer production also displayed a surprising US resilience, as the increasing-returns logic of the 'Win-tel' standard defined by Microsoft and Intel rippled outward to boxes. One indicator was the failure of Japanese microcomputers to make much of an inroad into the US market. Following a jump from 9 to 13 percent between 1989 and 1990, Japan's US share fell back to 6 percent in 1991. Commenting on this reversal, Steve Jobs observed in 1992, 'The United States computer manufacturers have re-invented themselves and are holding on to the most desirable market in the world' (quoted in Markoff 1992).

The eventual outcome found Japanese firms supplying US computer makers with flat screens and memory chips, but struggling to sell the US markets the actual computers. 'Dependence on US standards has trapped the Japanese computer industry in the decreasing returns segments of the PC industry,' blocked from the 'large increasing returns markets for software and microprocessors' (Dedrick and Kraemer 1998, p. 89).

Figure 17.2 shows that by 1999, six of the world's seven top PC manufacturers were US-headquartered. To be sure, firms like Apple and IBM had widely scattered production sites (notably in Singapore and China). But Dell (number two and rising) and Gateway represented top-seven firms that also sited much of their production within the US.

At the same time, the top seven accounted for only half of the estimated 114 million PCs sold in 1999. In the background, local no-name producers in Taiwan and China were producing more and more of the world's IT output. Most of it, however, remained at the hard-scrabble end of the IT spectrum, marked by intense competition and thin profit margins.

Software

As to software, point one was the demise of Japan's Fifth Generation project. After ten years, MITI gave up the ghost in mid-1992. 'The problem for Japan is that the computer industry shifted so rapidly that the

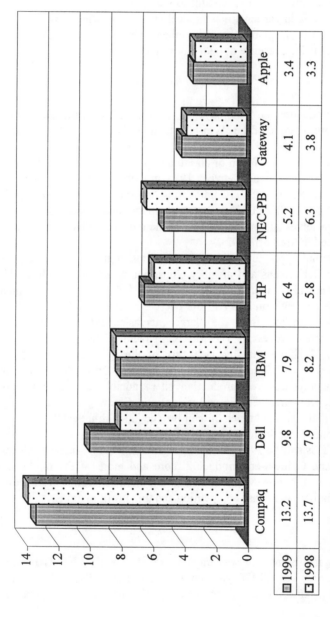

	Compaq	Dell	IBM	HP	NEC-PB	Gateway	Apple
■1999	13.2	9.8	7.9	6.4	5.2	4.1	3.4
□1998	13.7	7.9	8.2	5.8	6.3	3.8	3.3

Note: Preliminary estimates. Share of top 7 was 50.0 percent of 1999 total of 113,521,000 units.
Source: Dataquest, January 24, 2000.

Figure 17.2 Global PC market shares in 1999 (percent)

technological path the Fifth Generation took – which seemed a wise choice in 1982 – turned out to be at odds with the computer industry's direction by 1992' (Andrew Pollack 1992). The lack of interest in the software that resulted led MITI to give it away free, though few took them up on the offer.

Equally important was the triumph of Microsoft's Windows platform, an exercise in cumulative standard-setting that gave an edge to US computer companies relative to, say, NEC or Toshiba, which were late to commit to the standard.

The upshot for the US software industry was an explosion of high-paid employment, as Chapter 19 will document in some detail.

HDTV

As with the Fifth Generation project's commitment to the wrong technological trajectory, so too with HDTV. US companies developed digital approaches that leapfrogged Japan's analog approach:

> [E]nlightened federal regulation, rapidly advancing digital technology and cooperation between competing organizations have combined to vault the late-starting United States into a clear lead in the race to develop practical high-definition television. (Cook 1992, p. 14)

In 1994 the director general of broadcasting in Japan's Ministry of Posts and Telecommunications conceded as much. He created a furor by revealing that his ministry was contemplating withdrawing support for Japan's HDTV program. The announcement was taken to signal 'The triumph of American-style HDTV, something almost unimaginable five years ago. . . .' (Pollack 1994)

In any case, HDTV still waits in the wings years later. The fear in the late 1980s was that HDTV constituted a 'strategic technology.' But the new standard has yet to approach the network dynamic that gave, for example, DVD (the digital video disk) recent widespread adoption.

Industrial Policy: A Heavy Hand?

These four distinct sectors seemed to suggest that industrial policy can retard change in a dynamic technological environment. Pollack comments that the HDTV episode is especially telling: '. . . Japan's plan for HDTV showed the drawbacks in [its] system of Government-backed cooperative industrial development. The system allows for great staying power and steady progress down a particular path, but does not adjust well when the technological road turns.'

More generally, of the major government-sponsored R&D consortia from the 1980s, the Fifth-Generation project was not alone in its lackluster results. The others were the Supercomputer Project; a software campaign called the Sigma Project; and TRON, an attempt to attain widespread use of smart building components and appliances. All were attempts to wrest standard-setting power from the US. For diverse reasons, notably a lack of enthusiastic participation by key players, none came to much (Dedrick and Kraemer, pp. 106-109).

Such failures, combined with Japan's distant lag in its over-regulated telecommunications sector, seemed to point up the extent of the sea change in the world's IT industry. What had worked so well for Japan in the automotive and consumer-electronics sectors in the 1970s and 1980s looked shopworn by the mid-1990s.

THE GEOGRAPHY OF THE NEW BUSINESS MODEL

To sum up: In Chapter 15 we considered six examples of tensions between the old computer industry of the US Northeast and more entrepreneurial actors in the West. Now we have compared the dismal 1989 prospects and startling US comebacks during the 1990s in computers, software, semi-conductors (more specifically, microprocessors), and HDTV. The counterparts were surprising setbacks for Japanese efforts in each of the four components of IT, as well as in a related sector, telecommunications (though we have not considered it separately here).

The logical link between these two sets of events is what Andrew Grove termed 'the breakup of the old computer industry' between about 1985 and 1990. The drumbeat of 18-month product cycles for chips given by Moore's (and Joy's) Laws required quick responses by players throughout the IT sector.

If that sounds deterministic, perhaps we need to leave room for the technology as an influence, not just an outcome. The technology's momentum in effect 'required' entrepreneurial agility. Agility's nemesis is bureaucracy – which in the mainframe culture of IBM would slow decision-making to a standstill as Microsoft heated up the system-software design wars of the late 1980s. In a parallel quest, Intel's radical bet-the-company makeover after 1985 cleared the path to standard-setting leadership for microprocessors that has yet to be overthrown.

The new business model that took hold after 1985 spawned competition via open (published) systems, compatible components, and uniform technical standards across vendors. In addition, the characteristic PC firm was specialized in a particular slice of the sector:

[T]he PC industry from its earliest beginnings adopted a purely horizontal supplier structure. Companies such as Intel, Microsoft, Novell, Lotus, Compaq, Seagate, Oracle, 3Com, Electronic Data Systems, and many others thrived by being specialists in particular layers of a newly emerging IT industry value chain. *By focusing on just one technology area, the horizontal companies moved with a speed, deftness, and openness that the older systems companies simply couldn't match* (Moschella 1997, pp. x-xi, emphasis added).

The competitors that succeeded under the new rules were not only American, but from the West. 'From a global perspective, this change in vendor business models led to an even more dominant US competitive position. Most of the companies that mastered the horizontal model turned out to be American, usually from the western half of the country' (Moschella p. xi).

Without the regional realignment, the history of the US computer sector might well have remained the preserve of IBM and Route 128 (the aging upstarts). Japan would then have taken outright leadership in the IT sector from the US. Its great electronics companies, notably Fujitsu and Hitachi, but also Toshiba and NEC, gave every indication in the 1970s of knowing how to catch and overtake Big Blue. Instead, that would fall to such specialized standard-setters as Intel and Microsoft.

JAPAN'S IT STRATEGY IN THE YEAR 2000

To be sure, some observers still viewed the US resurgence as only transitory. Eamonn Fingleton, for example, wrote a 1995 book with the uncompromising title, *Blindside: Why Japan Is Still on Track to Overtake the US by the Year 2000.*

But as 2000 arrived, Japan's IT Strategy Council (led by Nobuyuki Idei, president of Sony) had a different view. The Council concluded that 'Our country must aim to accomplish a new period of rapid economic growth by stimulating new businesses and existing industries, and overtaking the United States within five years as a major high-speed Internet nation' (AP 2000, *SiliconValley.com,* September 1, 2000, on-line).

Japan's hopes lay in the possibility of a leapfrog-action around PCs to a wireless or telephonic mode of connectivity. As the world moved from a PC-based to a wireless mode of communication, the US looked increasingly vulnerable. The point was brought home by the startling success of a subsidiary of Japan's privatized telephone company (NTT, for Nippon Telephone and Telegraph). In a nation with relatively few PCs, Internet access has increasingly come through NTT DoCoMo, a wireless Internet delivery system that by mid-2000 had quickly found 10 million subscribers.

The next chapter takes a closer look at such changes in the IT landscape.

18. The Internet decade

> Put simply, the story of computer industry competition has been one of new
> waves of technology, led by new waves of vendors, rapidly overpowering much
> of the existing order . . . [T]he network-centric era will result in market and
> supplier restructuring every bit as great of those of the PC revolution.
> (Moschella 1997, pp. vi-vii)

As American computing evolved from the mainframe and minicomputer to
the PC and the Internet, the centers of design, strategy, and control that
were initially combined at IBM's headquarters at Armonk, New York,
would scatter far and wide. Table 18.1 lists stylized 'home-regions' for the
mainframe, mini, and PC eras. These are New York State for mainframes,
Boston's Route 128 for minicomputers, and the West generally for the PC
era.

The Internet stage began about 1994, the year that saw the removal of
the last major barriers to the creation of a 'network of networks.' Whether
it, too, can be said to have a home-region is one of the questions to be
considered now.

Table 18.1 *Changes in regional advantage over the life cycles of mainframe, mini, PC and internet-enabled systems*

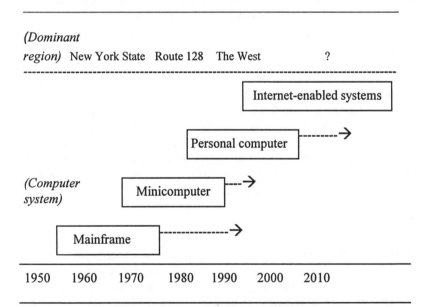

(Dominant region) New York State Route 128 The West ?

Source: Adapted by the author from Morgan Stanley Research Estimates as reported in Meeker
and DePuy (1996, p. 1-9).

OFFICIAL ORIGINS

What even the briefest sketch of the Internet's origins reveals is its non-commercial – and international – pedigree. It thus differs decisively from the PC. The PC was spawned by certified 'geeks and freaks' from the far West and by a corporate 'skunk works' in Boca Raton, Florida. The Internet has a more mainstream institutional lineage. And unlike the PC, it shows continuity between the Cold-War R&D regime and the infrastructure of the Digital Age. A complete account of this evolution may be found in Hafner and Lyon (1996). Here we note some highlights.

ARPAnet

The Defense Department's ARPAnet had been around since 1969. Right from the start it used packet-switching and routers, thanks to Leonard Kleinrock's inspired application of the queuing theory he had developed in his 1961 MIT doctoral dissertation. Bolt, Baranek, and Newman (or BBN, also of Cambridge, Massachusetts) contracted with the Pentagon to build ARPAnet. A router the size of a refrigerator was installed at the University of California at Los Angeles (UCLA), where Kleinrock was a professor, and packet-switching became a reality. Packet-switching technology was then long ignored by both IBM and AT&T as impractical.

TCP/IP

By the mid-1980s the National Science Foundation had helped ARPAnet evolve into a university research network based on the Pentagon's software standard. One of Kleinrock's graduate students at UCLA, Vinton Cerf, had written the original network protocol for ARPAnet and with Robert Kahn later wrote TCP/IP (Transmission Control Protocol/Internet Protocol). This network communications software operates as a traffic cop to allow the digital packets to fly across the Internet in all directions and reconnect as (usually) coherent messages or images.

WWW

Then came the Web – from Europe. By 1989 Tim Berners-Lee (a British physicist from Manchester and the son of two mathematics teachers), working at the European particle physics research lab CERN in Switzerland, had devised the hyperlink system of document linkage and access. (Before that, hypertext mark-up language or *html* had languished in literary applications.) Another deceptively simple breakthrough he made was the system of Internet addresses now known as URLs. On these and other counts, Berners-Lee emerges as the inventor of the World Wide Web. He got a pilot system up and running at CERN in December 1990, just in time to get the decade off to a good start (Berners-Lee 1999).

MOSAIC

The next step was a good graphical user interface (GUI) browser, MOSAIC, as devised in 1993 by programmers at the University of Illinois (where another public-spirited programmer had designed the widely used free e-mail program, Eudora). No sooner had the Illinois researchers got the bugs out than their team leader, Mark Andreeson, decamped for Silicon Valley and helped launch Netscape Navigator for profit in 1994.

At this juncture Metcalfe's Law came into play. It says that the costs of adding users to a network increase linearly, while the benefits expand quadratically. If a network's users increase in number from 99 to 100, for example, the costs to the network go up by the incremental cost per node, the same as if the number increased from two to three users. But the number of additional two-way connections goes up by 99, compared to only three more when a third subscriber is added. The larger the network, the greater the incremental benefit.

The smaller, closed proprietary business networks of the 1980s (MCI or AT&T, for example) had failed to break through to the threshold that was now accessible via the Internet and a Mosaic-class browser. That all changed quickly after 1994.

1997 LOCATIONS OF THE WORLD'S TOP 100 IT FIRMS

The Internet permitted a blending of computing, communications, and entertainment in the mid-1990s that, like the PC before it, changed the rules.

To get a sense of the changes the Internet brought, we can turn to a 1997 list of the world's top IT firms, then look at specific firms and their locations. The July 1997 *PC Magazine* list of the world's 100 'most influential' IT firms appears as Table 18.2.

The main point is that 81 of the top 100 in that year were American, and 54 from the West. Indeed, 43 of the top 50 were American. The role of US firms was thus even more dominant than the 81 percent share suggests, since most of the 19 non-US firms ranked below number 50.

In addition, the ages of the 100 firms become younger as we move west. Those predating 1960 tend to be from the Northeast – or outside the US.

Table 18.2 PC Magazine's 100 most influential PC companies in the world in 1997

1 Microsoft Corp.	41 GT Interactive Software Corp.
2 Intel Corp.	42 Ascend Communications Inc.
3 IBM Corp.	43 Sony Corp. **(Japan)**
4 Netscape Communications	44 Cyrix Corp.
5 Sun Microsystems Inc.	45 Diamond Multimedia Systems
6 Compaq Computer Corp.	46 CUC International Inc.
7 Hewlett-Packard Co.	47 Computer Associates Intl.
8 Cisco Sytems Inc.	48 AT&T Corp.
9 Oracle Corp.	49 Texas Instruments Inc.
10 Toshiba Corp. **(Japan)**	50 International Data Group
11 Dell Computer Corp.	51 Seiko Epson Corp. **(Japan)**
12 Apple Computer Inc.	52 Xerox Corp.
12 Adobe Systems Inc.	53 Iomega Corp.
14 Gateway 2000 Inc.	54 Dialogic Corp.
15 Novell Inc.	55 Samsung/AST Research **(Korea)**
16 3Com Corp.	56 Logitech International SA
17 Corel Corp. **(Canada)**	57 Matsushita Electric Industrial **(Japan)**
18 America Online Inc.	58 National Semiconductor Corp.
19 PointCast Inc.	59 PC Connection Inc.
20 Packard Bell NEC Inc.	60 Sharp Corp. **(Japan)**
21 Softbank Corp. **(Japan)**	61 Fujitsu Ltd. **(Japan)**
22 Intuit Inc.	62 Hitachi Ltd. **(Japan)**
23 Digital Equipment Corp.	63 NEC Corp. **(Japan)**
24 Silicon Graphics Inc.	64 Borland International Inc.
25 Symantec Corp.	65 MetaTools Inc.
26 US Robotics Corp.	66 Matrox Graphics Inc. **(Canada)**
27 Canon Inc. **(Japan)**	67 Sybase Inc.
28 Progressive Networks Inc.	68 MCI Communications Corp.
29 Macromedia Inc.	69 Motorola Inc.
30 id Software Inc.	70 Hayes Microcomputer Products
31 Seagate Technology Inc.	71 Adaptec Inc.
32 Advanced Micro Devices Inc.	72 Philips Electronics NV **(Netherlands)**
33 S3 Inc.	73 Western Digital Corp.
34 Acer Group **(Taiwan)**	74 Activision Inc.
35 Marimba Inc.	75 Cirrus Logic Inc.
36 McAfee Associates Inc.	76 Cabletron Systems
37 Micron Technology Inc.	77 ATI Technologies **(Canada)**
38 Autodesk Inc.	78 Aimtech Corp.
39 Bay Networks Inc.	79 Computer Discount Warehouse
40 Creative Technology **(Singapore)**	80 Quarterdeck Corp.

Table 18.2 PC Magazine's 100 most influential PC companies (continued)

81	CompuServe Inc.	91	Number Nine Visual Technologies
82	idealab!	92	Eastman Kodak Co.
83	DeLorme Mapping Co.	93	The Santa Cruz Operation Inc.
84	Informix Software Inc.	94	ViewSonic Corp.
85	Lexmark International Inc.	95	Rockwell Semiconductor Systems
86	Madge Networks Inc. **(UK)**	96	SAP AG **(Germany)**
87	Broderbund Software Inc.	97	The Learning Company Inc.
88	Phoenix Technologies Ltd.	98	Tektronix Inc.
89	Power Computing Corp.	99	Yahoo! Inc.
90	Be Inc.	100	Firefly Network Inc.

Source: Kirchner (1997).

Most Non-US Companies Were Old

Among Japan's ten entries, for example, eight were founded before World War II, and the average founding date is 1927. The remaining elder statesman on the list is the creator of the compact disk, Philips Electronics of the Netherlands, founded in 1891.

In all 19 of the top 100 firms were from outside the US, and Toshiba, at number ten, was the highest ranking among them. The nationalities of the 19 firms were mainly Asian, with Canada and Europe hosting three each. Japan accounted for ten listings: Toshiba (number 10), Softbank (21), Canon (27), Sony (43), Seiko (51), Matsushita (57), Sharp (60), Fujitsu (61), Hitachi (62), and NEC (63). Canada had three: Corel (17), Matrox Graphics (66), and ATI Technologies (77).

Europe also had three (the Netherlands' Philips Electronics, the UK's Madge Networks, and Germany's SAP), but none in the top 50. In Asia outside Japan, Taiwan's Acer was ranked at 34, Singapore's Creative Technology at 40, and Korea's Samsung/AST Research at 55.

The Vision Thing

To return to the question posed at the beginning of the chapter: Did the coming of the Internet have much impact on the pattern of regional specialization in IT? The events of late 1998 offered a new angle on this question, in that they revealed the inability of Silicon Valley companies to set the agenda for the Internet era.

By that time, of course, PC production was centered in Texas, and Microsoft set the software standards from Seattle. Then in 1998 it became clear that the struggle for commercial leadership on the Internet would take place between Microsoft and a company based in Virginia: America Online. Such was the implication of AOL's $5 billion takeover of Netscape, a warm-up for its much larger 1999 merger with Time-Warner.

As a columnist for the San Jose *Mercury News* observed in 1998,

> Before Marc Andreesen co-founded Netscape Communications Corp. in 1994, he'd moved from Illinois to Silicon Valley. . . . *It is the nerve center of visionary technology. But it sometimes lacks vision, or the ability to sustain it.* . . . Silicon Valley has long disdained AOL as an East Coast pretender. . . . But America Online is not a technology company. It is a media company, and an online shopping mall. . . . Every person, and place, has limitations. It's no slam on Silicon Valley to note that its imagination has sometimes been limited to techno-whizzery (Dan Gillmor, November 23, 1998, emphasis added).

A perverse implication (though not a meaning intended by Gillmor), was that the world may have needed Microsoft as a successor to IBM to set uniform standards for IT. Intel aside, Silicon Valley was a fluid assemblage of technology, creativity, and capital that at the same time never quite produced strategic grandmasters on the order of Bill Gates or Steve Case.

Such was the sense of things, at least, circa 1998. By 1999 anti-trust and technological challenges (true open-systems software, exemplified by Linux) gave every indication of destroying Microsoft's dominant position as a standard-setting natural monopoly.

More generally, the shift from a PC-based to a network-based playing field implied new competitive positions for Europe and Japan.

EUROPE'S POTENTIAL IN THE NET-CENTRIC ERA

In the long view, how did the rise of the newcomer western companies compare to earlier crises of national competitiveness? This book has described the US as a nation of country-sized regions at different stages of economic development. In that light, America's IT sector experienced an internal, regionally focused maturity crisis in the Northeast à la nineteenth-century Britain (Chapters 8 and 9). But now the newcomer companies, created by entrepreneurs in younger regions, were still American.

From the 1950s through the mid-1980s, IBM had made the rules, and the rest of the world largely adapted to them. By the late 1980s, it looked as if Japan's great electronics companies would replicate earlier triumphs in home electronics and automobiles. But that did not happen.

Once again by the mid-1990s the US held a clear lead in IT. The difference was that the sector's dynamism came not from a company with a dress code (IBM), but from a variegated spectrum of younger enterprises in the West.

The Entrepreneurship Gap, Revisited

As we saw in Chapter 10, one reason for the eclipse of Europe's IT sector in the 1980s and 1990s was the smaller role played by entrepreneurs, relative to mature firms. In a 1998 newspaper column, Lester Thurow regarded this as the reason Europe had dropped behind Japan and the US in the world's growth industries:

> *When breakthrough technologies occur, it is very difficult for old large firms to lead.* They have to cannibalize themselves to save themselves, and that is simply very difficult to do. If one looks at the 25 biggest firms (based upon stock market capitalization) in the United States in 1960 and again in 1997, six of America's twenty-five biggest firms either did not exist in 1960 or were very small. In contrast, in Europe all of the twenty-five biggest firms in 1997 were big in 1960. In the past four decades Europe has been able to grow no new big firms that could lead the world technologically (emphasis added; for a slightly different comparison, see also Thurow 1999, p. 23).

The Net-Centric Era: New Rules?

The changes now occurring in Europe may help open up new possibilities for entrepreneurial creativity. Moschella, for example, made a strong case in his 1997 book (chapter 12) for the resurgence of European companies with the shift to the 'net-centric era.'

One characteristic of the transition is the shift in what he termed 'supplier structure' away from the horizontal value chain toward a communications chain. He saw a corresponding shift in supplier leadership from US-made components to national telecommunications carriers.

In other words, Moschella assumed that national governments would retain control over major telecommunications suppliers, preventing complete globalization in this sector. The prospect was for a localization of the then unified global market, in which competitive advantage was gained through sheer design or cost efficiency.

Applying Porter's diamond model of national competitiveness, Moschella assigned number grades (in the form of stars) to the US, Japan, and Europe in a variety of categories he deems important for the next few years. The detailed evaluations are listed in Table 18.3.

Table 18.3   Competitor scores on Porter's diamond in IT

	Europe	Japan	US
Average score	3½	2½	4½
Factor conditions (telecommunications infrastructure)	4	3	5
Related industries	3	3½	4½
Demand sophistication	3½	2	4
Domestic rivalry	3	2	4½

Source: Compiled from ratings in Moschella (1997, Ch. 12).

The implication was a better outlook for Europe than for Japan. Summing over Porter's categories of (1) factor conditions, (2) related industries, (3) demand sophistication, and (4) domestic rivalry, Moschella computed aggregate ratings. The scorecard finds the US with 4½ stars (out of a maximum of five), Europe 3½, and Japan 2½.

In the event, both Europe's and Japan's prospects came to depend increasingly upon common standards and wireless technologies. As the net-centric era moved gradually from PC's to telephones, US producers seemed trapped in a maze of incompatible protocols.

SEEING THE WORLD THROUGH WIRELESS LENSES

A mid-2000 update on the top 100 IT firms tends to bear out the idea that non-US firms have new opportunities in the net-centric era. Table 18.4 shows *Business Week's* list of 'The Information Technology 100,' as of June of that year. In a nutshell, it reveals an increase in the number of non-US companies from 19 (as listed in Table 18.2) to 23 a few years later.

While an increase of four firms may not seem surprising, their placement on the list finds non-US firms moving up in the hierarchy. Now 15 of the top 50 are from outside the US, including the number-one firm on the list, Finland's Nokia!

Table 18.4 An avant-garde list of the 100 top IT firms in the net-centric era
(Business Week's 'Information Technology 100' as of June 2000)

Rank	Company	Sector	Country
1	Nokia	Telecom Equipment	Finland
2	Siebel Systems	Software	
3	Oracle	Software	
4	Nvidia	Semiconductors	
5	Taiwan Semiconductor	Semiconductors	Taiwan
6	CDW Computer Centers	Services	
7	PC Connection	Services	
8	Legend Holdings	Computers & Peripherals	Hong Kong
9	Xilinx	Semiconductors	
10	Analog Devices	Semiconductors	
11	Sun Microsystems	Computers & Peripherals	
12	Amdocs	Software	
13	Network appliance	Computers & Peripherals	
14	Micron Technology	Semiconductors	
15	Yahoo Japan	Internet Companies	Japan
16	CTS	Semiconductors	
17	Broadcom	Semiconductors	
18	Powerwave Technologies	Telecom Equipment	
19	S3	Semiconductors	
20	Stmicroelectronics	Semiconductors	France
21	China Telecomm (Hong Kong)	Telecom Services	China
22	Cypress Semiconductor	Semiconductors	
23	JDS Uniphase	Telecom Equipment	
24	Dell Computer	Computers & Peripherals	
25	Cisco Systems	Networking	
26	EMC	Computers & Peripherals	
27	Hon Hai Precision	Computers & Peripherals	Taiwan
28	Symantec	Software	
29	Ericsson (LM) Telephone	Telecom Equipment	Sweden
30	Internet Capital Group	Internet Companies	
31	Flextronics International	Services, Resellers, Dist.	Singapore
32	Netcom AB	Telecom Services	Sweden
33	Amkor Technology	Semiconductors	
34	Broadvision	Internet Companies	

Table 18.4 An avant-garde list of the 100 top IT firms (continued)

35 Kemet	Semiconductors	
36 Advanced Micro Devices	Semiconductors	
37 LSI Logic	Semiconductors	
38 Scientific-Atlanta	Telecom Equipment	
39 AVX	Semiconductors	
40 NTT Docomo	Telecom Services	Japan
41 ADC Telecommunications	Telecom Equipment	
42 Logitech International	Computers & Peripherals	Switzerland
43 Veritas Software	Software	
44 I2 Technologies	Software	
45 Getronics	Services	Netherlands
46 Infineon Technologies	Semiconductors	Germany
47 Murata Manufacturing	Telecom Equipment	Japan
48 IDT	Telecom Services	
49 Jabil Circuit	Services	
50 Texas Instruments	Semiconductors	
51 Computer Associates	Software	
52 Altera	Semiconductors	
53 SK Telecom	Telecom Services	South Korea
54 Celestica	Services	Canada
55 Nortel Networks	Telecom Equipment	Canada
56 Integrated Device Technology	Semiconductors	
57 Chartered Semiconductor	Semiconductors	Singapore
58 Apple Computer	Computers & Peripherals	
59 Asustek Computer	Computers & Peripherals	Taiwan
60 Tokyo Electron	Semiconductors	Japan
61 Tech Data	Services	
62 Titan	Services	
63 Atmel	Semiconductors	
64 ATI Technologies	Computers & Peripherals	Canada
65 Network Solutions	Internet Companies	
66 Tellabs	Telecom Equipment	
67 Citrix Systems	Software	
68 Nextel Communications	Telecom Services	

Table 18.4 An avant-garde list of the 100 top IT firms (continued)

69 Voicestream Wireless	Telecom Services	
70 Comverse Technology	Telecom Equipment	
71 Sprint PCS Group	Telecom Services	
72 Bea Systems	Software	
73 Rational Software	Software	
74 Netcreations	Internet Companies	
75 Microsoft	Software	
76 Cognos	Software	Canada
77 Conexant Systems	Semiconductors	
78 America Online	Internet Companies	
79 Lexmark International	Computers & Peripherals	
80 SCI Systems	Semiconductors	
81 Ciena	Telecom Equipment	
82 Compuware	Software	
83 Gateway	Computers & Peripherals	
84 Lattice Semiconductor	Semiconductors	
85 Sanmina	Services	
86 Solectron	Services	
87 Viant	Internet Companies	
88 Art Technology Group	Internet Companies	
89 Vignette	Internet Companies	
90 SBC Communications	Telecom Services	
91 Sapient	Internet Companies	
92 Maxim Integrated Products	Semiconductors	
93 Take-two Interactive Software	Software	
94 Yahoo	Internet Companies	
95 Micromuse	Internet Companies	
96 Verisign	Internet Companies	
97 Worldcom	Telecom Services	
98 Hewlett-Packard	Computers & Peripherals	
99 Burr-Brown	Semiconductors	
100 Infospace	Internet Companies	

Source: *Business Week*, 'The IT 100,' June 19, 2000 (pp. 138-54).

All such lists need to be appraised in context, of course, and this one in particular should come with red flags attached. For one thing, the selection process behind it remains a black box. For another, it omits Amazon, IBM, Intel, and eBay, while ranking AOL at number 78, right behind Microsoft (75th). It would seem that the criteria for such decisions are different from an assessment of the current crop of the most powerful or influential IT companies.

Instead, the designers of the list have looked into a crystal ball to discern a post-PC paradigm of 'The Second Coming of Software.' In that world, 'Corporations are moving their entire operations online' and turning over the management of their web-based activities to outside IT specialists (*Business Week* 2000, p. 88).

As a corollary, any shift away from traditional fully featured PCs to more network-based modes will elevate 'applications service providers' (ASPs). To that extent, software firms like Oracle (number 3) or hardware companies like Sun (11) will thrive.

The worldview that flows from such an exercise highlights consulting and web-based software firms – because all companies, new and old, will tend to rely on them. Also prominent are firms doing chip design and production where the application enhances wireless communications, adds bandwidth, or in some other way breaks through network bottlenecks.

Accordingly, Table 18.4 is tagged an 'avant-garde' list, meaning one that seems to place more emphasis on prospects than on current performance. Still, and in that light, it provides a valuable antidote to any tendency in this chapter to look back, or to place too much emphasis on a PC revolution now fading into the distant recesses of the twentieth century.

By the same token, the list provides a brisk reminder that US hegemony in IT may not survive the shift to the wireless and telephone-based delivery systems in which northern Europe and Japan now excel.

19. Postscript: State IT roles

> The evidence is suggestive of the emergence of a new set of locational influences, involving entrepreneurial climate, environmental amenities, and lower costs of living and doing business. (Holly and Clarke 1998, p. 1)

What happened to state technology profiles between 1986 and 1996, the decade covering the 'break-up of the old computer industry' (Grove 1993, p. 57)? For an answer, we draw on employment data for the three core components of the IT sector: computers, electronics, and computer services (including software) (see Figure 19.1).

The three industries are selected by virtue of their position at the heart of the digital revolution.[1] As per Chapter 6, we thus use a strictly digital measure of IT, one distinctly this side of the more inclusive 'knowledge-based' cluster of computers, telecommunications, and biosciences.

IT employment, so defined, was not a source of large-scale job growth for the nation as a whole, accounting for a net gain of 600,000 jobs. Separate and self-contained logics of competition and location prevailed.

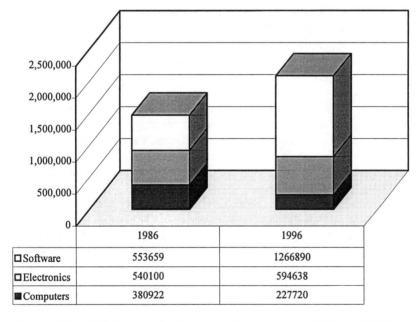

	1986	1996
□ Software	553659	1266890
□ Electronics	540100	594638
■ Computers	380922	227720

Figure 19.1 US job counts in three core IT components, 1986 and 1996

In computer production (SIC 357), the US job count peaked in the mid-1980s then plunged by 40 percent over the interval 1986-96, as mainframe and minicomputer production gave way to the PC's leaner production systems here and abroad (see Table 19.1). In electronics (SIC 367), both Asian competition and domestic defense cutbacks held US employment in check.

Table 19.1   US employment changes in three IT components, 1986-1996

	1986	1996	Change	(%)
Total	1,474,681	2,089,248	614,567	42
(357) Computers	380,922	227,720	-153,202	-40
(367) Electronics	540,100	594,638	54,538	10
(737) Services	553,659	1,266,890	713,231	129

Source: US Department of Commerce, *County Business Patterns* for 1986 and 1996.

Only in computer services (SIC 737) did rapid national job growth spur employment in all states. Software and other computer services more than doubled to 1.3 million, giving this component some 60 percent of the IT sector's jobs by 1996.

Silicon Elsewhere

Whatever IT jobs lack in numbers they more than make up for in prestige. At issue is the evolution of state employment structures toward (or away from) the Holy Grail: becoming 'the next Silicon Valley.' In virtually every state, of course, policies are pushed to expand the IT base, in hopes of reaping the harvest of high-wage jobs. (This is one reason we track employment rather than output.)

A 1997 list, 'Silicon Elsewhere,' from Silicon Valley's San Jose *Mercury News*, thus documented the aspirations of newcomer rivals ranging from Silicon Mountain (Colorado) to Silicon Dominion (Virginia) and beyond to Silicon Plateau (Bangalore, India) and Silicon Island (Taiwan).

Who excelled in the quest, and why? In general, as Figure 19.2 shows, the states that increased their shares of US IT employment between 1986 and 1996 were 'elsewhere,' meaning not California or New York or Massachusetts, the initial leaders.

To get at an explanation for differences in growth and in 1996 employment structures, we posit a model to test for post-1986 dispersal. We test for *the spatial dispersal of employment from the states that were most*

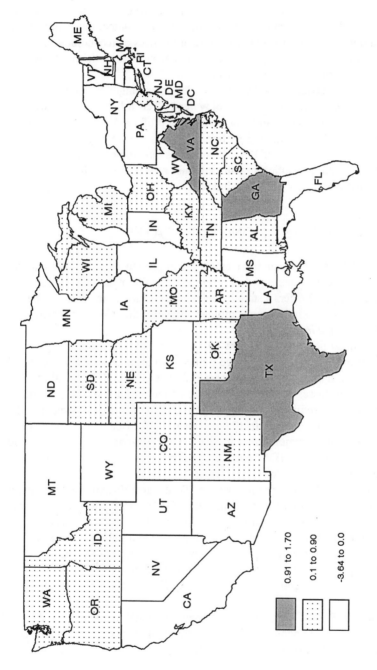

Figure 19.2   Changes in total IT shares by state, 1986-1996

0.91 to 1.70

0.1 to 0.90

-3.64 to 0.0

specialized in each activity in 1986, as measured by location quotients. A companion variable is regional, to designate whether a state is in the Northeast, the initial center of the mainframe and minicomputer industries. In addition, variables are added for such influences as technology linkages, education, unions, and wages. One version or another of the model is then fitted to each of the three components.

The next section provides an overview of changes in aggregate state shares of the nation's total IT employment. The following three sections scan the determinants of state job changes and of 1996 roles in each of the three sectors. The concluding section integrates the findings as to the new IT roles for the states as of 1996. It compares our findings, which are based on 1996 location quotients, with another recent study, the Progressive Policy Institute's New Economy Index.

REALIGNMENTS AMONG THE STATES

While all states participate in IT employment growth by virtue of computer services, some have increased in prominence while others have lagged. As noted, Figure 19.2 offers a state-by-state look at changes in shares of the US totals for the three industries combined. It shows that *Georgia, Texas, and Virginia had the largest gains*.

For added perspective, Figure 19.3 lists the 12 states that had gains or losses of more than 0.5 percentage points. Owing largely to its huge initial share of the nation's IT employment (22.4 percent in 1986), California's hardware job losses meant that its share of national IT fell by 3.6 points. The next most prominent states in 1986 were New York (7.8 percent of the 1986 total) and Massachusetts (7.0 percent). Each lost about 1.5 percentage points. The other major losers in share were Arizona, Pennsylvania, and Minnesota (where IBM had a facility and Cray Computing, a supercomputer firm, failed).

The brisk relative gains in Georgia, Texas, and Virginia set them apart from most of the South (or Southwest). For Virginia, the 1.7 point gain reflects a software expansion fueled by America Online and by the dispersal of federal government activities to both private and public agencies across the Potomac (Haynes et al. 1997). Texas's gain of 1.6 points was driven by rapid expansion in its electronics sector. Georgia's rise signals its emergence as a regional center – and a winner relative to neighboring Florida.

On the West Coast as well, internal regional realignments can be discerned. Both Oregon (with an expanding Intel facility in the Portland area) and Washington (home of Microsoft) gained more than 0.5 points.

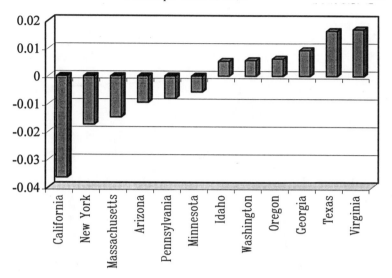

Figure 19.3 Swing states in the IT realignment, 1986-1996
(changes in shares of US total IT)

Within the Pacific division, in other words, a dispersal north from California rearranged the landscape.

As my anecdotal comments imply, the reasons for such outcomes lie in the separate logics of competition, growth, and dispersal in each of the three IT components. A sketch of each follows, beginning with computer production.

COMPUTERS . . . THE HARDER THEY FALL

Between 1977 and 1984, as the Apple II and then the IBM PC entered the picture, computer employment in the US soared 70 percent, from 302,500 to 515,000 (see Figure 19.4). But by 1984 Compaq had reverse-engineered the BIOS chip of the PC, which otherwise could easily be assembled from Microsoft and Intel components. That opened the door to the clone-makers.

When You Have Something, You Have Something to Lose

After 1984 a cost-driven dispersal then scattered production, including US-headquartered production, abroad. US employment has drifted downward since, though buoyed recently by Dell and Gateway. Today it stands at about 380,000.

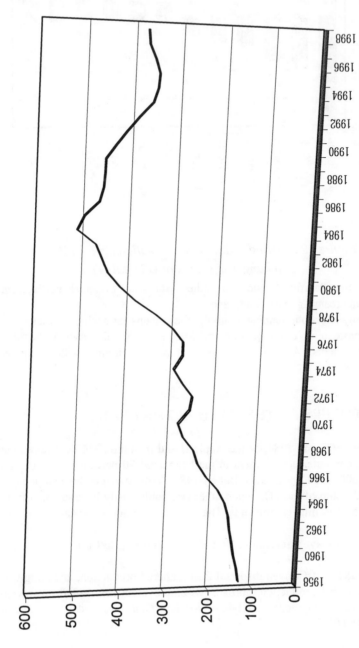

Figure 19.4 US computer manufacturing employment, 1958-1998 (SIC 357, in thousands)

The states that had the largest stake in computer production (SIC 357) in the mid-1980s had most to lose – and proceeded to do so. Which states were they? A standard measure of specialization is the *location quotient*. It is computed here as the ratio of (1) a state's percentage share of nationwide SIC 357 employment to (2) the state's share of total US employment. A location quotient of 1.0 thus indicates a state's share of computer employment that is the same as its share of the nation's total employment. A ratio above 1.0 indicates specialization.

In 1986 the states with computer employment over twice their share of the national average were Minnesota (4.8), Idaho (3.2), Massachusetts (3.2), Colorado (3.1), Utah (3.1), New Hampshire (2.8), Arizona (2.7), California (2.3), and South Dakota (2.1). These indicators show that some western states were already specialized in computer production at the beginning of the period.

In other words, the big losers were not only the states of the Northeast but other established producers: California (-44,000), Minnesota (-18,000), Arizona (-12,000), Florida (-11,000), and Texas (-9,000). Together with Massachusetts (-32,000) and New York (-19,000), they accounted for virtually all the decline in US computer employment during the interval.

The star performers were the handful of states that gained employment in the face of such widespread job losses. South Dakota, paced by Gateway, led the list with about 6,000 jobs.[2] Oregon also added over 5,000. Idaho, home of Micron, added nearly 4,000. Alabama (3,700) and North Carolina (2,900) also gained jobs.

An appendix to this chapter lists a regression equation (19A.1) to explain this difference. The equation as a whole accounts for about half the variation among states in computer-job losses over the period. It might be interpreted as follows. A state's predicted losses were larger (1) the more specialized it was in 1986, (2) the higher its manufacturing wages, (3) the faster its population growth in the 1980s, (4) the larger the share of its population in poverty in 1990, and (5), the larger the decline in its business establishments during the early 1990s (see appendix Table 19A.1).

What the variables document is a shift from established coastal centers to smaller, less urban states away from the Northeast and California.

Changes in Computer Location Quotients

The realignments that occurred also register as changes in the location quotients for computer production from 1986 to 1996. Table 19.2 shows that *all of the nine states with the largest gains in location quotients were in the South and West*, led by South Dakota (home to Gateway Computers) and Idaho (home to Micron). At the other end of the spectrum, the states

The revolution

Table 19.2 Computer location quotients: changes and 1996 values

A. Change in location quotients, 1986-1996

Top 10		Change		Bottom 10	Change
1	South Dakota	10.08	41	New York	-0.41
2	Idaho	5.20	42	Florida	-0.49
3	Oregon	2.34	43	Nebraska	-0.65
4	Alabama	1.46	44	New Hampshire	-0.66
5	North Carolina	1.28	45	Maine	-0.94
6	Kentucky	0.80	46	Utah	-0.95
7	Wyoming	0.77	47	Minnesota	-1.34
8	Oklahoma	0.71	48	Vermont	-1.37
9	Washington	0.56	49	Massachusetts	-2.12
10	Delaware	0.49	50	Arizona	-2.37

B. Values and employment in the most specialized states, 1996

		Quotient	Employment
1	South Dakota	12.19	7,500
2	Idaho	8.42	7,500
3	Oregon	3.63	10,174
4	Minnesota	3.47	16,745
5	Colorado	3.32	12,030
6	North Carolina	2.95	20,406
7	Kentucky	2.42	7,500
8	Alabama	2.30	8,155
9	California	2.22	56,021
10	New Hampshire	2.15	2,349
11	Utah	2.12	3,750
12	Connecticut	1.82	5,896
13	Washington	1.40	6,368
14	Oklahoma	1.35	3,313
15	Massachusetts	1.10	6,940
16	Wyoming	1.05	375
17	Texas	0.84	13,210

hit hardest by the collapse of the mainframe and minicomputer markets registered negative changes. *New York and Florida, as well as four of the six New England states, occupied the bottom ten slots.*

The conclusion? The decline of IBM and the Route 128 companies registered in larger job losses for the states of New England and the Mid-Atlantic region, as the struggles of IBM and the mini-makers would lead us to expect. In addition, as initial specialists in PC production, California and Texas also experienced sizeable losses, apparently as a result of the movement of the industry to Taiwan and other low-cost centers of production offshore. And a few smaller states like South Dakota and Idaho managed to add jobs, as smaller PC companies expanded production within their borders.

Since 1996, of course, competition within the industry has seen a strengthening of Texas's role as the nation's new, unrivaled center of computer production. The acquisition of Route 128's Digital Equipment Corporation by Houston's Compaq and the bid by Austin's Dell to dislodge Compaq as the world leader make the point. The Lone Star State is now the PC State – and one of the four or five preeminent technology states in the US.

ELECTRONICS: INTEL ET AL.

As with computers, US electronics employment peaked in 1984 at about 660,000 (See Figure 19.5). This level would not to be seen again until 1998. In the latter year 284,000 of the 660,000 jobs in category 367, Electronic Components and Accessories, were semiconductor-related. The other 376,000 jobs were partly medium-tech (for example, printed circuit boards) and partly traditional components like resistors and capacitors.

The reasons for job losses after 1984 differ as between semiconductors and other activities in SIC 367. The timeline for semiconductor employment is in large part the story of Intel's bold decision in 1985 to let memory chips go to more efficient Japanese competitor – and to focus entirely on microprocessors.[3] The line for other electronics activities is more directly defense-dependent, as indicated by the loss of nearly 100,000 jobs nationwide between 1988 and 1992, with the end of the Cold War.

Mapping State Gains and Losses

Changes in state electronics employment between 1986 and 1996 thus reflect (1) global semiconductor competition and (2) the impact of defense-linked electronics cutbacks. They are also tied to (3) changes of fortunes of

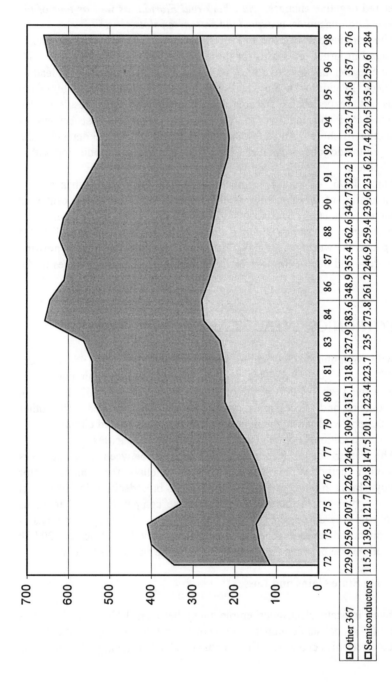

	72	73	75	76	77	79	80	81	83	84	86	87	88	90	91	92	94	95	96	98
□ Other 367	229.9	259.6	207.3	226.3	246.1	309.3	315.1	318.5	327.9	383.6	348.9	355.4	362.6	342.7	323.2	310	323.7	345.6	357	376
□ Semiconductors	115.2	139.9	121.7	129.8	147.5	201.1	223.4	223.7	235	273.8	261.2	246.9	259.4	239.6	231.6	217.4	220.5	235.2	259.6	284

Figure 19.5 Electronics (including semiconductor) employment, 1972-1998 (SIC 367, in thousands)

a state's *computer* sector. These three influences combined to hit certain states especially hard after 1986. In practice, the most defense-dependent states, such as California, Massachusetts, and New York, also tended to have high profiles in computer production in the mid-1980s – and to miss out on Intel's branch-plant start-ups.

As a result, most major producer states in the Northeast had brisk job losses in electronics employment between 1986 and 1996 (See Figure 19.6). Connecticut, New Jersey, New York, and Pennsylvania each lost from 28 to 38 percent of their 1986 job counts. In the Midwest, Illinois (the home of Motorola, which in addition to telephones makes microprocessors for the Macintosh), lost 13 percent. Florida, where the IBM PC had been created and brought to market in 1981, also had a slight decline for the decade after 1986.

Location quotients for SIC 367 thus fell in much of the Northeast, even as they rose sharply in a number of western states. The new line-up at the end of the period can be seen in Table 19A.2 in the appendix. The 1996 rankings thus reflect *both legacy (especially in the East) and novelty (as in some smaller western states)*. An example of legacy might be Massachusetts, with a value of 2.2 in 1996.

Newcomer specialists in electronics tend to be located away from both coasts. Consider New Mexico, at 2.8 – that is, nearly three times as much employment in electronics as its share of total US employment would predict. Idaho has a computer location quotient above 8, partly because it is home to Micron. South Dakota has a computer location quotient of 12, because of Gateway. As winners in the PC wars, they were also among the top ten states with the greatest specialization in electronics.[4]

Determinants of Electronics Roles in 1996

While linkages to a computer role give us one explanation for a state's electronics profile, Intel's predominance within semiconductor manufacturing points up a second key influence. That is, a major influence on the dynamics of electronics employment is *where Intel sites its production facilities*. But which states had Intel facilities?

In 1996, California-based Intel also had production sites in Massachusetts, Arizona, New Mexico, and Oregon (Blanton 1999). (Since then a new Intel 'fab' or fabricating plant has been introduced in rural Washington State, near Olympia, but it was not yet in operation in 1996.) These sites are consistent with a strategy of expanding Intel's growing base away from Silicon Valley, building fab plants at $1-2 billion apiece in smaller western states. As to the Massachusetts site, the state once had a minicomputer industry and can still lay claim to MIT.

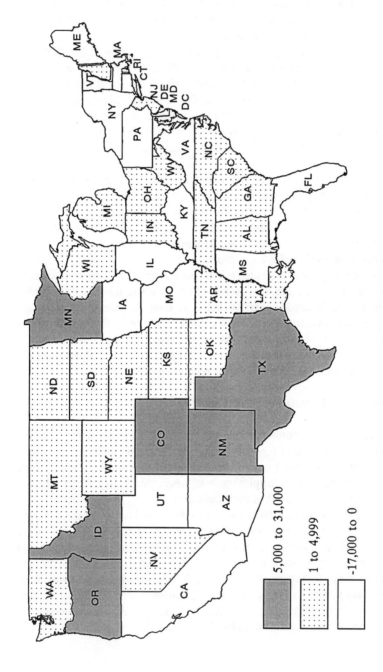

5,000 to 31,000

1 to 4,999

-17,000 to 0

Figure 19.6 Changes in electronics employment by state,1986-1996

As Table 19A.2 shows, *all five states with Intel plants in 1996 show up in the top ten*, the states most specialized in electronics. Combining Intel's plant locations and the linkage effects of a state's computer role gives us a workable explanation of the 1996 pattern of electronics specialization by state. Equation 19A.2 in the appendix accounts for 60 percent of the variation in location quotients for 367 in 1996.

In sum, the pattern of electronics specialization, a function not only of semiconductors but of the economy's now smaller defense sector, is more checkered than that of computer production. Nevertheless the tilt westward and to less urban-industrial states emerges as a pronounced tendency in this sector.

SOFTWARE: THE LANDSCAPE THICKENS

The main job-generator within IT is SIC 737 (see Figure 19.7). Between 1986 and 1996 employment here jumped nationwide by 713,000, an increase of 129 percent. Every state enjoyed job growth in 737, 'software and other computer services.' The slowest rate (for Mississippi) was still 27 percent, the next slowest (for Michigan), 52 percent. All but eight states at least doubled their initial job counts.

Computer services jobs are thus *the attainable prize* in the competition among states for IT employment. While many service activities are adding jobs rapidly, this sector is different. Unlike the rapid increase in, say, retail jobs, computer services employment tends to command impressive salaries. At the high end, the average 1996 earnings in pre-packaged software companies were $70,431 (Thurm 1997). Such prodigious salaries, which make software second only to financial services in pay levels, are perhaps still not the limit. In the land of Microsoft in 1998, 'the average Washington state software company worker earns $118,000' (Seattle *Post-Intelligencer*, 1998).

Holding on to the High End

Just as for computers and electronics, the prognosis for American software employment was at times dire in the late 1980s and early 1990s. The biggest threat seemed to be the abundance of well-educated but lower-paid programmer-types in such countries as India, the Philippines, and the post-Soviet economies. Given the low cost of data transmission via ever-improving telecommunications links, the implication was that US programmers would suffer something like the fate of the hand weavers in the face of the power loom two centuries ago. If such pessimism is hard to

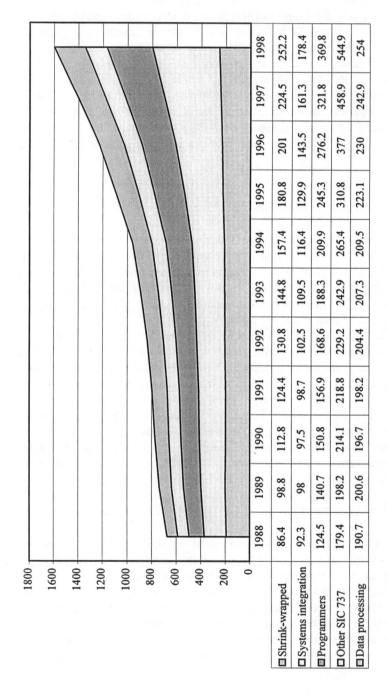

	1988	1989	1990	1991	1992	1993	1994	1995	1996	1997	1998
▣ Shrink-wrapped	86.4	98.8	112.8	124.4	130.8	144.8	157.4	180.8	201	224.5	252.2
□ Systems integration	92.3	98	97.5	98.7	102.5	109.5	116.4	129.9	143.5	161.3	178.4
▣ Programmers	124.5	140.7	150.8	156.9	168.6	188.3	209.9	245.3	276.2	321.8	369.8
□ Other SIC 737	179.4	198.2	214.1	218.8	229.2	242.9	265.4	310.8	377	458.9	544.9
▣ Data processing	190.7	200.6	196.7	198.2	204.4	207.3	209.5	223.1	230	242.9	254

Figure 19.7 Computer services employment in the US, 1988-1998 (SIC 737, in thousands)

believe today, one might recall such seemingly authoritative accounts as *The Decline and Fall of the American Programmer* (Yourdon 1993).

To be sure, between high US salaries, labor shortages, and the Internet, we can expect to find some milder version of this product-cycle dynamic – that is, a parceling out of software and programming jobs off-shore. A prominent example is Bangalore, India's 'Silicon Plateau' (See Wolman and Colamosca 1997, ch. 5). Stories abound of the US-Bangalore division of labor, in which sophisticated tasks can be 'zapped' to India late in a Silicon Valley afternoon, to be completed 'overnight' during Bangalore's workday and show up on California desktops at 9 a.m. the next morning.

By the same token, and as Figure 19.7 shows, the only major component of SIC 737 not to add much employment was routine data-processing – an activity that can readily be performed in low-cost remote sites around the world.

But it turns out that the globalization of computer services leaves plenty for US-sited workers (foreign and native alike) to do at the more creative high end. Between 1988 and1998 *employment in shrink-wrapped software roughly tripled, as did the job count for programmers.* Computer services employment has thus flourished, first with the PC revolution and now with the Internet.

Agglomeration versus Dispersal ... Within US Borders

In any case, there is a similar issue as to the location of software activity within US borders. Manuel Castells makes an eloquent case for the continuing concentration of software production in major urban centers. He contends that as a quintessential brainy activity, software design and production needs a large, high-density, diverse, university-enriched milieu to flourish (Castells 1996).

In this view, such mobility-enhancing tendencies as mechanization, standardization, and the high costs of initial centers are held at bay in the churning and competitive environment of the software sector. The value of face-to-face communication, the need for quick access to research institutions, and the constancy of change – all are thought to favor large metropolitan areas.

On the other hand, the researchers Brian P. Holly and Audrey E. Clarke saw a somewhat different tendency in their study of trends in computer services employment between 1988 and 1993. In their words,

Recent growth tends to favor less urbanized regions and larger metropolises on either coast. There is evidence that computer services activity is decentralizing to more peripheral areas and to medium sized metropolitan regions in interior parts of the country. The evidence is suggestive of the emergence of a new set of locational influences, involving entrepreneurial climate, environmental amenities, and lower costs of living and doing business. (1998, p. 1)

Their findings seem consistent with Figure 19.8, which portrays 1986-96 percentage changes in SIC 737 by state. There we can see that the largest relative gains occurred mainly in less urban, inland states. Statistical tests also confirm that *the higher a state's initial location quotient, the smaller its subsequent percentage gain in jobs.* To be sure, part of this apparent relative dispersal reflects larger percentage gains in states with small initial bases and to that extent is a misleading artifact of the measurement.

But it is clear that something else was going on as well to create a new regional tapestry. In particular, *location quotients fell in much of the South and Upper Midwest,* 1986-1996. Conversely, not only Microsoft's Washington State but also the Pentagon's and AOL's Virginia became more specialized.

A Gaggle of 1996 Software Roles

As a result, the 1996 division of labor found a regional bloc ranging from Wisconsin and Michigan in the North to Louisiana, Mississippi, and Alabama in the South whose employment structures were under-represented in SIC 737. (This bloc can be seen in Figure 19.9, which shows the states with 1996 location quotients below 1 in white.)

The specific 1996 values of location quotients for computer services by state are given in Table 19.3. Considering the 14 states in the table with values of the location quotient above 1, no one explanation will suffice – if only because SIC 737 has the distinct functional components displayed in Figure 19.7. (For a look behind this new pattern of specialization, see equation 19A.3 in the appendix.)

The least surprising entries, perhaps, are California, Massachusetts, Utah, and Washington. Connecticut and New Jersey are relatively specialized in computer services because they contain headquarters facilities for large numbers of Fortune 500 and other corporations. Minnesota and Texas may specialize in software in part because of their past and present roles as centers for computer production. Nebraska's surprising appearance toward the top of the list may reflect its prominence as a center for telemarketing. Maryland and Virginia benefit from their proximity to the nation's capital and its data-dependent activities. Rhode Island's defense complex near Newport (including the Naval Undersea Warfare Center) helps explain its software presence.

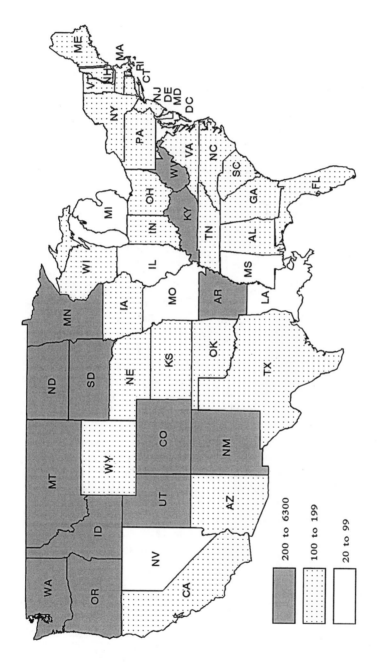

Figure 19.8 Percent change in computer services jobs, 1986-1996

200 to 6300

100 to 199

20 to 99

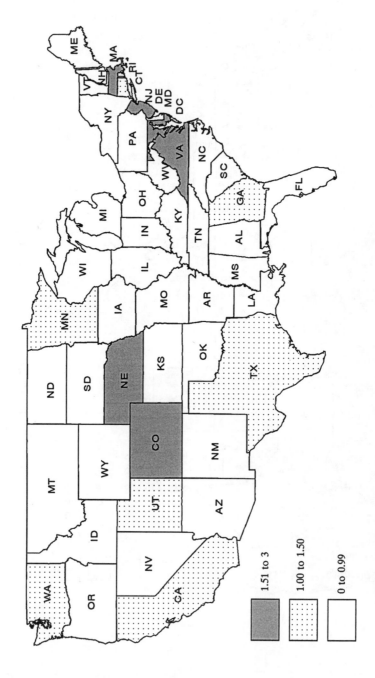

Figure 19.9 Software location quotients in 1996

ME

MA

VT

NH

RI

CT

NY

NJ

DE

MD

DC

PA

VA

WV

NC

OH

KY

SC

MI

IN

TN

GA

IL

AL

WI

MS

MO

AR

LA

IA

MN

OK

KS

TX

NE

ND

SD

CO

NM

WY

MT

UT

AZ

ID

NV

OR

CA

WA

1.51 to 3

1.00 to 1.50

0 to 0.99

Table 19.3 Software and total IT location quotients in 1996

	Software LQ		IT LQ
1 Virginia	2.71	1 Idaho	2.49
2 Massachusetts	2.15	2 South Dakota	2.14
3 Maryland	1.95	3 Massachusetts	2.04
4 Colorado	1.60	4 Vermont	1.98
5 New Jersey	1.55	5 Virginia	1.83
6 Nebraska	1.53	6 New Hampshire	1.79
7 California	1.43	7 California	1.72
8 Utah	1.38	8 Colorado	1.70
9 Georgia	1.21	9 Minnesota	1.43
10 Connecticut	1.10	10 Oregon	1.38
11 Minnesota	1.10	11 Arizona	1.34
12 Texas	1.06	12 Maryland	1.29
13 Rhode Island	1.02	13 Utah	1.27
14 Washington	1.01	14 Texas	1.18
15 New Hampshire	1.00	15 Connecticut	1.17
16 New York	0.96	16 New Jersey	1.14
17 Illinois	0.96	17 Rhode Island	1.10
18 Michigan	0.94	18 Nebraska	1.09
19 Pennsylvania	0.80	19 New Mexico	1.07
20 Missouri	0.80	20 Washington	0.96
21 Arizona	0.80	21 North Carolina	0.93
22 Oregon	0.78	22 New York	0.92
23 Florida	0.76	23 Georgia	0.83
24 Iowa	0.74	24 Illinois	0.83
25 Ohio	0.72	25 Alabama	0.82
26 Delaware	0.67	26 Pennsylvania	0.79
27 Kentucky	0.63	27 Kentucky	0.70
28 Alabama	0.62	28 North Dakota	0.69
29 Vermont	0.58	29 Michigan	0.68
30 Kansas	0.55	30 Florida	0.66
31 North Carolina	0.55	31 South Carolina	0.65
32 North Dakota	0.54	32 Missouri	0.62
33 Oklahoma	0.51	33 Maine	0.60
34 Wisconsin	0.49	34 Ohio	0.58
35 Idaho	0.48	35 Oklahoma	0.57
36 Arkansas	0.48	36 Wisconsin	0.54
37 Indiana	0.44	37 Iowa	0.53
38 New Mexico	0.43	38 Delaware	0.51

Table 19.3 Software and total IT location quotients (continued)

39 Montana	0.41	39 Indiana	0.49
40 South Carolina	0.40	40 Kansas	0.44
41 Tennessee	0.39	41 Arkansas	0.42
42 South Dakota	0.34	42 Tennessee	0.33
43 Maine	0.26	43 Montana	0.28
44 West Virginia	0.25	44 Nevada	0.23
45 Louisiana	0.24	45 Wyoming	0.22
46 Nevada	0.24	46 West Virginia	0.18
47 Mississippi	0.16	47 Louisiana	0.16
48 Wyoming	0.09	48 Mississippi	0.13

NEW ECONOMY ROLES

The results for the three industries combine to create new IT profiles for the states. Our results provide a basis for an informal taxonomy of emerging state roles in the New Economy. To that end, we can refer to the 1996 state location quotients for combined IT employment. The focus in this last section is on the states occupying *the top half of the ladder*, the 25 states with location quotients in total IT above 0.80 in Table 19.3. The top 25 are depicted graphically as the shaded states in Figure 19.10.

On what basis can we ignore the bottom half of the list – the states rendered in white in Figure 19.10? In general, it seems reasonable to conclude that the 25 states *below* the mid-point (including Alaska and Hawaii, which are not shown) have no particular IT foothold in the new scheme of things. To say as much is not to describe them as also-rans. It is merely to recognize that they have either faded from an earlier prominence (as with Pennsylvania and Florida) or (like Montana or Tennessee) have yet to make their presences felt on the IT front. The assumption is that they tend to react to the Internet revolution rather than to have much part in shaping it.

As to the top 25 states, they can be viewed as occupying three distinct positions:

- *Hardware specialists*: Idaho, South Dakota, Vermont, New Hampshire, New Mexico, Oregon, Arizona, and North Carolina.
- *Software specialists*: Virginia, Maryland, Nebraska, New Jersey, Georgia.

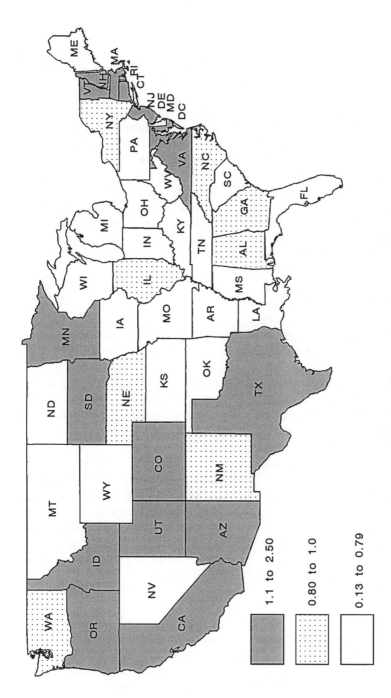

Figure 19.10 State IT location quotients in 1996

1.1 to 2.50

0.80 to 1.0

0.13 to 0.79

- *Balanced IT economies*: Massachusetts, California, Colorado, Minnesota, Utah, Texas, Connecticut, Rhode Island, Washington, New York, Illinois, and Alabama.

The premise for the categories needs to be made explicit. These classifications are derived entirely from 1996 location quotients. Hence they depend only on state employment structures. They reflect the share of a state's total private payroll employment that is accounted for by the several IT industries, singly and combined. The implicit assumption, therefore, is that most states in the top half of the IT ladder in Table 19.3 are there because of above-average past performance and above-average current IT resources.[5] But the indicator itself measures only the 1996 share of IT jobs in a state's economy, nothing more.

Given that caveat, we can now derive the three distinct IT orientations for the top 25 states.

(1) Hardware in the Hinterlands

Software's growing employment role within IT may seem to suggest that a state's location quotient for combined IT will depend on SIC 737 alone. Not so.

A useful exercise to get at the array of new state roles is as follows. Let us ask which states among the 25 (that is, with location quotients in IT at 0.8 or more in 1996) had markedly lower values for location quotients in software. In other words, *which states have now become specialized in IT mainly by virtue of their hardware roles?*

If we adopt a mechanical decision rule of selecting the handful of states whose location quotients in IT exceeded those for computer services by 0.4 or more, a clear pattern emerges. As Figure 19.11 illustrates, the eight states with the largest differential are all less urbanized, smaller states: Idaho, South Dakota, Vermont, New Hampshire, New Mexico, Oregon, Arizona, and North Carolina. The implication? For hardware manufacturers, these states seem to offer 'wide-open spaces,' in terms of economic cultures no less than of available land and labor.

(2) Software in the City

The states for which location quotients in software and other computer services exceed those for combined IT by more than 0.4 are fewer in number (see Figure 19.11). Most specialized by this measure are Virginia and Maryland, followed by Nebraska, New Jersey, and Georgia. With the

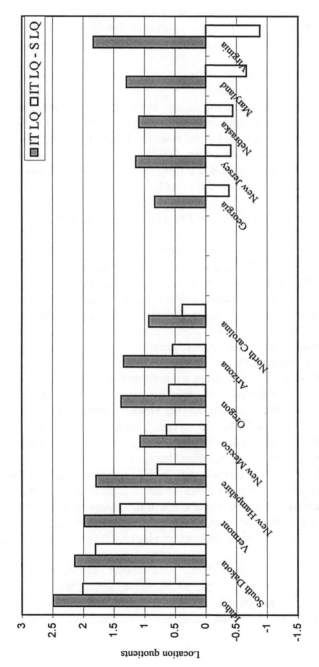

Figure 19.11 Hardware and software specialists in 1996

possible exception of telemarketing center Nebraska, software and other computer services are concentrated in the most urban portions of these states, which for three of them means the suburbs of Washington, DC, and New York City.

(3) Balanced IT Economies

The remaining states in the top 25 can be thought of as having hardware-software balance – as well as balance in the sense of shares of combined IT employment near or above the US average. Under heading (3) in the list, we begin with Massachusetts because within this group, it has the highest combined IT location quotient, 2.04. By the same token, Alabama, the last state listed, has the lowest indicator, 0.82.

Structure versus Potential: The PPI's New Economy Index

For perspective on the value and limitations of the labels thus derived, we can compare the top 25 states to a similar list compiled by the Progressive Policy Institute in *The State New Economy Index* (Atkinson et al. 1999). In contrast to the single-variable approach used here, the PPI proposes a weighted average of 17 different variables. These are grouped under the headings of 'knowledge jobs,' 'globalization,' 'economic dynamism,' 'the digital economy,' and 'innovation capacity.'

The two top-25 lists are compared in Table 19.4. The overlap is considerable: 20 of the 25 states are the same in both lists. But the few states that differ in the two lists point up contrasts in the two approaches. The PPI list includes Delaware, Florida, Nevada, Pennsylvania, and Kansas, none of which makes the top 25 derived from location quotients. It omits South Dakota, Rhode Island, Nebraska, North Carolina, and Alabama, each of which appears in the list developed here.

The PPI index thus elevates such mature industrial states as Delaware and Pennsylvania over such states as South Dakota and North Carolina. The 17-variable composite would seem to tilt toward education and patent variables, rather than employment outcomes. In contrast, the use of the single variable, the location quotient, emphasizes the production system *per se*.

Intuitively, the contrast may also reflect differing weights for entrepreneurship and new enterprise formation, as brought out by the two pairs of states just mentioned.

As it happens, these are the topics to be explored in the next few chapters.

Table 19.4 Top 25 states: location quotients versus the PPI New Economy Index

Rank		IT LQ 96	PPI rank	PPI rank		PPI index
1	Idaho	2.49	23	1	Massachusetts	82.3
2	**South Dakota**	2.14	43	2	California	74.2
3	Massachusetts	2.04	1	3	Colorado	72.3
4	Vermont	1.98	18	4	Washington	69.0
5	Virginia	1.83	12	5	Connecticut	64.9
6	New Hampshire	1.79	7	6	Utah	63.4
7	California	1.72	2	7	New Hampshire	62.4
8	Colorado	1.70	3	8	New Jersey	60.9
9	Minnesota	1.43	14	9	**Delaware**	59.9
10	Oregon	1.38	15	10	Arizona	59.2
11	Arizona	1.34	10	11	Maryland	59.2
12	Maryland	1.29	11	12	Virginia	58.8
13	Utah	1.27	6	13	Minnesota	56.5
14	Texas	1.18	17	14	Oregon	56.1
15	Connecticut	1.17	5	15	New York	54.5
16	New Jersey	1.14	8	16	Texas	52.3
17	**Rhode Island**	1.10	29	17	Vermont	51.9
18	**Nebraska**	1.09	36	18	New Mexico	51.4
19	New Mexico	1.07	19	19	**Florida**	50.8
20	Washington	0.96	4	20	**Nevada**	49.0
21	**North Carolina**	0.93	30	21	Illinois	48.4
22	New York	0.92	16	22	Idaho	47.9
24	Illinois	0.83	22	24	Georgia	46.6
23	Georgia	0.83	25	23	**Pennsylvania**	46.7
25	**Alabama**	0.82	44	25	**Kansas**	45.8

Note: Bolded states in each list are staes omitted from the other list's top 25 ranks.
Source: Progressive Policy Institute New Economy Index from Atkinson et al. (1999).

NOTES

1. A fourth candidate, communications equipment, is omitted because it was only beginning to 'go digital' in these years. The three core digital industries also differ from the traditional category of 'high-tech' activities. High-tech was typically defined in terms of a high proportion of engineers and R&D as inputs (Norton and Rees 1979). Today the issue resolves itself around the digital revolution: the expression and communication of all information in terms of 0's and 1's.
2. Gateway has moved its headquarters from Sioux Falls to San Diego, where the founder hopes to find it easier to attract skilled technical people.
3. That there is more to the story than Intel is made clear in Schoonhoven and Eisenhardt (1992), who compare the experiences of semiconductor start-up firms in Silicon Valley with those of comparable firms elsewhere.
4. The limits to the assumption of spatial linkages are also apparent. Semiconductor chips are the ultimate illustration of Alan Greenspan's 'Weightless World' theory of advanced development (Coyle 1998). Value is so high in relation to weight that overnight air shipment of chips adds little to the price. An example is the production by Illinois's Motorola of the microprocessor for Apple computers. Virtually from the start Apple computers were assembled in Singapore. Apple is thus a Silicon Valley computer manufacturer that takes its chips from an Illinois source, manufactures the boxes in Asia, then ships many of them back to the US market.
5. To cite a (literally) border-line entry, Rhode Island is on the list not because of rapid growth in IT employment, but because IT employment is about as prominent in its economy as in the nation's.

APPENDIX 19A

This appendix reports regression results for the three sectors profiled in the body of the chapter. A glossary following the equations provides definitions of the variables.

Equation 19A.1: Absolute Changes in Computer Employment, 1986-96

$$COMPJOBS = 26600 - 4049\ LQC86 - 2109\ WAGES - 288\ DPOP80 - 576\ POVT$$
$$\quad\quad\quad (2.4)\quad (4.6)\quad\quad\quad (2.5)\quad\quad\quad (3.1)\quad\quad\quad (2.3)$$

$$+ 3399\ DESTABS,$$
$$(5.0)$$

$R^2 = 0.49$ (adjusted for degrees of freedom), $F = 10.2$, $n = 48$.

The absolute values of the t-ratios are parenthesized under their coefficients, which are all significant at $p = 0.05$. The number of observations is 48; Alaska and Hawaii are omitted.

The dependent variable, to repeat, is the absolute change in a state's computer employment, 1986-96. *LQC86* is the location quotient for a state in SIC 357 in 1986. *WAGES* is average hourly earnings of a state's production workers in manufacturing in 1990. *DPOP80* is the change in state population, 1980-90. *POVT* is the percentage of a state's 1990 population with incomes below the poverty line. *DESTABS* is the per capita net change in the number of a state's private non-farm payroll business establishments, 1990-94.

An interpretation of the results appears in the body of the chapter.

Equation 19A.2: Electronics Location Quotients in 1996

$$LQE = 2.2 + 1.0\ INTEL + 0.15\ LQCOMP - 0.002\ DENSITY$$
$$\quad (3.7)\ (3.3)\quad\quad (4.5)\quad\quad\quad\quad (4.1)$$

$$- 0.05\ UNION85 + 1.6\ NEAST - 0.8\ NON\text{-}UNION,$$
$$(2.6)\quad\quad\quad\quad (2.7)\quad\quad\quad (3.0)$$

adjusted $R^2 = 0.60$, $F = 12.7$, $n = 48$.

Four of the variables support what might be termed a 'hinterland' interpretation. They show a positive association with an Intel plant and a computer production role. They show a negative connection with state population density and with high unionization rates in manufacturing in 1985. On the other hand, and as lingering *legacies*, a Northeast dummy (set to 1 for the nine states in the Northeast, 0 otherwise) has a positive coefficient. And a dummy set to 1 in the 20 right-to-work or anti-union states (all of which are outside the Northeast and away from the Pacific Coast) has a negative sign.

Equation 19A.3: Software Location Quotients in 1996

$$SLQ = -0.9 - 0.40NEAST - 0.03FORINV + 0.001DENSITY + 0.13BA,$$
$$(2.9) \quad (2.2) \qquad\qquad (3.1) \qquad\qquad (3.3) \qquad\qquad (5.4)$$

$$\text{adjusted } R^2 = 0.51, F = 13.7, \ n = 48.$$

The first two coefficients reflect tendencies toward dispersal from established centers. One is a dummy for the nine states in New England and the Middle Atlantic region, and its negative sign indicates a lower rate of software specialization than would otherwise be expected. The second is the per capita accumulated stock of foreign investment in a state in 1990. Its negative sign seems to indicate a higher degree of computer services specialization in states away from the industrial heartland and from California.

Working in the opposite direction, the other two variables signal tendencies in software specialization in *more urban* states with *more college graduates*. The density variable refers to a state's 1990 population per square mile; it takes on higher values in states with large urban settlements. BA refers to the percentage of the state's population that has a four-year college degree.[1] Examples of states with both high densities and high proportions of college graduates might be the Northeastern states of Connecticut, Maryland, and New Jersey.

Glossary

Variables in the equations, in order of appearance, dependent variables in **bold**:

COMPJOBS: 1986-96 absolute change in computer production employment (SIC 357).

LQC86: The 1986 location quotient for computer production (SIC 357) in a state.

WAGES: 1990 average hourly earnings of production workers in manufacturing.

DPOP80: Percent change in a state's population, 1980-90.

POVT: Percent of a state's 1990 population below the poverty line.

DESTABS: Per capita 1990-94 change in private non-farm establishments.

LQE: 1996 location quotients for electronics, including semiconductors (SIC 367).

INTEL: A dummy taking a value of 1 in the five states with Intel 'fab' plants in 1996.

LQCOMP: 1996 location quotient for computer manufacturing employment.

DENSITY: State population density in 1990.

UNION85: Percent share of manufacturing payroll employees unionized in 1985.

NEAST: A dummy set to 1 for the nine states in the Northeast, 0 otherwise.

NON-UNION: A dummy taking the value of 1 in the 20 'right-to-work' states.

SLQ: 1996 location quotient for computer services employment (SIC 737).

FORINV: Book value of accumulated foreign investment per 1,000 residents in 1990.

BA: Percent share of a state's 1990 population holding a four-year college degree.

NOTE

1. While it is tempting to test PhDs as an explanatory variable, the circularity of doing so would overwhelm the modest capacity of our OLS (ordinary-least-squares regression) technique. Once a software center emerges, it might draw PhDs from outside a state. This is the chicken-and-egg issue familiar in the migration literature.

Table 194.1 Explaining changes in computer employment by state, 1986-1996

	Abs. change, SIC 357 emp.	1986 location quotient, 357	1990 earnings/hour in manufacturing	Pop. ch (%), 1980-90	Poverty %, 1990	Business estab. p.c. 1990-94
California	-44,465	2.26	11.48	25.8	13.9	-0.34
Massachusetts	-32,713	3.22	11.39	4.9	10.7	-0.04
New York	-19,031	0.85	11.11	2.5	14.3	-0.24
Minnesota	-18,376	4.81	11.23	7.4	12.0	2.57
Arizona	-12,339	2.73	10.21	34.9	13.7	2.87
Florida	-10,939	0.87	8.98	32.8	14.4	2.43
Texas	-9,227	0.87	10.47	19.4	15.9	2.09
Colorado	-5,170	3.13	10.94	14.0	13.7	5.23
Pennsylvania	-5,058	0.46	11.04	0.2	11.0	0.20
Connecticut	-4,203	1.56	11.53	5.8	6.0	-0.62
New Jersey	-3,577	0.41	11.76	5.2	9.2	0.44
Utah	-3,094	3.07	10.32	17.9	8.2	4.15
New Hampshire	-2,938	2.81	10.83	20.4	6.3	0.56
Ohio	-2,599	0.25	12.64	0.5	11.5	1.11
Illinois	-1,846	0.39	11.44	0.0	13.7	1.40
Maine	-1,582	0.95	10.59	9.1	13.1	0.61
Nebraska	-1,575	0.76	9.66	0.5	10.3	1.83
Iowa	-1,375	0.45	11.27	-4.7	10.4	1.67
Vermont	-1,193	1.39	10.52	10.1	10.9	0.86
South Carolina	-1,149	0.27	8.84	11.7	16.2	1.77
Missouri	-1,026	0.21	10.74	4.1	13.4	1.56

Maryland	-1,010	0.24	11.57	13.4	9.9	1.15
Virginia	-860	0.41	10.07	15.8	11.1	1.51
Kansas	-789	0.37	10.94	4.8	10.3	1.60
Tennessee	-673	0.24	9.55	6.2	16.8	1.79
New Mexico	-638	0.44	9.04	16.3	20.9	2.84
Nevada	-375	0.42	11.05	50.2	9.8	4.75
Mississippi	-315	0.13	8.37	2.2	25.7	1.27
Indiana	-251	0.10	12.03	1.0	13.0	1.87
Wisconsin	-180	0.39	11.11	3.9	9.3	1.94
Michigan	-129	0.19	13.86	0.4	14.3	1.33
North Dakota	0	0.01	9.27	-2.2	13.7	1.80
West Virginia	0	0.00	11.53	-8.0	18.1	1.42
Kentucky	0	1.62	10.7	0.7	17.3	1.40
Louisiana	0	0.01	11.61	0.4	23.6	1.62
Georgia	7	0.26	9.17	18.6	15.8	2.42
Montana	12	0.01	11.51·	1.5	16.3	4.17
Rhode Island	68	0.30	9.45	6.0	7.5	-0.26
Arkansas	200	0.06	8.51	2.8	19.6	2.39
Wyoming	200	0.29	10.83	-3.5	11.0	4.67
Delaware	365	0.01	12.39	12.1	6.9	2.58
Oklahoma	622	0.65	10.73	4.0	15.6	1.86
Washington	968	0.85	12.61	17.8	8.9	3.64
North Carolina	2,906	1.67	8.79	12.8	13.0	1.77
Alabama	3,710	0.84	9.39	3.8	19.2	1.90
Idaho	3,750	3.23	10.6	6.6	14.9	5.33
Oregon	5,143	1.30	11.15	8.0	9.2	3.66
South Dakota	5,750	2.12	8.48	0.7	13.3	2.71

Table 19A.2 Determinants of electronics location quotients in 1996

	SIC 367 location quotient	Intel dummy	Right-to-work state	Dummy = 1 for Northeast	Population density	% of mfg workers in unions 1985	1996 357 location quotient
Vermont	5.74	0	0	1	60.8	14.9	0.02
Idaho	4.47	0	0	0	12.2	21.5	8.42
New Hampshire	3.34	0	0	1	123.7	9.3	2.15
Arizona	2.87	1	1	0	32.3	7.8	0.37
New Mexico	2.82	1	0	0	12.5	15.2	0.10
Massachusetts	2.19	1	0	1	767.6	20.2	1.10
California	2.15	1	0	0	191.0	18.6	2.22
South Dakota	2.06	0	1	0	9.2	19.3	12.19
Oregon	1.78	1	0	0	29.6	26.9	3.63
Maine	1.57	0	0	1	39.8	26.5	0.01
Texas	1.55	0	1	0	64.9	9.8	0.84
South Carolina	1.42	0	1	0	115.8	6.7	0.05
Rhode Island	1.42	0	0	1	960.3	16.2	0.69
Minnesota	1.33	0	0	0	55.0	23.1	3.47
Colorado	1.29	0	0	0	31.8	9.3	3.32
North Dakota	1.28	0	1	0	9.3	17.4	0.02
Connecticut	1.06	0	0	1	678.5	20.4	1.82
New York	1.01	0	0	1	381.0	28.7	0.45
North Carolina	0.96	0	1	0	136.1	7.0	2.95
Pennsylvania	0.94	0	0	1	265.1	35.1	0.34
Indiana	0.74	0	0	0	154.6	42.0	0.12

State							
Illinois	0.70	0	0	0	205.6	30.9	0.50
Utah	0.69	0	1	0	21.0	8.6	2.12
Washington	0.68	0	0	0	73.1	37.8	1.40
Alabama	0.65	0	1	0	79.6	25.2	2.30
Wisconsin	0.62	0	0	0	90.1	36.5	0.55
New Jersey	0.59	0	0	1	1044.3	28.4	0.27
Florida	0.57	0	1	0	239.9	8.2	0.38
Nebraska	0.52	0	1	0	20.5	22.4	0.11
Virginia	0.46	0	1	0	156.3	18.7	0.50
Missouri	0.43	0	0	0	74.3	32.0	0.15
Ohio	0.43	0	0	0	264.9	39.9	0.16
Oklahoma	0.41	0	0	0	45.8	21.0	1.35
Arkansas	0.40	0	1	0	45.1	20.4	0.18
Maryland	0.31	0	0	0	489.1	28.7	0.18
Michigan	0.28	0	0	0	163.6	42.3	0.30
Kansas	0.27	0	0	0	30.3	23.7	0.25
Tennessee	0.24	0	1	0	118.3	16.9	0.22
Iowa	0.23	0	1	0	49.7	37.7	0.14
Nevada	0.20	0	1	0	10.9	13.7	0.23
Wyoming	0.19	0	1	0	4.7	15.0	1.05
Georgia	0.19	0	1	0	111.8	13.8	0.39
Delaware	0.18	0	0	0	340.8	23.5	0.50
Kentucky	0.17	0	0	0	92.8	37.1	2.42
West Virginia	0.12	0	0	0	74.5	40.3	0.00
Montana	0.11	0	0	0	5.5	38.2	0.04
Mississippi	0.09	0	1	0	54.9	15.0	0.03
Louisiana	0.04	0	1	0	96.9	21.4	0.02

PART IV

Networks

Roadmap:

This is a section on spatial, electronic and financial networks, as they overlap and coalesce to shape the current positions of America's largest metropolitan areas.

The next three chapters represent separate modules on cluster theory, venture capital, and Internet business models.

Readers in a hurry can go directly to Chapter 23, 'Strategic Cities,' where the implications of Chapters 20-22 show up in the analysis. Part IV concludes with an informal list of a dozen urban centers deemed to offer the right chemistry for entrepreneurial creativity.

20. Clusters: a primer
21. Venture capitalism
22. IPOs and Internet business models
23. Strategic cities

20. Clusters: a primer

Most of the growth is from the new companies. The big guys aren't driving it.
(Craig Moore on the Massachusetts software revival, quoted in Crum 1998)

Spatial, electronic, and financial networks are key ingredients in the recipe for entrepreneurial creativity. By way of introduction, this chapter sketches a few basic issues from the avalanche of recent writings on spatial clusters.

PROXIMITY AND SPATIAL SPILLOVERS

Neoclassical approaches to clusters derive from Alfred Marshall's century-old theory of industrial districts (Marshall 1890, 1920, pp. 267-277).

A recent *New Yorker* magazine piece on the bunching of new restaurants in a particular block in Brooklyn illustrates the logic. Whether for restaurants today or for Manchester's cotton mills in the nineteenth century, the same processes can be seen.

Marshall's basic point about why companies in the same industry congregate still holds: *industrial districts enjoy the same economies of scale that only giant companies normally get.* Specialized suppliers arrive. Skilled workers know where to come to ply their trade. And everyone involved benefits from the spillovers of specialized knowledge. As Marshall put it, 'The mysteries of the trade become no mysteries, but are as it were in the air.' (Surowiecki 2000, p. 68, emphasis added)

Localization vs. Urbanization Effects

Opinions differ on the roles of localization economies (à la Marshall) and the more diverse urbanization economies that come with large city size, often identified with Jane Jacobs (1969, 1984). As suggested in Chapter 8, the resolution of this issue can be found in a product-cycle or industry-maturity perspective. As a recent *World Development Report* puts it,

Whether an industry benefits most from urbanization or localization economies depends on how innovative it is. *New, dynamic industries are likely to locate in large urban centers* where they can benefit from the cross-fertilization provided by diverse actors. Older, mature industries concentrate in smaller, more specialized cities, where congestion costs are low and localization economies can be high. (World Bank 2000, p. 117, emphasis added.)

When an industry matures, in other words, its initial centers become vulnerable to competition from newcomers and specialization becomes not an advantage but a burden.

Porter: Rivalry and Information Flows

By the same token, however, innovation can maintain a specialized cluster's competitive advantage. As Michael Porter puts it, 'Successful firms are frequently concentrated in particular cities or states within a nation' (1990, p. 29). Offering detailed maps of the Italian and German cluster landscapes (pp. 155-6), he cites a variety of additional examples as well.

Porter explains such agglomerations in terms of his 'diamond.' Its four corners are demand, factor conditions, rivalry-strategy, and industry clusters. That is, an industry becomes internationally competitive because of

- favorable home conditions in the markets it sells to,
- the quality of its factor inputs,
- the competitive pressures encouraging excellence within its industry, and
- the supplier and customer linkages specific to the industry, which in practice are often traced out within specific urban agglomerations.

On this last point, a tight geographical locale intensifies (1) information flows and (2) rivalry between competing firms. Local media, banks, universities, bars, and eateries enhance communication. The spatial proximity of rivals – whether they communicate and cooperate or not – spurs competition and innovation.

Second Thoughts: Can Clustered Firms Also Be Less Adaptive?

Porter himself now recognizes that participation in an established cluster may not always help a firm adapt to new circumstances. In this recent passage, for example, it is hard to miss the influence of Porter's Harvard Business School colleague, Clayton Christensen (1997):

> When a cluster shares a uniform approach to competing, a sort of groupthink often reinforces old behaviors, suppresses new ideas, and creates rigidities that prevent adoption of improvements. Clusters also might not support truly *radical innovation*, which *tends to invalidate the existing pools of talent, information, suppliers, and infrastructure*. In these circumstances, a cluster participant . . . might suffer from greater barriers to perceiving the need to change.... (Porter 2000, p. 24, emphasis added)

RETHINKING CLUSTER LOGIC

Beyond such concerns, there are other criticisms of research that purports to measure information flows within the static-externality framework.

One might be termed 'the invisibility problem,' as described by Krugman:

> Knowledge flows . . . are invisible; they leave no paper trail by which they can be measured and tracked, and there is nothing to prevent the theorist from assuming anything about them she likes. . . . So while I am sure that true technological spillovers play an important role in the localization of some industries, one should not assume that this is the typical reason – even in the high technology industries themselves. (Krugman 1991, p. 54)

The literature contains numerous studies claiming to find empirical validation of neoclassical static externalities as a source of localization – when such evidence can often be interpreted equally well as showing increasing returns.

A second issue stems from the assumption that firms must rely on face-to-face communication to remain efficient or innovative. 'Despite these claims, there is in fact abundant evidence that information and knowledge networks that influence business efficiency can be and often have been widely diffused geographically' (Hansen 2000, p. 4). Hansen, among others, believes that competing firms within a given cluster or region often try *to maintain secrecy locally*, while networking aggressively with distant partners or allies.

A third doubt about proximity as a sufficient or measurable condition for competitive advantage comes from Saxenian. She disavows the neoclassical notion of spatial spillovers in favor of a related but distinct concept of regional industrial networks among non-hierarchical firms.

Network-Based Industrial Systems

The first round of post-neoclassical theorizing began with Piore and Sabel (1984). What distinguished the New Industrial District (NID) theory they launched were twin emphases on (1) Italianate trust and (2) flexible or post-Fordist production systems (see Chapter 9).

In a similar spirit, Saxenian contrasted Silicon Valley's adaptability with Route 128's decline in the 1980s as a minicomputer center. Her 1994 work, *Regional Advantage: Culture and Competition in Silicon Valley and Route 128*, highlighted differences in communication within the two clusters.

Rejecting external economies as a way to understand clusters, Saxenian contends in a subsequent work that 'this approach cannot account for the divergent performance of' Route 128 and Silicon Valley in the 1980s (1996, p. 42). She continues, 'The simple fact of spatial proximity evidently reveals little about the value of firms to respond to the fast-changing markets and technologies that now characterize international competition' (p. 44).

What does explain the divergent performance of the two clusters in her view is the relative importance of regional information networks. In contrast to Route 128, the Valley's 'dense social networks and open labor markets encourage entrepreneurship and experimentation' (p. 45).

To develop this argument, she compares two start-ups (Apollo from Route 128, Sun from the Valley) and two mature firms (Digital Equipment Corporation and, in the West, Hewlett-Packard). Each pair started from similar positions in the early 1980s, but in each the Silicon Valley firm opted for the open-systems (non-proprietary) approach that would fit in with the then-unfolding PC revolution. The result: Sun triumphed over Apollo and H-P over DEC in work-stations and servers.

The lesson Saxenian draws is that regions should be viewed 'as networks of relationships rather than as collections of atomistic firms' (p. 57). Accordingly, she views the Valley as a 'network-based industrial system.' The term refers to a project-oriented adaptive mode of production that may be seen not only in Silicon Valley but also to the south, in Hollywood. As she put it in a 1998 interview,

> You have these very fluid labor markets and these communities of highly skilled people who recombine repeatedly. *They come together for one project – in this case a new film, in Silicon Valley it would be a new firm – and then they move on.* The system allows a lot of flexibility and adaptiveness. . . . Information about new markets and new technologies flows very quickly. This sustains the importance of geographic proximity, despite the fact that, theoretically, the technology allows you to be anywhere. (Cassidy 1998, p. 125, emphasis added)

Don't Know Much about the Rise and Fall . . .

Still, the industrial-networks explanation for Route 128's failure after 1985 feels incomplete these days. The reason: the Boston area achieved an impressive comeback around software and other advanced services in the 1990s, placing it on a growth trajectory comparable to the Valley's. Moreover, Silicon Valley itself has seen computer production go elsewhere.

Two charts reveal the timing and dimensions of the Boston area's comeback. Figure 20.1 shows that across a broad spectrum of high-technology activities, the two clusters each registered comparable

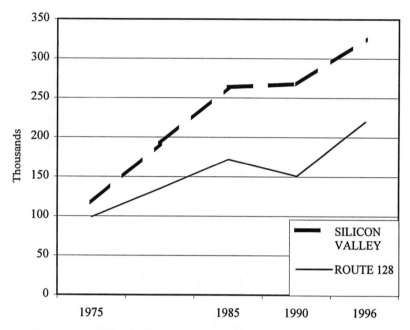

Employment in SIC codes 283, 348, 357, 361-7, 369, 376, 379, 381-7, 737, 871, 873 (1980 interpolated)

Figure 20.1 High-tech job growth in Route 128 and Silicon Valley, 1975-1996

employment growth between 1990 and 1996. Figure 20.2 narrows the focus to three core IT lines (electronics, computers, and software).

The latter chart finds surprisingly similar patterns of structural change in each area over the interval 1986-1996. Each area had large losses in computer production, little change in electronics, and rapid growth in software.

The implication is that Route 128 has managed to convert from the devastating collapse of its minicomputer sector and to rebuild around software and Internet activities. Between venture capital and MIT, the Boston area has seen two radical make-overs in three decades: minicomputers in the 1970s, and a broader base of elite services in the 1990s: software, medical, and financial.

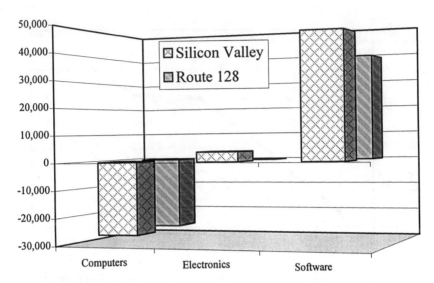

Source: *County Business Patterns*, machine-readable data for 1986 and 1996.

Figure 20.2 Similarity of job growth in the two clusters: three IT industries (SIC 357, 367, 737), 1986-1996

Path Dependency and Techno Lock-Ins

Saxenian's question can thus be turned on its head. She asked why Route 128 failed to adapt in the 1980s. Now the question becomes, how did it manage to overcome that failure and move on? Any answer to this question would then also need to provide an alternative explanation for the initial failure.

Just this sort of alternative scenario can be found in 'Technology, Entrepreneurship and Path Dependence: Industrial Clustering in Silicon Valley and Route 128,' Martin Kenney and Urs von Burg emphasize the importance of the microprocessor as a general-purpose technology:

> The evolution of each region displays path-dependent characteristics as Route 128 evolved into the center of the minicomputer industry and Silicon Valley became the center of the semiconductor industry. The semiconductor would become the fundamental input to every product with an electronics function, whereas the minicomputer was a much more limited artifact. (Kenney and von Burg 1999, p. 68)

Kenney and von Burg's analysis can thus be understood as a spatial application of Christensen's *Innovator's Dilemma* (1997). So much also helps explain Porter's second thoughts on the advantages of proximity among competing firms. Route 128's firms turned out to be locked in to a narrow technology, unable to recognize necessity until it was too late. Something like Porter's 'group-think' appears to have set in.

ECONOMY 2: THE PRIMACY OF VENTURE CAPITAL

Moreover, Route 128's bounce-back can also be understood in the framework Kenney and von Burg develop. They contrast what they term Economy 1 (established firms and their supporting institutions) and Economy 2 (the institutions nurturing new-firm formation). Recall that Saxenian's account of Silicon Valley's superior performance in the 1980s emphasized better information flows among the Valley's more open firms.

The authors observe, 'Undoubtedly, information sharing and interfirm cooperation have been important in Silicon Valley's success, as they were in Route 128. . . . [But this view] does not address the ultimate reason for the industrial success of both regions – new firm formation' (p. 71).

The participants in Economy 2 have as their goal 'discovering market discontinuities created by technological advances' (p. 95). Start-ups can thus be viewed as Economy 2's products. Start-ups contain 'discrete packets of knowledge,' which can be brought to the test of market profitability with the help of Economy 2's institutions (p. 73).

The central players in this drama are entrepreneurs and venture capitalists. Other supporting institutions include specialized law firms, consulting firms, and investment banks (p. 75).

As a link to the next chapter, and with the solemn phrases 'path-dependency' and 'first-mover' in mind, we should recall how Route 128 and Silicon Valley emerged as the two initial venture-capital centers.

Historically, venture capital was invented in the Boston area at the end of World War II with the formation of American Research and Development, or ARD (Adams 1977, chapter 9). But the term 'venture capital' was coined only later by Arthur Rock, a pivotal figure in the creation of Silicon Valley's venture-capital industry (Jackson 1997, p. 22).

When the Traitorous Eight resigned from William Shockley's two-year-old semiconductor company in 1957, they turned to Rock, an investment banker in New York, for help finding backing. Rock visited the Eight in California before getting financing from inventor Sherman Fairchild back in New York. Before long he himself moved to San Francisco and set up a new investment bank specializing in financing new companies.

Then spin-offs from Fairchild Semiconductor came to include other local venture capital firms as well. These soon replaced East Coast investors in the financing of local start-ups (Kenney and von Burg, p. 84).

In sum, the emergence of a local venture-capital industry gave the Valley a system that enabled it to continue to reproduce itself around new activities. Now a similar financial fountain of youth, along with a steady stream of MIT and other top talent, has refreshed Route 128 as well.

21. Venture capitalism[1]

> If you have a sound business idea and you live in the New England area, you can get money. (Patrick Gray, of PricewaterhouseCoopers, quoted in Healy 2000, p. C15)

Venture capital is one of the two or three basic ingredients in Economy 2, along with research centers and existing IT companies. Not to be over-looked is the money itself, which as Figure 21.1 shows has reached floodtide proportions. Just as important is the management expertise venture capitalists provide to engineers and other would-be entrepreneurs.

The face-to-face nature of the relationship shows up in the tendency for venture capital (VC) firms to cluster in a few specific US metropolitan areas. Clustering follows from the local access VC managers must have if they are to monitor and assist the early-stage firms they are funding.

In turn, localization combines with a network logic (that is, positive feedback) to create higher rates of VC placements and eventual initial public offerings (IPOs) in seedbeds like Silicon Valley, Route 128, Denver, and northern Virginia.

THE CAPITAL-GAP HYPOTHESIS

The spatial clustering of venture capital and IPOs points up a possible missing link in the innovation process in such economies as Germany and Japan, relative to the US, Canada, or (more recently) the UK. In the absence of venture capital, banks and governments are left to fill a 'capital gap.' For reasons to be considered now, neither institution is right for the task.

Transaction Costs, the Gap, and Micro-lending

The point can be illustrated in terms of the capital-gap hypothesis suggested by Laughlin and Digirolamo in a 1994 article arguing for government loan guarantees. They contended that commercial banks are only equipped to handle loans with an annual default rate of two percent or less, regardless of the interest rate they can charge (see Figure 21.2).

At the other end of the risk-return spectrum, the VC-IPO market invests in the tiny minority of start-ups that offer expected returns of 35-50 percent a year or more. For returns that high, the VC industry accepts default (more accurately, failure) risks of 50 percent and higher.

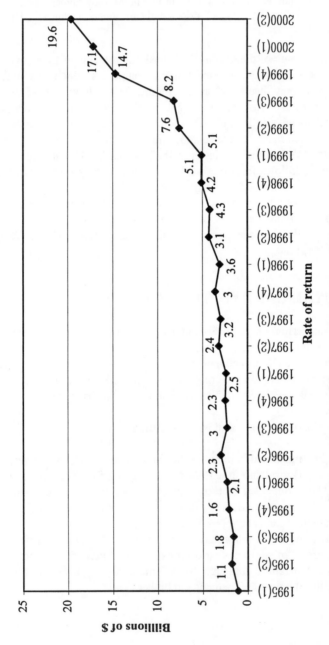

Source: Data from PricewaterhouseCoopers, 'Money Tree Highlights: Q2 '00,' www.pwcglobal.com.

Figure 21.1 Venture capital funding soars, 1995-2000 (quarterly commitments in billions of $)

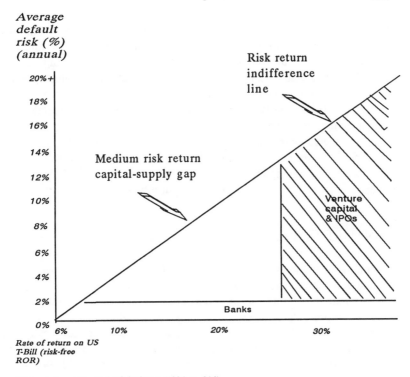

Source: Laughlin and Digirolamo (1994, p. 316).

Figure 21.2 The capital-gap hypothesis

In this view transaction costs (the time and money it takes to assess a small-loan application) destroy the financing market for intermediate small firms. In the lurch are companies with default rates above two or three percent but rates of return below about 20 percent. These are the countless micro-enterprises and small businesses the authors contend fail to find financing in the private capital market.

The authors conclude that non-profit and governmental organizations have a role to play to fill in the gap. The programs they advocate include not only Small Business Association (SBA) loan guarantees but also 'capital-access-programs' at the state and local level.[2] Whatever one's view on that, the analysis is consistent with the worldwide spread and documented successes of the micro-lending movement during the 1990s.[3]

Do Bank-dependent Financial Systems Discourage Start-ups?

This analysis holds interest here for a different set of reasons. First, Figure 21.2 sharpens the contrast between a commercial bank's universe of projects, on the hand, and the projects of interest to venture capitalists. Second, the capital-gap hypothesis underlines the drawbacks of financial systems in countries that rely mainly on banks for start-up financing.

Both Germany and Japan rely less on equity markets and more on long-term relationships between corporations and individual large banks. Lacking traditions of venture capital, their systems have favored established companies over newcomers.

Hence the conclusion noted in Chapter 10 that VC is a primary reason for higher US rates of new-business formation. By extension, the higher US rate of entrepreneurship and innovation in IT since the mid-1980s appears to derive in part from the flexibility and creativity of its capital markets.

VENTURE CAPITAL IN THE START-UP CYCLE

The point can also be made in terms of Figure 21.3's 'valley-of-death' schema of the financing challenges facing US technology-based start-ups.

Through the initial stage from concept to working model and engineering prototype, sources of funding remain informal and personal. In the second stage, development of a production prototype, seed capital is obtained from *angels* (a term derived from investors in Broadway plays) and other informal investors, typically in amounts of under $500,000.

While the nature of this informal market makes measurement elusive, one recent estimate is that friends, family, own-sources, and angels combined now exceeds $50 billion. As an estimate, perhaps half, or $25 billion, is supplied by some 250,000 angels (Zacharakis et al. 1999). Such informal support also plays a large role in the next stage, moving toward product introduction, where financing needs may range to $1 million.

This is also the stage where formal venture capital firms may enter the picture. At recent rates, as reported in Figure 21.1, VC placements have overtaken informal sources in volume. While survey estimates differ, VC funding in the first half of 2000 alone seems to have exceeded $35 billion.

In exchange for putting up financing and adding management skill, the venture capitalist hopes to bring the assisted firm to an IPO at a stock price that will give the VC a high rate of return.

For its part, in accepting the agreement (and signing the so-called *term sheet*) the supported firm agrees to share management duties and power in exchange for the infusion of capital. It surrenders some equity and allows the venture capitalist to step in and have a voice in the firm's operations.

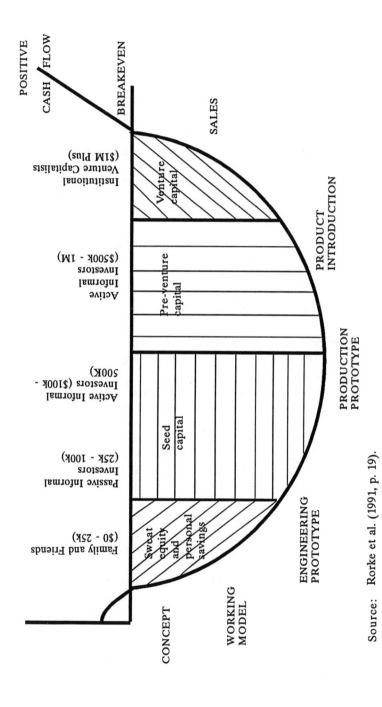

POSITIVE CASH FLOW

BREAKEVEN

SALES

Family and Friends ($0 - 25K)

Passive Informal Investors (25k - 100k)

Active Informal Investors ($100k - 500K)

Active Informal Investors ($500k - 1M)

Institutional Venture Capitalists ($1M Plus)

Sweat equity and personal savings

Seed capital

Pre-venture capital

Venture capital

CONCEPT

WORKING MODEL

ENGINEERING PROTOTYPE

PRODUCTION PROTOTYPE

PRODUCT INTRODUCTION

Source: Rorke et al. (1991, p. 19).

Figure 21.3 Valley of death

IMPROVING THE ODDS

The function of the venture capitalist within the larger spectrum of US financial intermediaries is to reduce the risks faced by investors in new businesses (Berlin 1998).

Like a commercial bank, in other words, a VC partnership is a financial intermediary.[4] It raises money from investors, about two-thirds from corporations and institutions, notably pension funds.[5]

The difference is that the venture capitalist provides funds to a company just beginning to show revenue, let alone earn profits. And instead of making a loan to a fledgling firm with an uncertain future, the venturist buys a stake in it.

Then it tries to improve the odds by providing technical, financial, and strategic expertise based on its experience in the early-stage company's particular field.

Decentralized Specialization in VC 'Funds'

The primacy of technical expertise is one reason most VC partnerships run separate 'funds' or bundles of supported firms. Each specialized fund includes a number of early-stage firms in a specific line of activity, such as biotechnology or telecommunications. This decentralized structure enables the VC firm to employ individual experts to oversee and assist the various start-ups in a given domain.

Some larger VC partnerships may operate five, ten or even more funds at any one time. Each fund will have a finite life-span, perhaps five years, after which the supported start-ups will have been brought to an IPO, shut down, or sold. Then new funds will be created, in the same or another activity.

Both VC partnerships and their component funds are highly concentrated within a few major centers. Whatever the precise linkages, the *destinations of VC placements* are also spatially concentrated.

More specifically, Figure 21.4 shows that of the $20 billion in new placements in the second quarter of 2000, over a third went to supported firms in Silicon Valley. Another 30 percent went to the next four locations: Route 128, the DC metro, New York, and the Texas complex. Nearly two-thirds of the soaring volume of placements thus landed in only five areas.

The localized geography of the VC sector is one of the ingredients helping to reduce investors' risk. While VC placements may have participation from around the US, the on-the-scene 'lead' player in a syndication will need commuting access to supported firms.

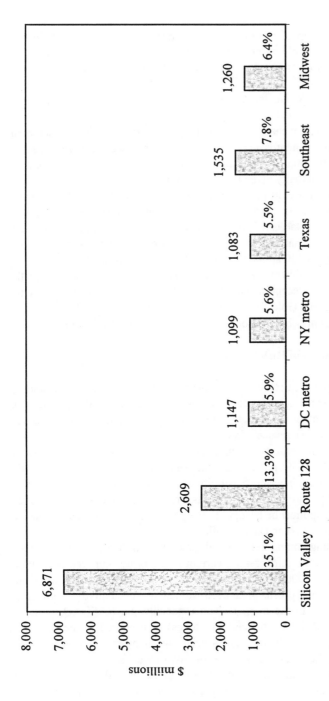

Source: Data are from PricewaterhouseCoopers 'Money Tree Highlights: Q2 '00,' www.pwcglobal.com.

Figure 21.4 Destinations of VC placements, Quarter 2 of 2000 (amounts and percent of total US estimated placements of $19.6 billion)

In short, the capital can be raised anywhere, but hands-on participation remains local. The old bumper sticker (Think global, act local) may have a new application: Raise the money globally, but mind the store at home.

100 Pitches...10 VC Deals...2 IPOs?

A more obvious mechanism to reduce investors' risk is the selection process. While standards may have eased in the recent hot IPO market, only about 10 in 100 of the presentations ('pitches') made by entrepreneurs to venturists are actually given the green light.[6]

Of the ten successful pitches perhaps five of the supported companies will fail. Three more might be sold in some manner, say through an acquisition by an established firm, perhaps at a price giving the VC a break-even investment. That leaves only about two of the original ten firms (or two of the original 100 applicants) to go through the full cycle to an IPO.

While these numbers are approximations, they give some idea of the stringency of the decentralized search and selection mechanism. At the same time, both the Gold Rush atmosphere of recent years and the resulting influx of capital may have eased the odds of acquiring VC funding.

Other Dimensions of Risk Reduction

The VC brings an entrepreneur's concept to the point where the start-up enterprise can show sales revenue. To that end the specialists from the VC partnership try to guide the start-up around three types of hazards. The process works in a sequence of steps or stages.

Risks arise in connection with *technology, marketability, and profit potential* (Berlin 1998). That is, the first step is to demonstrate the technological or engineering feasibility of a start-up's concept. The second is to show that the product or service has a ready market at a plausible price. Third, the start-up must be brought to the point where a convincing case can be made that the firm can earn a profit.

Among young companies that had gone through the complete cycle and had recent IPOs, the third issue – current profitability – proved decisive in March and April 2000. During the 'dot-com bubble,' seemingly promising companies without profits had been valued at speculatively high stock prices. Sentiment in the markets (and especially the NASDAQ, which is heavily weighted toward technology stocks) then shifted to the view that current profits should matter. Stock prices on many recent issues fell to a third or less of their peaks in a matter of days or weeks.

This episode points up a fourth and more immediate risk that VC participation can ameliorate: *running out of cash*. However, that blade cuts both ways. As part of the popping of the bubble in early 2000, VC partnerships decided to say no to additional rounds of funding for some money-losing start-ups, effectively putting them out of business.

The larger lesson is that the intimate relationship between the venturist and its supported firms is fraught with ups and downs.

COUNTERPOINTS

In any case, some of the heroes of the PC revolution did it on their own. Despite what is sometimes heard, Microsoft got off the ground with virtually no VC participation. In the first place, Gates and Allen did not seek it, but preferred to 'bootstrap' the company's launch, meaning to finance its expansion from within.

Beyond that, as Amar Bhide observes, its daring and novelty meant that Microsoft at its inception was not a good candidate for VC:

> [W]hen Gates and Allen launched Microsoft in 1975, only a small number of hobbyists even knew about personal computers. Microsoft's first product did not have the potential to generate significant revenues. . . . Gates was still a teenager, and Allen was only two years older . . . [I]t took about nine years for Microsoft to book the same revenues that Lotus did in its first year, and ten years for it to go public (Bhide 2000, pp. 147-8).

In these respects and others, says Bhide, Microsoft was neither an attractive target for VC, nor would it have known what to do with VC funding. Accordingly, 'For Gates and Allen, therefore, start-up financing from VCs was neither feasible nor useful' (p. 148). The result was that Bill Gates personally retained substantial equity in the company (the value of his holdings reached $100 billion in 1999, before falling with the firm's stock price in 2000), and Paul Allen held another massive chunk, as we saw in Chapter 5.

Firing the Founder

Moreover, from the standpoint of a start-up based on an entrepreneur's new idea, *VC financing can be a mixed blessing*. In exchange for investing in the start-up, the venture-capital firm receives ownership in the form of convertible bonds (convertible into stock at the time of the IPO) or preferred stock (which has priority in dividend-payment over the founder's common stock).

The accumulated, separate-stage infusions of venture capital into a start-up or early-stage firm often give venture capital majority ownership and control through participation on its board of directors. VC ownership confers a management voice, not only in an advisory role, but sufficient to fire the original entrepreneur.

Examples include the firings by a VC-dominated Board of Directors of Mitch Kapor at Lotus, Steve Jobs at Apple (the first time around), and Rod Canion at Compaq (Schwert 1999). Still, as Compaq's rebound after the firing of its founder suggests, the power VC-based directors acquire may at times be needed to help turn troubled companies around.

CAPITAL GAP, MISSING LINK?

As a rule, however, the goal is not to manage the start-up company as a going concern but to nurture it to the point where it can be sold for a high rate of return. To sum up: the target return will exceed 35-50 percent a year on equity to compensate for the failure of perhaps half the partnership's portfolio of firms before any profit or sale to other owners. The desired outcome, a successful IPO, will happen for perhaps one in five of the start-ups in the VC portfolio.

In a comparative framework, the VC sector in the US fills what in most other advanced economies is a missing link in the innovation process. This is the crucial stage for a start-up or early-stage firm before the company can show much in the way of sales revenue, but after informal sources of financing have been exhausted.

The geographical clustering of the venture-capital industry helps reduce investors' risk in the financing of early-stage companies.

The next chapter scans Internet IPOs in particular and interprets the recent Gold Rush as a search for workable Internet business models.

NOTES

1. This chapter (and the next) owe a great deal to Chip Elitzer, of Elitzer Associates, a consulting specialist in the field of mergers and acquisitions and an authority on US capital markets. Any remaining errors are my own.
2. The Small Business Administration *guarantees* (not extends) bank loans to small businesses. The volume of SBA loan guarantees reached about $16 billion in 1999. Most are for loans to 'going concerns,' existing small businesses that can show revenue and profit – or, failing that, adequate collateral. The typical technology-based start-up has neither one and thus fails to qualify for a loan. That is why bank loans seldom go to start-up firms.
3. Initiatives ranging from Bangladesh to the Andes to poverty neighborhoods of American cities have demonstrated the value of small loans (as small as $1,000 or even $100) to help individual micro-businesses get off the ground. Not surprisingly, commercial banks have played little if any direct role in allocating micro-loans for street-front eateries or textiles shops. Instead, that task has fallen to community-development and other non-governmental organizations.

4. In this context, the term 'partnership' refers to the legal form of organization most venture capital companies use, as distinct from either a proprietorship or a corporation.
5. In the development of the VC industry, a key regulatory event was the relaxation in 1979 of the 'prudent man' rule governing institutional investors. (The concept: 'Would a prudent man using his own money invest in this project?') From then on life insurance companies and pension funds could place some small part of their vast pools of savings into high-risk venture capital projects. Pension funds illustrate why some large institutions would want to seek out high-risk projects. Their participation in high-risk venture capital is typically a small percentage of their total assets, and they can wait: they are 'patient capital.' More recently, companies like Intel, Microsoft, and Oracle have joined the fray, starting their own venture projects as subsidiaries. Among large banks, Chase has long operated Chase Capital Partners, a separate and highly successful venture-capital unit within its corporate family, prompting other banks, including Bank Boston, to follow suit.
6. Pitches occur in all kinds of settings, of course – public, private, or personal. See Don Peppers (1995), *Life's a Pitch Then You Buy*.

22. IPOs and Internet business models[1]

> The best growth/value proposition is among the 'old new industrials,' that is, the companies that are today generating strong earnings growth by selling the products used to build the infrastructure of the Information Age. (Kerschner et al. 2000, p. 2)

In 1999 there were 399 IPOs in the US, an estimated 271 of them backed by venture capital. Functionally, about 250 of the total were Internet-related or in some other sense digital. As for the money raised, some $47 billion in stock was issued for the year, more than double 1998's $21 billion. In the last quarter of 1999 alone, the offerings added up to $22 billion, or more than the 1998 total (Mahoney 2000, p. 4).

When the financial markets gave up on money-losing Internet-based recent issues in the spring of 2000, the market for new issues cooled. This chapter surveys the post-Gold Rush landscape to see what priorities survived. The whole sequence can be understood as a search for workable Internet business models – or strategies for making money.

PRELUDE: IPO PRICE RUN-UPS, 1995-1998

One reason it was called an Internet Gold Rush can be seen in Table 22.1. The table shows that from 1995 to February 1999 a growing number of Internet-related IPOs had prices at least double by the end of the stock's first day on the open market. (The table is adapted from Ritter 1999[2].)

For perspective, in all of the 1980s only seven IPOs saw the stock price double in the opening day of trading. None, of course, was Internet-related. This relatively languorous pace extended into the first half of the 1990s, with three more such offerings.

But by 1994 MOSAIC was being repackaged as the commercial browser Netscape, and the Internet was poised to break out of its academic niche. Thus 1995 saw 11 big run-ups (as many as in the prior 15 years combined), and most were Internet-related. Among the class of 1995 were such solid performers as Netscape and Citrix Systems, as well as Tivoli Systems.

Disappointments after the First Day

On the other hand, fully eight of the 11 big run-up IPOs of 1995 had lower stock prices in early 1999 than they had at the end of the first day's trading

Table 22.1 Ritter list of IPOs that doubled in price the first day, 1990-1998

Company	Offer date	Offer price ($)	Closing price ($) First day	02/12/1999	Change (%)
Net Worth	11/25/1992	16.00	32.00	42.00	31.2
Boston Chicken	11/08/1993	*20.00	48.50	0.50	**-97.9**
Shiva	11/17/1994	*15.00	31.50	5.88	**-62.7**
Tivoli Systems	03/10/1995	14.00	30.75	47.38	54.1
Premisys Comms.	03/05/1995	*16.00	35.00	8.75	**-50.0**
Arcsys	06/06/1995	13.00	26.50	18.25	**-31.1**
Netscape	08/08/1995	*28.00	58.25	66.94	129.8
Triatholan	09/07/1995	5.50	11.75	11.63	**-1.1**
Arbor Software	11/06/1995	17.00	39.25	16.69	**-57.5**
Sync Research	11/09/1995	*20.00	44.00	0.69	**-98.4**
Secure Computing	11/17/1995	16.00	48.25	19.38	**-59.8**
Objective Systems	11/30/1995	19.00	41.25	3.31	**-92.0**
Citrix Systems	12/08/1995	*15.00	30.00	82.38	723.8
Extended Stay Amer.	12/13/1995	*13.00	27.50	9.19	**-33.2**
Xylan	11/11/1996	26.00	58.38	20.00	**-65.7**
Yahoo!	04/12/1996	*13.00	33.00	151.00	2645.5
Edify	05/02/1996	15.00	33.75	6.63	**-80.4**
Open Market	05/22/1996	18.00	39.88	13.69	**-65.7**
Rambus	05/14/1997	12.00	30.25	74.13	145.0
Great Plains Software	06/20/1997	16.00	32.38	41.00	26.6
Broadcom Class A	04/17/1998	*24.00	53.63	125.63	134.3
Inktomi	06/10/1998	*18.00	36.00	68.50	280.6
Broadcast.com	07/17/1998	*18.00	62.75	68.88	119.5
Geocity	08/11/1998	17.00	37.31	95.13	154.9
eBay	09/24/1998	*18.00	47.38	236.00	398.2
Earthweb Tech.	11/11/1998	14.00	48.69	39.81	**-18.2**
theglobe.com	11/13/1998	*9.00	63.50	48.13	**-24.2**
E-Tek Dynamics	12/02/1998	12.00	26.75	27.25	1.9
Ticketmaster Online	12/03/1998	14.00	40.25	36.50	**-9.3**
uBid	12/04/1998	15.00	48.00	62.50	30.2
Xoom.com	12/09/1998	14.00	34.44	51.44	49.4
Artificial Life	12/17/1998	8.50	23.50	12.50	**-46.8**

Note: *Stock has subsequently had one split.   **Bolded:** declined from first-day close.
Source: Jay R. Ritter, 'Big IPO Runups of 1975-99' (for on-line details, see note 2).

back in 1995. That was an interval when the broader stock indexes (the Dow, NASDAQ, and S&P 500) more than doubled.

For new issues through 1998, a similar pattern holds. Of the 32 big IPO run-ups from the 1990-1998 interval, over half had experienced outright declines in the stock price (adjusted for stock splits) by February 12, 1999, an arbitrary end-of-period date used by Ritter.

That is, each of the 32 had at least doubled in price on the first day of the offering, but then about half would back off from the price at the end of the opening day, trading lower in February 1999. Since the broader market averages were doubling during this period, even stocks whose prices rose slightly (like Great Plains Software or E-Tek Dynamics) turned out to be under-performers after the first day.

The Staying-Power of Infrastructure IPOs

Then there were the big winners: Citrix Systems (up 723%), Yahoo! (up 26-fold), Inktomi (nearly quadrupling in price), and eBay (up 398%, roughly quintupling in price).These few issues with staying-power underline a far more general pattern of price declines.

What, then, do the big winners among the pre-1999 Internet-based IPOs do? *Each of the four provides what could loosely be termed 'infrastructure'* for the Internet.

- Fort Lauderdale-based Citrix Systems makes software to improve the operation of Windows-based networks.

- Yahoo! began in 1995, had an IPO in 1996 as a search service, and has now expanded its role as a premier Internet portal.

- Inktomi provides Yahoo! and other major web sites with its search engine and also makes Traffic Server, a network bottleneck-breaker sold to America Online, among other companies.

- eBay (like Yahoo! and Inktomi a Silicon Valley firm) is not technically an infrastructure enterprise, but as the leading on-line auction service, it might as well be, since it handles purchases and sales for its millions of registered users.

Hence the frequently heard observation about the parallel between this and the original Gold Rush of 1849. The first time around, few miners got rich – or at any rate few stayed rich. Instead, it was the people who sold the miners whiskey, equipment, and Levi's who wound up with the gold. The obvious parallel today would find the firms who provide infrastructure in the form of network-enhancements for e-commerce making the most money.

The 20 Best-Performing IPOs of 2000

Similarly, a list of the 20 biggest IPO price run-ups of the first six months of 2000 consists mainly of digital issues, most of which are in some sense for companies with ideas for increasing bandwidth. Such schemes for speeding data and voice transmission over networks also fall under the rubric of infrastructure services (see Table 22.2). The implication is that neither business-to-business (B-B) nor business-to-consumer (B-C) issues held up through the popping of the dot-com bubble. Instead, that honor was reserved for companies that offer solutions to network problems, devices for photonic systems, or other fiber-optic applications.

Once we recognize this simple conclusion about infrastructure, however, where does that leave us? Three further points are worth making here:

1. Biotech companies attracted over $22 billion (from all sources) in the first half of 2000, thus joining Internet infrastructure companies as the hot investments to survive the popping of the bubble (Pollack 2000, p. C1).

2. The quest for workable Internet business models can be understood by combining traditional economic concepts of market power (or market structure) and new concepts of increasing returns through network effects.

3. The dot-com shake-out of spring 2000 pointed up the contrast between 'old' or profitable New Economy companies and 'new,' much more speculative ventures.

The resurgence of interest in biotech companies as the Human Genome Project reaches fruition is beyond our scope here. (For a gifted explanation of what is at stake see Ridley 2000.) But items two and three in the list can be touched upon now.

THE SEARCH FOR PROFITABLE BUSINESS MODELS

As noted, the Gold Rush seemed bizarre because billions of dollars were being paid for companies that had yet to earn a profit. By April and May of 2000, reality caught up with the bubble-supporting stories as to why profits no longer mattered. A classic shakeout ensued, in which most or all 'story-based' Internet companies saw their stock prices fall off the table.

What was left, after the fall? Peter S. Cohan offers one approach to sorting out the profit prospects for Internet-related firms (Cohan 1999). In his view, companies must fulfill three requirements for future profitability:

Table 22.2 IPOs from 2000 with largest rates of return, by product line (as of July 25, 2000)

Company name	Product or industry	IPO date	Offer price ($)	Current price ($)	Return (%)
Sonus Networks	Voice via packet networks	05/24/00	23.00	237.00	930.4
Nuance Communications	Voice software for the Web	04/12/00	17.00	135.44	696.7
New Focus	Products for optical networks	05/17/00	20.00	124.44	522.2
Orchid Biosciences	Health-Biomed/Genetics	05/04/00	8.00	43.13	439.1
StorageNetworks	Data storage utility	06/29/00	27.00	139.63	417.1
ONI Systems	Optical networks	06/01/00	25.00	120.50	382.0
Quantum Effect Devices	Embedded chips for networks	02/01/00	16.00	75.44	371.5
Turnstone Systems	Loop mgmt. software systems	02/01/00	29.00	135.88	368.5
Bookham Technology	Chips for fiber-optic networks	04/10/00	15.83	74.13	368.3
Centillium Communications	Chips for DSL equip. vendors	05/23/00	19.00	85.88	352.0
Pixelworks	Chips for broadband display	05/18/00	10.00	43.63	336.2
Stanford Microdevices	Radio frequency components	05/24/00	12.00	49.50	312.5
Ulticom	Wireless network software	04/04/00	13.00	53.44	311.1
webMethods	Web-based B-to-B e-com	02/10/00	35.00	133.13	280.4
Exelixis	Health-Biomed/Genetics	04/10/00	13.00	49.25	278.8
Embarcadero Technologies	Mgmt. software, e-com	04/19/00	10.00	37.50	275.0
Capstone Turbine	Energy-Alternatives	06/28/00	16.00	59.13	269.5
Numerical Technologies	Software to design chips	04/06/00	14.00	50.06	257.6
Avanex	Photonics for optical networks	02/03/00	36.00	127.63	254.5
Marvell Technology	Circuits for data storage	06/26/00	15.00	52.69	251.3

Source: Renaissance Capital on-line (http://www.ipo-fund.com/topfive.htm).

- One is economic 'leverage,' meaning the ability to hold on to a specific niche or position by virtue of brand identification, patent rights, or the advantages of standard-setting.
- A second is a 'closed-loop solution' to customer needs, meaning that the company can fulfill all the steps related to the product.
- A third is competent and (above all) agile management.

Management aside, what Internet business lines are candidates for the first two criteria: that is, leverage and completeness? Cohan develops the answers by means of nine separate business segments, grouped in three tiers or levels. The three are 'lossware,' 'brandware,' and 'powerware.'

As the tags suggest, certain lines of activity have little if any prospects for profitability (see Table 22.3).

Table 22.3 Cohan's hierarchy of Internet profitability

Level III: Powerware

- Network infrastructure
- Web consulting
- Internet venture capital

Level II: Brandware

- Internet security
- Web portals
- Electronic commerce
- Web content

Level I: Lossware

- Internet service providers (ISP's)
- Web commerce tools

Source: Cohan 1999 (p. 19).

Lossware: ISPs and Web Commerce Tools

These are businesses where entry costs are low and the quest for brand identity can devour endless funds for advertising with no real effect. Internet service providers (ISPs) are one such segment, principally because initial entry costs are low, but also because the attempt to gain a foothold nationally can be expensive.

The other lossware segment, web commerce tools, includes brochure designers, broadcast software, 'cookie' software, and the like. Examples of companies in this group are DoubleClick, Macromedia, and Open Market. Entry costs are low, switching costs are low, and competition keeps prices at or below operating costs.

Brandware: Portals, Web Content, E-commerce, and Security

Brandware turned out to be the sector where the shakeout hit hardest, leaving only one or a few survivors in some cases. An example is web portals, some of which originated around search engines. Once portal sites realized they could charge for advertising, the competition took the form of attracting the highest 'ratings,' or traffic.

Eventually, consumers settled into tastes, habits, and loyalties. Then a portal like Yahoo! emerged as a leader, while others fell away. Owing to the great expense of maintaining a portal, barriers to entry (along with loyalty to leaders) discourage newcomers. (Less successful portals were theglobe.com for 20-somethings, and iVillage.com for women.)

Web content firms monitor and analyze the Internet, and perhaps other media as well. Examples include CNET, the Gartner Group, and Ziff-Davis.

The best-known example of e-commerce is Amazon.com, a classic example of a successful branded identity, but facing increasing doubts by mid-2000. The category also includes eBay, the on-line auction house, and E-Trade, the brokerage.

Internet security firms are currently prominent (as a genre, if not by name) because of fears of 'cyber-terrorism' and of hackers generally – and, reciprocally, of government and private surveillance. The service they offer is to protect corporate and government networks from hostile invasion. Examples are Network Associates and Security Dynamics.

Brandware is thus characterized by the sort of positive feedback, operating through customer loyalty and brand identity, that erects barriers to entry and creates economic leverage.

On the other hand it was Brandware logic that created the feverish efforts by profitless unknown companies to spend vast amounts of venture capital on expensive ad campaigns (as for the Super Bowl in late January 2000). In retrospect, this amounted to throwing money away, a form of decadence that may have ended with the popping of the dot-com bubble.

Powerware: Internet VC, Web Consulting, and Network Infrastructure

In Cohan's framework, profit potential lies with firms that can establish *leverage* and offer *closed-loop* solutions. Leverage, once again, reflects a scarce resource. A closed-loop solution is an integrated package for which the costs of switching are prohibitive (as with an operating system).

Internet VC firms are an example of firms that moved from brandware to powerware by virtue of network effects. Once a few VC partnerships had outstanding records for high returns, suppliers of capital tended to seek them out, which in turn gave the emerging lead firms the ability to attract the best talent and link to the best underwriters. The result is a commanding position and high rewards for a few Internet-specialized VC partnerships.

Web consulting centers on strategy and tactics for companies across the spectrum to improve their positions by means of Internet tools. Examples include the Peppers and Rogers Group, Sapient, and Viant. It might be noted however, that by September 2000, as reported earnings in this category fell sharply, market valuations of stocks moved down apace. Evidently the de-mystification of the story-stocks weakened the market for consultants.

Network infrastructure, as noted above, provides goods and services to improve the Internet as a delivery system. The best known firms are those making telecommunications equipment, such as 3Com or Cisco Systems. In the parlance to be considered now, such established and successful New Economy companies are known generically as the 'old new industrials.'

NEW METRICS, OLD NEW INDUSTRIALS

In an influential and timely series of reports in 1999 and 2000, analysts at PaineWebber predicted and interpreted the shift against the dot-coms, meaning companies that had recently gone public in the hot market for Internet-related IPOs. They describe such 'new new industrials' as having been over-valued by virtue of a misapplication of the 'new metrics.' The latter term refers to an approach to stock valuation that predicts future earnings in companies that have as yet to make profits. Then the stock in question is valued as a high multiple of the as-yet only imagined earnings.

As we saw in Cohan's framework, much of the story-telling for recently public Internet-related companies pivoted on establishing a brand identity, then reaping the increasing-returns that might result.

Since few of the companies had such identities, their strategies got down to buying them through advertising. The limits of such excess could be seen in the extremely expensive dot-com ads for unknown companies during the January 2000 Super Bowl. Similarly, the Internet magazines grow ever heavier, fattened by advertising from relatively unknown companies. The winner-take-all logic and the absence of current profits or plausible strategies eventually combined to frighten investors and pop the bubble.

In contrast, the PaineWebber analysts argue that the 'old new industrials' remain good investments, worth their high price-earnings multiples (Kerschner et al. 2000, p. 4). They advance a method for calculating stock values for currently profitable companies that leads to much higher acceptable P-E ratios than the traditional limit, about 20.

The basis for higher than traditional valuations, in their view, is low inflation (p. 7). If inflation equals four percent a year, for example, then a company with 15 percent annual earnings growth should be valued at about 20 times earnings. But if inflation equals only two percent, the valuation for the same earnings growth soars to a P-E ratio of 65 (Kerschner et al., Chart 8).

In short, some form of 'new metrics' is suggested for what the analysts see as a new environment: low inflation, rapid productivity growth. And the firms that survive the popping of the bubble are the 'old new industrials.'

By this as well as by Cohan's approach, then, bandwidth-boosting and other infrastructure stocks are deemed worthy survivors of the shakeout.

NOTES

1. This chapter (like the preceding one) owes a great deal to Chip Elitzer, of Elitzer Associates. Any remaining errors are my own.
2. Professor Ritter's table, 'Big IPO Runups of 1975-1999,' is on-line at http://bear.cba.ufl.edu/ritter/ritterbi.htm.

23. Strategic cities

> The ultimate irony in the placeless world is that some places organize the rest.
> (Castells 1998, p. 188)

The purpose of this chapter is to consider which American cities are spearheading the New Economy's next round of development – and to ask how they have emerged as centers of innovation.

STRATEGIC INFORMATION

By way of introduction, we can combine several strands from earlier chapters around the theme of 'strategic information.'

In Chapter 13 we noted that at the crest of the Old Economy's development, John Kenneth Galbraith declared the individual entrepreneur obsolete, saying 'only the group has *the information that decision requires*' (Galbraith 1967, 1985, p. 104, emphasis added). Today, in the light of history, things look different. In retrospect, 'the group' in the traditional managerial corporation looks more like a stultifying bureaucracy, where the safest tactic was the non-decision (Farrell 1993).

By the same token, the IT case study in Part III illustrated the vital role played by newcomers, acting as entrepreneurs, to overthrow the established order and blast through the tendencies toward stagnation that past success seems to breed. From that standpoint, the difference between the US economy, on the one hand, and those of Japan or France or Germany, on the other, has seemed to lie in the superior opportunities the US has afforded newcomers – geeks, freaks, immigrants, and other outsiders.

Networks versus Hierarchy

Yet the basis for Professor Galbraith's verdict remains of interest. New technologies are not necessarily easier to understand today than in 1967. Group (or, in today's parlance, 'team') cooperation, consulting, and coordination are often as crucial to product development and innovation today as they were then.

What has changed, it would seem, is the legitimacy of hierarchy. A primary lesson of the last third of the twentieth century was that hierarchy is antithetical to the free and open flow of strategic information, 'the information that decision requires.' This, as many people have observed, is the impression one might glean from the fates of the USSR and of US corporate dinosaurs (like Sears or General Motors) alike.

More recently, of course, the proliferation of computer networks both within and between organizations has also made hierarchy less tenable. As a result, the 1990s saw powerful tendencies toward flatter organizations; burgeoning alliances between large and small firms; and deepening networks between firms and venture capitalists, universities, and governments.

Information flows remain vital, in other words. But now PC networks and spatial proximity provide increasingly complementary channels for the horizontal transmission of strategic information. One result, as manifested most vividly in the US in perhaps a dozen large and mid-sized cities, is a new framework for innovation, marked by partnerships between knowledge workers and venture capitalists.

Hence our current point of departure. In terms of networks, spatial access, and strategic information, which metropolitan areas offer the best environments for innovation? Naturally, any such inquiry needs to begin with a deep bow to Silicon Valley.

CULTURES OF COMMUNICATION

In Chapter 20 the point was made that Boston's Route 128 has re-joined Silicon Valley as a preeminent technology center. Meanwhile, its telecommunications role has catapulted the National Capital Region ('Silicon Dominion') to a similar position of leadership (see Chapter 12). If this is the new technology triumvirate, however, Silicon Valley remains first among equals – as this chapter will re-confirm.

As so many have asked before us: What is it about Silicon Valley, anyway? A good overview of the question is 'The Valley of Money's Delight' (*The Economist*, March 29, 1997). There John Micklethwait cites economic cultures as the catalysts that determine whether networks communicate. As he observes, 'Research has increasingly concentrated on clusters – places (such as Hollywood or Silicon Valley) or communities (such as the overseas Chinese) where there is "something in the air" that encourages risk-taking.'

He lists ten features of Silicon Valley's economic culture that help explain the area's dynamism (Micklethwait, pp. 7-12):

1. Tolerance of failure.
2. Tolerance of treachery.
3. Risk-seeking.

4. Reinvestment in the community.
5. Enthusiasm for change.
6. Promotion on merit.
7. Obsession with the product.
8. Collaboration.
9. Variety.
10. Anybody can play.

This list points up the fluidity of the Valley as an economic environment. One of the qualities it conveys is a sense of loyalty to the place, rather than to the firm. By extension, it suggests a milieu conducive to spin-offs and start-ups.

The picture that emerges is of a sizable cast of specialized characters within commuting-range of one another, capable of connecting if need be to turn new ideas into start-up businesses – perhaps as much for the adventure as for the money.

As noted in Chapter 20, strategic communication can also occur over long distances, especially where secrecy is a priority locally. But the focus at this point is on the spatial chemistry for innovation within a given area.

THE US SYSTEM OF CITIES: COMPETING VISIONS

Which other places in the US display similar characteristics? It will help to begin with a few framing points about the US system of cities – where by 'cities' we refer not to central cities alone but to their larger metropolitan areas.

(1) City Roles in the World Economy

In a conference announcement from the University of Newcastle (England) in 1998, the organizers proposed a typology of cities based on ten distinct city types. The conference theme was 'Cities in the Global Information Society,' so the taxonomy can be understood in that light. Here, then, is *their* list, along with examples they mention:

1. Old-industrial (for example, Newcastle, Pittsburgh, Essen)
2. Global (London, New York, Tokyo, Singapore)
3. Second-tier regional and national capitals (Amsterdam, Dublin, Milan, Taipei, Toronto, Sydney)
4. Newly-industrializing (Pearl River Delta)
5. Former communist (Moscow, Warsaw, Budapest)

6. Globally marginalized (Soweto, sub-Saharan Africa generally)
7. Information-processing (Sunderland, Bangalore, Kingston)
8. Resorts and tourism (Palma, Orlando)
9. Logistics (North Carolina [sic], Rotterdam)
10. New planned (Malaysia's Multimedia Corridor and Japan's
    technopoles)

With a couple of obvious modifications, a similar taxonomy could be
applied to the US system of cities, using, say, categories 1-3 and 7-9.

(2) American Metropolitan Evolution

In particular, asking which of America's largest cities are 'industrial' in
origin (type 1) is a fruitful exercise.

For example, Table 23.1 links changes in manufacturing employment
after 1970 to the mid-century industrial legacies of 30 large US areas. It
reveals a record of large losses by industrially specialized areas.

As background, these are the 30 metro areas that contained the 30
largest cities in 1970, when large-scale losses of manufacturing jobs were
about to begin. The areas are ranked by their population sizes in 1910, at the
end of the nation's heavy industrialization and before the automobile or
electricity had had much impact. This historical approach (introduced in
Norton 1979) owes much to the geographer John R. Borchert's proposed
sequence of technology epochs in a classic 1967 article, 'American
Metropolitan Evolution.'

In Figure 23.1 the dozen areas that had reached the largest size by 1910
are termed 'industrial' and the dozen then smallest, 'young.' In between,
such areas as Los Angeles, Washington, DC and Seattle are 'anomalous,' in
that much of their growth had occurred after 1910 but before 1950. Among
the variables that then align by age-class are (1) population density, (2)
industrial structure, and (3) unionization rates (Norton 1979).

Regionally, as the figure shows, 11 of the industrial areas were in the
Manufacturing Belt, and ten of the younger areas outside it. At mid-century,
the dozen industrial areas still had an average 35 percent of their 1950
workforces in manufacturing jobs. In contrast, the dozen termed younger
had an average of only 19 percent.

Their roles as exporters of industrial goods to the rest of the US and
abroad left the mature metro areas of the northeast quadrant vulnerable to
huge losses in manufacturing employment after 1970. *The combined
manufacturing job losses from four of them – New York (down 658,000),
Chicago (326,000), Philadelphia (277,000), and Detroit (198,000) –
exceeded the entire US loss (1,395,000).* Most younger areas added manu-

Table 23.1 1950 Employment structure and post-1970 industrial growth (000)

Metro area by 1910 population	% of work-force in mfg. in 1950	Manufacturing employment		Absolute change	Percent change
		1969/1970	1998		
1 N.Y.-Nassau	30.8	1,086	428	-658	-61
2 Chicago	37.7	983	657	-326	-33
3 Philadelphia	35.6	583	306	-277	-48
4 Boston	28.7	322	224	-98	-30
5 Pittsburgh*	38.0	292	140	-152	-52
6 St. Louis	33.8	278	195	-83	-30
7 San Francisco*	19.4	80	78	-2	-3
8 Baltimore	30.9	206	100	-106	-51
9 Cleveland*	40.5	316	201	-115	-36
10 Buffalo*	39.7	107	77	-30	-28
11 Detroit	46.9	637	439	-198	-31
12 Cincinnati	33.4	173	142	-31	-18
13 Los Angeles	25.6	881	668	-213	-24
14 Washington	7.4	104	103	-1	0
15 Milwaukee	42.9	213	179	-34	-16
16 Kansas City	24.5	127	108	-19	-15
17 New Orleans	15.6	56	49	-7	-13
18 Seattle*	19.8	198	228	30	15
19 Indianapolis*	33.1	128	107	-21	-16
20 Atlanta	18.3	154	221	67	44
21 Denver	16.8	95	93	-2	-2
22 Columbus	25.0	100	104	4	4
23 Memphis	20.5	61	64	3	5
24 Nashville	22.9	72	96	24	33
25 Dal.-Fort Worth*	18.4	235	363	128	54
26 San Antonio	11.6	38	52	14	37
27 Houston	21.4	158	220	62	39
28 Jacksonville	13.1	29	40	11	38
29 San Diego	15.7	70	127	57	81
30 Phoenix	10.4	75	170	95	127
US		20,167	18,772	-1,395	-7

* Area had a major discontinuity in territorial definition. Figures are for incomplete timespan.

Source: R.D. Norton 1979, p. 19; US Bureau of Labor Statistics, 'Selective Access' on-line at http://www.bls.gov/sahome.html.

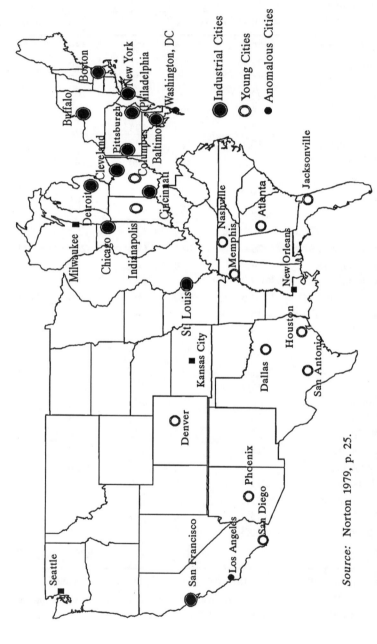

Source: Norton 1979, p. 25.

Figure 23.1 The regional clustering of the old cities

facturing jobs over the period, including a few (Atlanta, Dallas-Fort Worth, Houston, San Diego, and Phoenix) with sizable absolute gains.

As to changes in total employment, the contrasts between industrial and younger areas are milder, but still pervasive. The US added 55 million payroll jobs from 1970 to 1998, for a percentage gain of 78 percent. Relative to this national rate, three points about the 30 areas might be made:

- A few industrial areas (New York, Pittsburgh, Cleveland, Buffalo) had extremely low job growth – below 10 percent.
- The median figure for the 11 older areas in the Manufacturing Belt, 35 percent (for Chicago), was less than half the US rate.
- The median for the ten younger areas of the South and West was 157 percent, twice the national rate. Atlanta, Dallas, Houston, and Phoenix added more than 1 million jobs (as did a now resurgent Chicago, Los Angeles, and Washington).

Even in the late 1990s, with brisk job growth nationwide, the older areas still lagged. As Figures 23.2 and 23.3 document, aggregate job growth from 1995 to 1998 remained only about half the rate in most older areas as in most younger ones.

In sum, the specialized industrial roles of the mature areas led to large-scale losses of manufacturing and sluggish growth in total employment.

From the standpoint of cluster theory, we might put all this a different way: Specialization can be good for city growth – or not! It all depends on the nature of the activity, the pattern of demand from the rest of the world, and the chemistry between the activity and 'learning' on the part of the city's workforce and knowledge base.

(3) The Perils of Specialization, Continued: IT Hardware

Just as specialized roles proved a heavy load for industrial metros after 1970, so too did high profiles in computer production and electronics between 1986 and 1996 (see Table 23.2). The precipitants were declining US employment in computer production (SIC 357), slow job gains in electronics (SIC 367), and decentralization of both to rural states.

Thus the three areas with the greatest initial specialization in computer and electronics production accounted for over half of all hardware jobs lost nationwide from 1986 to 1996 (see Equation 1 in the chapter appendix). Phoenix, Boston, and Los Angeles combined for hardware losses of 73,000 jobs. Other big losses occurred in Chicago, Philadelphia, and New York.

How different is the lesson here from that of the de-industrializing 'industrial' cities after 1970? The two cases seem closely related, and not

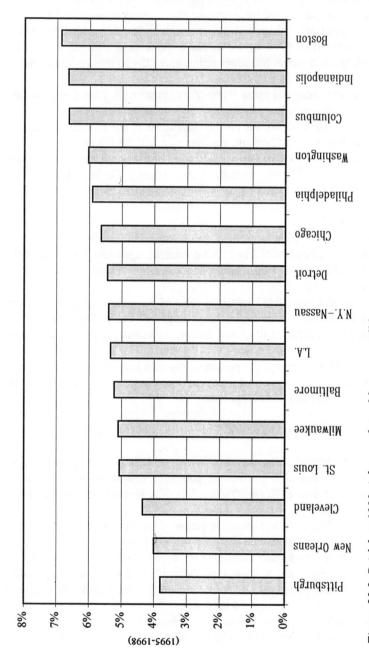

Figure 23.2 Brisk late 1990s job growth in older areas still lags . . . .

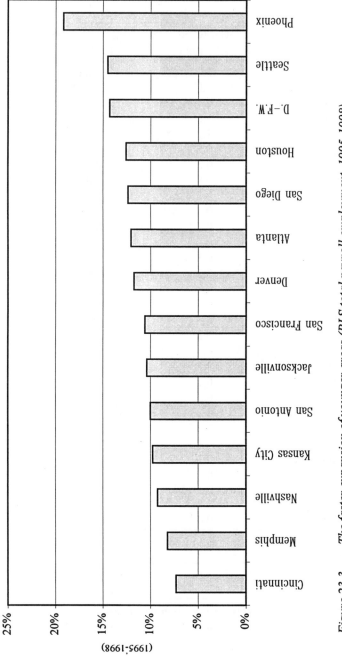

Figure 23.3 ... The faster expansion of younger areas (BLS total payroll employment, 1995-1998)

*Table 23.2 In hardware, specialized areas lost most (absolute
change in SIC 357 + SIC 367, 1986-1996)*

Area	Hardware LQ, 1986	Employment change 1986-1996
Phoenix	3.7	-13,864
Boston	3.0	-25,952
San Diego	2.1	-1,327
Los Angeles	1.6	-33,314
Dallas-Fort Worth	1.2	5,887
Chicago	0.8	-5,172
Philadelphia	0.8	-8,304
Kansas City	0.8	-3,427
San Francisco	0.6	-3,881
Seattle	0.5	2,752
NY-Nassau	0.4	-8,304
Milwaukee	0.4	415
Houston	0.3	3,765
Pittsburgh	0.3	666
Cincinnati	0.3	-49
Washington	0.3	-1,676
Columbus	0.3	-200
San Antonio	0.3	-1,190
Detroit	0.3	-365
St. Louis	0.2	1,400
Cleveland	0.2	497
Baltimore	0.2	155
Buffalo	0.2	450
Indianapolis	0.2	315
Denver	0.1	482
Nashville	0.1	408
Atlanta	0.1	48
New Orleans	0.1	150
Jacksonville	0.1	-40
Memphis	0.0	821
Total, 30 areas		-88,854
Exhibit: Silicon Valley	7.7	-22,940
Total, 31 areas		-111,794
US total		-126,123

Note: Area definitions are available on request from the author.

Source: Machine-readable *County Business Patterns* data for 1986 and 1996.

only because the IT hardware losses are one component of the larger losses in manufacturing employment in older areas.

In each story, initial production centers specialized in sectors that would add little or no employment nationally, a scenario that tends to be accompanied by rapid dispersal to competing domestic sites, including non-metro locations.

In a more positive light, one of the ways the US as a geographical entity retains employment relative to offshore locations is by offering both centers of innovation and lower-cost (including non-metropolitan) environments.

In any case hardware was at most half the story of metro IT job growth during 'the break-up of the old computer industry' (Grove 1993, p. 57). For most large cities the growth of IT employment depended much more on software, as we shall soon see.

(4) The Ladder of Influence

In the meantime, a stimulating alternative view – that older American cities remain on top, just as in Europe – comes from David Warsh, who writes an economics column for the Boston *Globe*. Prompted by the purchase of the Los Angeles *Times* by the Chicago *Tribune* in early 2000, Warsh proposed an informal ranking of the leading centers of US influence. His admittedly impressionistic list refers to 'education, finance, and media industries . . . and the capacity to absorb the latest streams of immigration. . . .' (Warsh 2000, p. E1)

By this reckoning, the three largest cities, New York, Los Angeles, and Chicago, are also the three most influential, the places where US opinions and attitudes are shaped. (See Table 9.3 for population counts.)

Then there are 'the other American cities of international importance – Washington, DC, Boston, Miami, San Francisco and, possibly, Seattle . . . world centers in certain fields.' In this reckoning, Washington qualifies only because it is the capital. Boston and San Francisco make the top eight by virtue of their financial and university strength. Miami qualifies as the gateway to Latin America and the Caribbean, and Seattle as a 'high-tech nursery.' Global cities in specialized realms, these five fall just below the top three, New York, Los Angeles, and Chicago.

Warsh's conclusion? 'This is not to rob a dozen other US cities of their significance. . . . But the hierarchy is well-established, and *here, as in Europe, the oldest cities tend to remain at the top*' (Warsh, p. E1, emphasis added).

This curious generalization may have some relevance to media and entertainment. Even on this front, it tends to miss the tensions portrayed in works of fiction like *Turn of the Century* (Anderson 1999), an account of the fear and loathing New York media moguls feel for digital yokels from Seattle. But to conclude that 'here, as in Europe, the oldest cities tend to remain at the top' also loses sight of a defining contrast between the US and Europe. To wit: the role of younger centers as technology seedbeds.

This latter process can be seen in a variety of indicators for the US system of cities – including not only the job growth noted already, but also IT roles and migration choices.

(5) Tech-Poles: The Milken Institute List

Consider, for example, the Milken Institute's 1999 ranking of 'Tech-Poles.' These are the US metropolitan areas that stand out by virtue of their size and specialization in a broad range of high-tech activities (DeVol 1999, p. 67). When an area's percentage share of US high-tech output is multiplied by its high-tech output location quotient, the result finds San Jose (Silicon Valley) the runaway leader, followed by Dallas, Los Angeles, Boston, and Seattle. The next five are Washington, DC, Albuquerque, Chicago, New York, and Atlanta.

In other words, four of the top five areas are from the South and West, as are three of the next five (once we recognize that the Washington, DC, area's high-tech center of gravity is northern Virginia). That adds up to *six of the top seven* metropolitan areas from the South and West, as measured across the gamut of high-tech activities.

An equally sharp regional watershed can be seen for domestic migration, which tends to shift technical talent away from the Northeast and California alike.

(6) Magnet Metros: The Seattle-Atlanta Line

Domestic migration flows in the 1990s may provide a good barometer of the economic opportunities offered by major metropolitan areas (Hansen 2000). The basis for this view is that domestic migration flows offer a better indicator of an area's success than per capita income growth, which may include a 'bribe' component in wages to offset urban disamenities (Glaeser et al. 1995). In addition, since perhaps three-fourths of the annual immigration into the US remains poor and unskilled, choices by *domestic* migrants are likely to give a better indication of opportunities, compared to points of entry into the country.

The areas with the largest 1990-1997 domestic in-flows can be found below what Hansen terms the Seattle-Atlanta line (see Figure 23.4). The numbers range from over 300,000 in Atlanta, Phoenix, and Las Vegas to

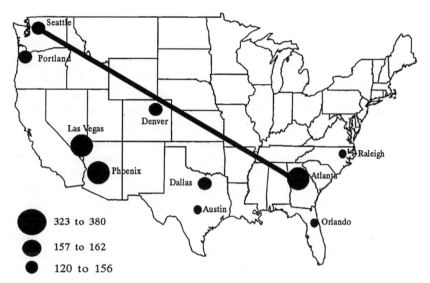

Source: Data from Hansen 2000, Table 2.

*Figure 23.4 The ten metro areas with largest net domestic
in-migration (000), 1990-97*

gains between 120,000 and 162,000 in Seattle, Portland, Dallas, Denver, Austin, Raleigh (which is just north of the line), and Orlando.

In terms of size, these 'magnet metros' had fewer than five million residents in 1995. The largest was Dallas, with 4.7 million. The next largest were Atlanta, 3.6 million, Seattle, 3.4, and Denver, 2.3. That meant that no magnet metro was as large as any of the eight largest areas: New York, Los Angeles, Chicago, Washington, San Francisco, Philadelphia, Boston, and Detroit. Each of these eight largest had over five million people, and each had net domestic outflows.

On the other hand, the map serves as a visual reminder that size is but one of several linked variables. It portrays a regional realignment from high-density, high-cost, older areas in the Manufacturing Belt and California to younger, low-density centers. In turn, this shows up in the data as a move from larger to smaller cities.

The net effect, Hansen concludes, 'has been a definite shift downward in the urban hierarchy in terms of where Americans want to live and work' (Hansen 2000, p. 12). As to innovation and entrepreneurship, the effect is to highlight the amenities drawing technically talented people to such rising centers as Portland, Denver, and Austin.

SEEDBED CLUSTERS

Where did concentrations of IT workers grow most rapidly between the mid-1980s and the mid-1990s? The answer turns largely on software and other computer services, where the story was opposite the one for hardware.

The places that specialized most in software and other computer services in the mid-1980s would then go on to record the largest software job gains over the next decade (see Table 23.3). Since software and other computer services added jobs at a rapid clip during this interval, for most of the 30 areas the employment gains easily outweighed computer hardware losses. (Exceptions were two hardware centers, Los Angeles and Phoenix.)

For example, of the 30 large areas, Washington, DC, was most specialized in SIC 737 (computer services) in 1986. Thanks in large part to the explosion of software and telecommunications in northern Virginia, the DC area also had the largest gain in computer services employment, over 50,000. At the other end of the spectrum, one of the least specialized areas in 1986, New Orleans, had the smallest increase in computer services employment.

How general was this tendency? Equation 2 in the chapter appendix indicates that every additional one point in an area's 1986 location quotient was associated with an increment of 10,000 computer-services jobs over the next decade. (As noted in Chapter 19, a location quotient above unity is a sign of specialization.) Whatever the bundle of variables represented by the initial location quotients, together they account for nearly 60 percent of the variation in job gains.

In contrast to IT hardware jobs, then, software and other computer services followed a virtuous circle. In a sector with rapid job growth nationwide, the initial centers tended to grow as rapidly in percentage terms as others, hence scoring larger absolute gains.

In turn, some of the initially specialized areas saw software expansion interact with the local venture-capital base to spur new technology-based business creation, as measured by initial public offerings (IPOs).

Measuring the Local VC Base

As a working hypothesis, we might surmise that IPOs in the late 1990s were most frequent where knowledge workers could hook up with venture capitalists – the suppliers not only of money, but of management expertise.

To measure the size and energy of an area's VC sector in the late 1990s, we can use survey estimates of the number of initial deals originating with the area's VC firms in 1997. Table 23.4 lists these comparisons for all areas

*Table 23.3 In software, specialized areas gained most
(employment changes in SIC 737)*

Area	Computer services LQ, 1986	Employment change, in SIC 737, 1986-96 (percent)	(absolute)
Washington	5.0	122.5	51,293
Atlanta	2.9	88.9	12,729
Boston	2.4	134.8	38,239
Dallas-Fort Worth	2.2	120.6	27,461
Detroit	2.1	52.4	11,134
Denver	2.1	101.5	10,561
San Diego	1.9	91.7	7,613
Chicago	1.6	58.7	19,105
Baltimore	1.3	108.9	4,834
Philadelphia	1.3	113.1	17,937
Los Angeles	1.3	71.5	28,109
St. Louis	1.3	129.6	7,183
Houston	1.2	93.7	9,431
San Francisco	1.2	225.3	10,113
Seattle	1.1	239.3	13,178
Cincinnati	1.1	108.9	3,985
San Antonio	1.1	22	655
NY-Nassau	1.0	80.4	23,046
Jacksonville	0.9	145.7	3,002
Indianapolis	0.9	141.2	4,218
Kansas City	0.8	230.7	7,508
Phoenix	0.8	187.1	9,783
Columbus	0.7	278.2	6,871
Pittsburgh	0.7	177.8	6,662
Cleveland	0.7	101.7	4,191
Milwaukee	0.6	204.1	5,128
Nashville	0.5	152.4	2,205
Buffalo	0.5	102.4	1,461
New Orleans	0.5	36.4	478
Memphis	0.0	(not app.)	3,833
Total, 30 areas			351,946
Exhibit: Silicon Valley	2.7	170.3	45,270
Total, 31 areas			397,216
US total			713,231

Note: Negligible base-year value precludes percent change for Memphis.
Source: Machine-readable *County Business Patterns* data for 1986
        and 1996.

Table 23.4 Areas with the most active VC base in 1997 (as
measured by the number of initial placements from
reporting VC partnerships in the Money Tree Report)

Area	Initial deals
Silicon Valley/San Francisco	500
Boston	351
New York	190
Minneapolis	62
Chicago	61
Los Angeles/Orange County	50
Dallas	42
Baltimore	30
Philadelphia	26
Denver	19
Seattle	18
DC/Northern Virginia	17
Charlotte	14
Austin	13
Pittsburgh	8
Detroit	8
Cleveland	7
Kansas	6
Portland, Me	6
Greenville, SC	6
Indianapolis	5
New Orleans	5
San Antonio	5
Tampa	5
Total	1,454

Note: Another 407 initial deals by 197 venture firms were not listed separately
    in the *Report* for 1997.
Source: Coopers & Lybrand *Money Tree Report* (1998, p. 12).

specified separately in the (then) Coopers & Lybrand *Money Tree Report* for 1997.

This indicator measures *where placements originate* – not where they land. Since the purpose of a VC placement is to bring the early-stage firm to a successful IPO, linking IPOs to where placements land would explain nothing. (That is, when a Chicago venture capitalist has a placement in Silicon Valley, the IPO is all but certain to occur in the Valley.)

In contrast, we are testing the proposition that lead or solo VC firms prefer to make their placements locally because of the need for frequent face-to-face contact with supported start-ups (see Appendix 23B).

The Clustering of IPOs in a Few Areas

Table 23.5 lists IPO counts for the 30 metros. From mid-1996 to November, 1999, 1,532 IPOs were launched in the US. That averages over 400 per year, or more than one a day. The three and a half years surveyed is the interval covered by the database in Hoover's on-line IPO directory (at http://www.hoovers.com/ipo/). The comprehensive data-base permits counts by industry, by state, and by metropolitan area.

Over that interval from mid-1996 about three-eighths of the total count were in some sense 'digital,' linked to computing, semiconductors, software, networks, or e-commerce. (The proportion rose sharply in 1999, as the Gold Rush gathered speed, to about 60 percent.)

In absolute terms a handful of areas dominated the metro landscape for IPOs over the period. New York and Silicon Valley each were home to about 200 IPOs. Adding Los Angeles's 94 and Route 128's 90 gives a figure for the four top metros of over half of the 30-area total – and about 40 percent of the US total (see Table 23.5). IPO activity thus tends to be concentrated in a few major centers, though not as concentrated as VC 'funds.'

In addition, the large number of IPOs for the New York area suggests a sharp increase in start-up activity, triggered in part by media-linked Internet firms. No longer does money raised by venture capitalists in New York go largely to other regions.

At the same time, some unexpected places also have high IPO rates, once we discount the effect of absolute population size.

Table 23.5 Areas ranked by digital IPOs per million residents

Rank	Area	Dig./mil.	IPOs/mil.	All IPOs	Digital IPOs
1	S.F.-San Jose	21.2	29.3	196	142
2	Denver CMSA	8.7	16.1	37	20
3	Boston	8.1	15.5	90	47
4	Seattle CMSA	6.5	10.3	35	22
5	Washington PMSA	6.1	12.8	59	28
6	New York CMSA	4.5	10.9	199	83
7	Atlanta	4.2	11.9	43	15
8	San Diego	3.7	11.5	31	10
9	Dal.-F.W. CMSA	3.0	9.6	45	14
10	Baltimore CMSA	2.4	6.8	17	6
11	Phil. CMSA	2.4	8.1	48	14
12	Los Angeles CMSA	2.2	6.0	94	35
13	Houston CMSA	2.1	14.2	61	9
	US	2.1	5.7	1,532	575
14	Kansas City	1.8	7.1	12	3
15	Pittsburgh	1.7	4.2	10	4
16	Chicago CMSA	1.5	5.6	48	13
17	Phoenix	1.4	4.6	13	4
18	Indianapolis	1.3	5.3	8	2
19	St. Louis	1.2	2.7	7	3
20	Jacksonville	1.0	6.0	6	1
21	Milwaukee CMSA	0.6	3.1	5	1
22	Cincinnati CMSA	0.5	3.7	7	1
23	Cleveland CMSA	0.3	2.8	8	1
24	Detroit CMSA	0.2	3.3	18	1
25	Buffalo	0.0	0.8	1	0
26	New Orleans	0.0	0.8	1	0
27	Columbus	0.0	3.3	5	0
28	Memphis	0.0	2.7	3	0
29	Nashville	0.0	5.5	6	0
30	San Antonio	0.0	1.3	2	0

Source: Hoover's on-line database www.hoovers.com/ipo/.

IPO Rates, Standardized for Population

Standardized for population, how do individual areas compare to the US averages of about six total IPOs, and about two digital IPOs, per million residents?

For total IPOs, the highest rate was Silicon Valley (approximated by combining the San Francisco and San Jose metropolitan areas). It had nearly 30 IPOs per million residents, about twice the rate of any other area. As in the Milken Institute ranking of high-tech output noted above, the San Jose/San Francisco region is in a class by itself.

A dozen other areas on the list came in above the US average. Other entries include second-place Denver (above Boston or New York), Seattle, Atlanta, San Diego, Baltimore, and Philadelphia.

In contrast, both the smaller areas in the South and West and the more 'heavy-metal' areas of the Midwest lagged the national averages.

For digital IPOs the top entries are *Silicon Valley, Denver, Route 128, Seattle, Washington, DC, New York, Atlanta, San Diego, and Dallas.* By contrast, Philadelphia, Houston, Kansas City, and Chicago are less prominent digitally than for IPOs in general.

Digital IPO Rates as a Function of Software Workers and VC

Besides 'the usual suspects,' then, this measure of IT generativity includes Denver, Atlanta, and San Diego. To what extent does this outcome reflect the proposed explanatory variables – the supply of venture capital and the relative size of an area's software sector? (The first variable is repeated in Table 23.6, along with the second, the percentage share of an area's total employment accounted for by computer services jobs in 1996.)

It turns out that three-fourths of the differences among areas in digital IPO rates per million residents can be statistically explained in this framework. (In Equation 3 in the chapter appendix, the adjusted R^2 is .73.)

The implication is that the areas just mentioned have unusually high rates of IPO activity because large numbers of technically talented people are concentrated in places offering relatively easy access to venture capital – including not only the funding, but the management expertise that comes with it.

Part Real, Part Surreal: The Internet Gold Rush

At the same time, this may be the dimension to the New Economy best described by Mark Zandi's term, 'part real, part surreal' (Zandi 1998). In

Table 23.6 The VC base and software employment as determinants of IPO formation rates, 1996-1999, in 30 large US metropolitan areas

Area	Rate per million population		No. of initial deals by area VC firms, 1997	1996 payroll employment in SIC 737 (%)
	All IPOs	Digital IPOs		
S.F.-San Jose	29.3	21.2	500	2.5
Denver CMSA	16.1	8.7	19	2.4
Boston	15.5	8.1	351	3.7
Seattle CMSA	10.3	6.5	18	1.7
Washington PMSA	12.8	6.1	17	6.4
New York CMSA	10.9	4.5	190	1.2
Atlanta	11.9	4.2	0	2.9
San Diego	11.5	3.7	0	1.8
Dal.-F.W. CMSA	9.6	3.0	42	2.6
Phil. CMSA	8.1	2.4	26	1.7
Baltimore CMSA	6.8	2.4	30	1.5
Los Angeles CMSA	6.0	2.2	50	1.4
Houston CMSA	14.2	2.1	0	1.2
Kansas City	7.1	1.8	0	1.5
Pittsburgh	4.2	1.7	8	1.1
Chicago CMSA	5.6	1.5	61	1.5
Phoenix	4.6	1.4	0	1.1
Indianapolis	5.3	1.3	5	1.1
St. Louis	2.7	1.2	0	1.6
Jacksonville	6.0	1.0	0	1.2
Milwaukee CMSA	3.1	0.6	0	1.0
Cincinnati CMSA	3.7	0.5	0	1.1
Cleveland CMSA	2.8	0.3	7	0.8
Detroit CMSA	3.3	0.2	8	1.9
Buffalo	0.8	0	0	0.6
New Orleans	0.8	0	5	0.4
Columbus	3.3	0	0	1.4
Nashville	5.5	0	0	0.7
San Antonio	1.3	0	5	0.7

Source: Same as for Tables 23.3, 23.4, and 23.5.

practice, an IPO can be viewed as an attempt on the part of promoters to 'sell' a new idea to the investment community. During the Internet Gold Rush of 1998 and 1999 some IPOs had more hype than content, as the shakeout of dot-com's in April and May of 2000 demonstrated (see Chapter 22).

To that extent, IPOs are an imperfect measure of innovation – an indicator of market fads as well as of genuine new ideas.

On the other hand, there are no perfect measures of innovation, as a look at patents makes clear.

PATENTS: OLD ECONOMY?

The question is whether we might find an alternative indicator with which to monitor changes in innovative performance in the US system of cities. An approach that is sometimes used is to compare patent rates by metropolitan area.

For example, O ' hUallachain (1999, p. 613) observes, 'Innovation is not the product of lone individuals nudging technology forward, but encompasses many interdependent people, firms, and institutions working within networks of social and economic relations.' It turns out, however, that the article is not about innovation at all, but about patents, tabulated relative to population in US metropolitan areas in 1996.[1]

In a similar spirit, Varga observes, 'This chapter, using a large data set of US patents, presents the first industrially and spatially detailed analysis of recent trends of innovative activity in the United States' (1999, p. 230).

Both studies monitor patent rates and tend to highlight the 'inventiveness' of traditional metros in the Manufacturing Belt. O'hUallachain, for example, finds that the 87 metros of the Manufacturing Belt accounted for half of all metropolitan patents in 1996, when they had only 44 percent of the metropolitan population. Accordingly, 'Metropolitan residents in the manufacturing belt remain the most industrious inventors' (p. 613).

That such an inference is misleading can be seen in Varga's findings, which monitor changes in patent activity from 1983 to 1992. He finds *a general shift in patent activity from the metros of the Manufacturing Belt to areas in the South and West*, led by patents registered for IT.

On the other hand, some centers in the Belt retained strong presences in chemicals and pharmaceuticals, and in high-technology machinery. Philadelphia, for example, remained strong in the former, and Chicago in the latter. Indeed, Chicago ranked second in 1992 among all areas in terms of high-technology patents (Varga, p. 225).

The Stellar Patent Performance of the Three Super-States, 1978-1998

Taken together, the two studies suggest that the strong patent performance of Manufacturing Belt metro areas in 1996 may have been a legacy effect, a sign of the continuing but fading presence of Fortune 500 R&D labs in the region.

This impression is confirmed when we compare *state* patent data over time. Consider, for this purpose, the ten states that had most patents in the late 1970s. Seven were from the Manufacturing Belt, and the other three were California, Florida, and Texas, the proverbial 'super-states' when it comes to population and employment growth. (The data set has been compiled and provided by Brian Ceh, who also alerted me to the increasing prominence of the latter three states.)

Among the ten major states, a surprising pattern shaped the increase in patents generated over the next 20 years. The national count doubled (from 44,762 to 90,676, up 103 percent). As Figure 23.5 shows, counts roughly tripled in Florida, California, and Texas. Massachusetts came in at the national average, while the remaining six states had increases of less than two-thirds the US pace.

A line is also included in Figure 23.5 to show state population changes over the same interval. With the possible exceptions of Massachusetts (where patents 'outperformed' population, as it were) and New Jersey (where the opposite can be seen), the two indicators show a remarkable correspondence.

The conclusion? For inventive activity as for population, the US experienced a pronounced shift away from the Manufacturing Belt in the 1980s and 1990s. On average, the three super-states had increases in patent activity at least triple that of such traditional industrial states as New York, Michigan, Ohio, Illinois, Pennsylvania, and New Jersey.

Synthesis: The Decentralization of Invention and Innovation

Interpreting such results in light of our discussion in Chapter 13, we might offer four tentative conclusions:

1. 'Per capita inventiveness' as a measure is likely to underestimate the speed of the regional transformation, because both patent activity and population have shifted at a rapid pace.
2. The widely noted US comeback in patent activity during the 1990s (which defied predictions by analysts such as Michael Porter) has depended directly on the supercharged patent performance of the

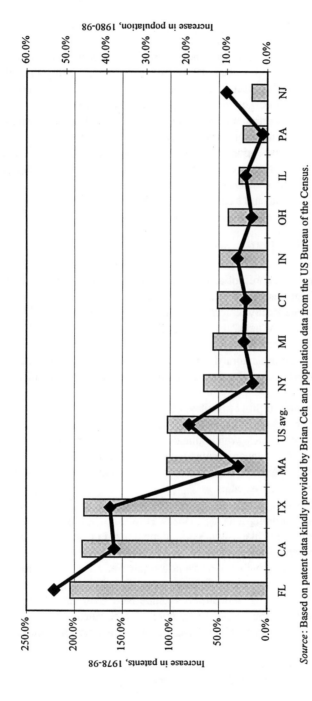

Source: Based on patent data kindly provided by Brian Ceh and population data from the US Bureau of the Census.

Figure 23.5 Patent growth rates, 1978-98, in the ten states with the most 1978 patents

Networks

growing states in the South and West, as symbolized here by Florida, Texas, and California.

3. In the end there may not be much difference in the geographical implications as between IPOs and patents as indicators of the geographical dispersal of creativity over the past few decades. Both indicators, the one of innovation, the other of inventiveness, point up the growing prominence of younger metros and regions within the economy as sources of technological advance.

4. The greatest exceptions to point (3) are the three resurgent industrial cities, Boston, New York (a major IPO seedbed), and Chicago, buoyed by 'high-tech' (but not IT) patent activity. Here the indicators give different results, and each must be respected.

STRATEGIC CITIES

'Large urban places are not anachronisms in the information age, they are the dominant places in the information age' (Drennan 1999, p. 314). But which ones, specifically, emerge from among our working list of 30 of the largest metropolitan areas? In Galbraith's phrase, which have emerged as strategic cities, places offering 'the information that decision requires'?

In light of the indicators we have considered, a dozen come quickly to mind (see Figure 23.6). One entry, Toronto, overrides the protocols.

- San Francisco/Silicon Valley, of course.
- Boston and Route 128, redux.
- Washington, DC, which thanks to northern Virginia is almost as prominent in telecommunications as in government.
- Dallas, especially when understood as the center of a soaring complex of Texas cities.
- Seattle, as symbolized by locals (Paul Allen, Bill Gates, Craig McCaw) and migrants (Jeff Bezos, Howard Schultz) alike.
- Los Angeles, like New York a media-rich location in an age of convergence between content and the Internet.
- Denver, a relatively unknown powerhouse and a regional capital.
- New York, by virtue of finance and media.
- Chicago, another 'industrial city' like New York and Boston, and a standout in terms of Old-Economy high-tech patents.
- *Toronto*, thanks to NorTel Networks and a thriving venture-capital sector.
- Atlanta, ascendant in its region and rising.
- San Diego, transcending its military legacy.

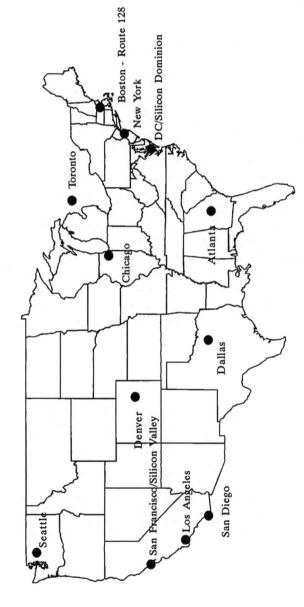

Figure 23.6 Strategic cities: 12 large North American centers shaping the New Economy in the post-PC era

Even while recognizing Toronto, however, the list omits such obvious smaller candidates as Albuquerque, Austin, Boise, Minneapolis, Orlando, Portland (Oregon), Rochester (New York), or the North Carolina complex – merely because of their smaller size. Then again, to note this defect in the selection protocol is also to recognize the entrepreneurial energy pervading the North American system of cities at the turn of the century.

DIVERSITY AND ADAPTIVE CAPACITY

As the New Economy moved into high gear in the mid-1990s around the Internet, most large US cities shared in the expansion, including some that had weathered decades of painful adjustment.

The underlying forces shaping place competition increasingly came to include media and finance, not just IT. Accordingly, the creation of technology-based start-ups would now depend on resources available to the more diversified of the former industrial centers. On the other hand, some younger cities may lack the education and research base required to stand out in the competition for IT functions.

In the larger picture, the diversity of the system of cities emerged as a spur to the US economy's adaptive capacity. As Clem Tisdell observes, 'Industrial diversity (more generally diversity of driving attributes in dynamic systems) can have value in increasing the likelihood that an economy (or system) can jump to a superior state' (1999, p. 163).

A superior state, not so much relative to the rest of the world, but relative to America's own earlier trajectory and apparent destiny.

The question remains, then, what went right?

NOTE

1. The basic objection to patents as indicators of innovation is that innovation is a separate step from invention (see Chapter 13). Innovation is the carrying out of a new idea to yield a new product or process. Invention is the registration of the idea itself, not its implementation.

   As O'hUallachain observes, there are additional caveats to be made about interpreting patent activity in *spatial* terms. One concerns the location of the discovery itself vs. the location of the patent's ownership. Tabulations that locate patent activity according to where the patent is owned, not where the inventor (or R&D lab) is located, tend to distort the picture, as when the 23 percent of Arizona's patent activity attributable to a Motorola facility there in 1996 might have been credited to the parent company's state, Illinois. Another is that patents have traditionally not covered software code, which instead comes under copyright laws. To that extent, patent counts will tend to slight metros specializing in IT (see O' hUallachain 1999, p. 628).

APPENDIX 23A REGRESSIONS FOR METROPOLITAN GROWTH AND IPO RATES

Equation (1)
The 1986-96 absolute change in hardware employment (SIC 357 and SIC 367), *DHARD*, as a function of the initial, 1986, location quotient in the same variable, for the 30 metropolitan areas:

$$DHARD = 1078 - 6273 \; LQHARD86,$$
$$(0.7) \quad (4.5)$$

$$N = 30, \text{ adjusted } R^2 = .41,$$

where the parenthesized terms are the t-ratios of the coefficient estimates.

Equation (2)
The 1986-96 absolute gain in computer services employment (SIC 737), *DSOFT*, as a function of a metropolitan area's location quotient in the same variable (*LQSOFT86*) in 1986:

$$DSOFT = -1395.4 + 9775 \; LQSOFT86,$$
$$(0.6) \quad (6.4)$$

$$N = 29, \text{ adjusted } R^2 = .59,$$

where Memphis is excluded because of a negligible base-year value.

Equation (3)
The number of digital IPOs per million area residents, 1996-99 (*DIGRATE*), as a function of (1) *VCBASE*, the number of initial deals done by a metro's VC partnerships (regardless of destination) in 1997; and (2) *SOFTSHARE*, the 1996 share of total payroll employment in computer services jobs:

$$DIGRATE = -.005 + .03 \; VCBASE + 1.0 \; SOFTSHARE$$
$$(0) \quad (7.3) \quad\quad (2.7)$$

$$N = 29, \text{ adjusted } R^2 = .73.$$

APPENDIX 23B DOES VC STAY LOCAL?

The assumption underlying the tests reported in this chapter is that *lead* VC firms tend to 'stay local.' The reason is their need for routine face-to-face contact with supported early-stage firms.

As a Silicon Valley journalist notes, 'If you need to meet with a company every week or other week to get it off the ground, you don't want to have to jump on a plane and cross three time zones to do it – especially if you generate high returns off companies based in your own proverbial backyard.' (Shawn Niedorf, 'New Yorkers Not Talk of Town,' San Jose *Mercury News*, on-line, March 7, 2000)

At the same time, Niedorf's qualifier ('especially . . .') points up the key premise in her argument. What if you cannot find promising companies right in your backyard? Which comes first, the VC chicken or the start-up egg?

In the old days, New York or Chicago venture capitalists might take part mainly in syndications, through 'co-investments' with lead VC firms elsewhere – Silicon Valley, Massachusetts, or more recently Texas, for example. This was the tendency documented in a 1992 study of VC's role in eight major centers. The authors classified the eight as technology-oriented (Silicon Valley and Denver), financial-oriented (New York and Chicago), or hybrids of the two (Boston, Minneapolis-St. Paul, Texas, and Connecticut). (Florida and Smith 1992, p. 201)

At that time they found that 'just 7 percent of the investments made by New York venture capitalists were made in-state,' vs. 70 percent in-state in California. In between was Massachusetts, whose VC firms made 40 percent of their placements in-state, and 30 percent to California start-ups (Florida and Smith, p. 193). (A different angle on the feasibility of long-distance relationships, as facilitated by airline connections between emerging and established centers, appears in a recent study of innovation in Texas cities. See Echeverri-Carroll and Brennan 1999.)

Florida and Smith's study of the eight VC centers appeared in 1992. In the meantime some things have changed, such as the rise of New York City's 'Silicon Alley,' which specializes in media-based Internet start-ups. One might therefore expect to find deepening ties between Wall Street venture capitalists and Silicon Alley entrepreneurs.

That, it turns out, is indeed what the evidence shows for recent years. By the late 1990s, the New York metro area had emerged as a major center for IPOs, a sign that New York-area venture capital was tending to 'stay local.'

PART V

What Went Right?

Roadmap:

These two concluding chapters take stock of corporate capacities for innovation and of the productivity debate.

Chapter 24 sketches answers to Schumpeter's classical questions about capitalism's 'laws of motion.'

Chapter 25 interprets research at the Fed linking the productivity surge of the late 1990s to improvements in technology.

24. Schumpeter's questions, revisited

> The mechanisms of economic change in capitalist society pivot on entrepreneurial activity. (Schumpeter 1947, p. 150)

The idea that a New Economy has pumped fresh energy into a system many people viewed as senescent accords with Schumpeter's view of economic change. This is a good place to recall some of his larger questions and then to suggest the outlines of some updated answers, 50 years after his death.

DO LIVING STANDARDS DOUBLE EVERY 40 YEARS?

In Schumpeter's view, this was capitalism's great achievement, to be set over and against its ills: instability, inequality, alienation, and vulgarity.

As Figure 24.1 shows, however, a doubling of per capita output did not occur automatically for every 40-year period in twentieth-century America. There was little increase in either the teens or the Great Depression of the 1930s. In the first half of the century, doubling thus sometimes took 50 years. *But from 1920 on, through the intervals ending in 1990, the 40-year rule held.*

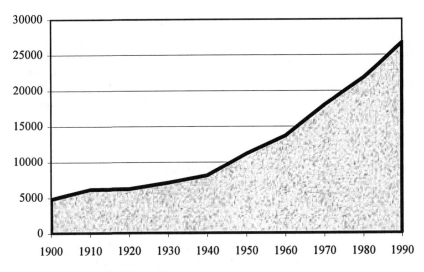

Source: Timothy Taylor 1996, p. 20.

Figure 24.1 US per capita GDP, 1900-1990, in constant (1995) dollars

Figure 24.2 updates the story with the most recent 40-year interval. Based on constant 1996 (chain-weighted) dollars, it tracks output per person from 1959 to 1999. The figure reveals several notable tendencies in the behavior of real per capita GDP since 1959:

- As each decade began, recessions kept per capita output flat.
- For the entire decade after 1973, there was little improvement.
- From 1966 ($16,274) to 1999 ($32,439), the figure about doubled.
- Over the 40 years, it rose from $12,985 to $32,439 (150 percent).

Viewing the century as a whole, the numbers mean *that average living standards were 6.7 times as high in 1999 as in 1900.* Some observers would dispute this finding. Beyond the crudeness of the measure, they might cite such setbacks as pollution and a weakened sense of community.

Among economists, however, many would argue that this measure falls short of the actual rise in living standards. It leaves out improvements such as increased leisure, the value of new products, and above all advances in medical technology. The latter helps explain a 30-year gain in life expectancies in the US since 1900 (Fogel 2000, p. 236).

LAWS OF MOTION

The theme of this book has been that unless entrepreneurs step forward to innovate, mature capitalist economies will succumb to deep inherent tendencies toward economic stagnation. Variations on this theme come through the answers to be given now to Schumpeter's classic questions.

In combination, the comments that follow could be read as an update of the themes from Marx, the classical economists, and Schumpeter himself on capitalism's 'laws of motion.'

Are There Long Waves of Creative Destruction?

Yes, if by long waves we mean not price swings or trends in output growth but technology regimes (Chapter 6). By the same token, however, the notion of 50-year technology regimes reminds us that this is far from the first 'new economy.' Whether one chooses to see it as a fifth long wave or 'The Third Industrial Revolution' will remain a matter of taste or emphasis.

And yes, Creative Destruction if we take account of the geographical obsolescence of places and their main industries (Chapter 11). Yes again, if we recognize how newcomers overthrow leaders, according to the Levinthal

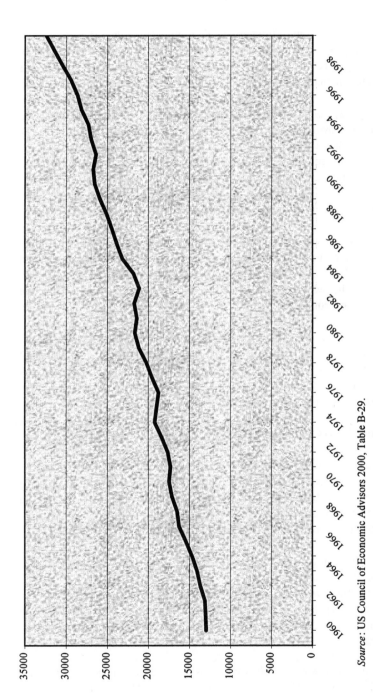

Source: US Council of Economic Advisors 2000, Table B-29.

Figure 24.2 Average living standards more than doubled in the 40 years, 1959-1999 (US GDP per capita in constant 1996 dollars)

speciation metaphor and Christensen's disruptive technologies .

Finally, yes Creative Destruction as a model of economic growth. Though neglected in this book, 'endogenous growth theory' interprets Schumpeterian innovation in terms of new 'recipes' (Romer 1993). Such concepts have led to formal models of Creative Destruction by Aghion and Howitt (1992) and Howitt (2000). The latter explains differences in productivity growth across countries as a function of national R&D levels, not just neoclassical capital accumulation. Instead of R&D, the analysis could perhaps equally well be made with reference to contrasts in entrepreneurship among countries.

Are There Economic Limits to Growth?

No, in the sense that in the long run there is no diminution of investment opportunities, and no falling rate of profit (Chapter 8). As Schumpeter put it in 1942, 'Technological possibilities are an uncharted sea' ([1942] 1962. p. 42). Here the record is clear. Whatever exhaustion of old possibilities had occurred, a new round was about to begin. Something similar might be said today.

The plausible current objection to the conclusion that there are no 'economic' limits is global warming, which falls outside the realm of Schumpeter's analysis. As China's planned reliance on its coal deposits makes clear, over the next half-century the world may face environmental limits to fossil-fuel-based industrialization

Can (American) Capitalism Survive?

In a famous paradox, Schumpeter agreed with Marx about capitalism's future. In *Capitalism, Socialism, and Democracy*, he predicted that capitalism's transition to socialism would occur not with a bang, but with a whimper – as a byproduct of its own success.

As he put it, 'capitalism is being killed by its achievements' (1942, p. xiv). To the question 'Can capitalism survive?' Schumpeter answered, 'No.' That is, 'My final conclusion does not differ . . . from that of all Marxists' (1942, p. 61).

In the mid-1980s, that answer was rejected by the authors of an economic-history text, who concluded that capitalism had more stamina than many had thought. On the other hand, they were not so sure about the American version:

> We are likely to see successful capitalisms and unsuccessful ones. We will have to wait and see whether the United States can overcome its present laggard condition to become, once again an adaptive and creative variant of a system

whose time within world history does not yet seem to have run its course. (Heilbroner and Singer 1984, p. 353)

Five years later, of course, the USSR and Eastern Europe began their rocky transitions to capitalism. It turned out to be communism that could not survive.

From one point of view, the reasons for the failure of centrally planned economies overlap with the more general problem of bureaucracy, whether public or corporate.

Can Socialism Work?

In other words, while this is not a question we have considered, it goes to the heart of the larger inquiry. Schumpeter's view was unequivocal: 'Can socialism work? Of course it can' ([1942] 1962, p. 167). If by socialism he meant a centrally planned economy, he was wrong.

In retrospect, Oscar Lange was also wrong, and Friedrich Hayek and Ludwig von Mises were right (Lange and Taylor 1938). The answer to their 'socialist calculation debate' of the 1930s and 1940s is that consumer preferences are not knowable or computable, but can only register through myriad, constantly shifting individual choices. Hence any mid-century idea that input-output analysis or mathematical programming could anticipate demand and resource requirements was an illusion.

In a succinct post-mortem on the theory of central planning, Robert Heilbroner brings out the primacy of the entrepreneurial mission: bold decision-making (Heilbroner 1993, pp. 163-4). To Mises' contention that planners would lack price signals showing what to produce or not to produce, Lange replied, in effect, 'We will watch inventories, to see whether they rise or fall, and that will tell us the same thing.'

Then Lange went on (verbatim this time), 'The real danger of socialism is the bureaucratization of economic life' (Heilbroner, p. 163). But he added that of course monopolistic capitalism faced the same problem.

In practice, notes Heilbroner, the prices-as-information problem was compounded by bureaucracy, to crippling effect. Even if prices or proxy signals got transmitted through the centrally planned system,

> A socialist ministry ignores changing inventories because bureaucrats learn that doing something is more likely to get them in trouble than doing nothing. . . .

Accordingly, Heilbroner concludes, 'The crucial missing element is not so much "missing information" as Mises and Hayak argued, as it is *the motivation to act on information*' (p. 164, emphasis added).

Still, with Lange, we might apply the same logic to the mature corporation. In a corporate bureaucracy, inaction is too often the safest decision. This, it should be added, is the point of departure for Larry C. Farrell's 1993 book, *Searching for the Spirit of Enterprise.*

Is the Individual Entrepreneur Obsolete?

No. US managerial corporations proved unable to capitalize on the technological possibilities discovered by their own R&D labs or by other people's discoveries in the 1970s and 1980s.

The PC revolution of the 1970s and 1980s was overwhelmingly the result of start-up companies. Some were spin-offs like Intel after 1968 (when the immigrant Andrew Grove would move to the center of the stage) or Compaq after 1984. Some were bootstrap firms by the archetypal geeks and freaks of the 1970s. Later, Internet-base start-ups would rely increasingly on venture capital, as at the Millennium.

What it all adds up to, as described by Paul Krugman, is 'the golden age of the individual entrepreneur' (Krugman 2000b, p.11).

Can Big Business (the Large Corporation) Innovate?

Here we might recall the Harvard Business School's current working definition of entrepreneurship: 'the pursuit of opportunities beyond means that are currently available.' This definition, as introduced in Chapter 13, has the pragmatic virtue of pertaining as much to Old Economy companies as to start-ups.

On balance, three kinds of answers might be framed to this question, ranging from (1) skeptical to (2) conciliatory to (3) culture-specific.

(1) Yes, but only to replace one sustaining technology by another, not in the face of a disruptive technology (Chapter 13). The only path Christensen suggests to equip established industry leaders to deal with a disruptive technology tells the tale. The established corporation has to create a smaller 'counter-company' within itself, a group of managers whose mission is *to simulate an attacking newcomer.* IBM's skunk works at Boca Raton, Florida, to create the IBM PC in 1980 was a successful example. But then the project was brought back to Armonk, New York, headquarters, and IBM was almost destroyed by the ruckus.

(2) Big and small companies are complementary in the innovation process. In Amar V. Bhide's view, big companies by their nature face certain constraints on the range of the possible.

Their advantages include superior access to capital and the ability to solve large-scale coordination problems. But conventional internal control systems '*limit the firm's capacity to pursue small, uncertain initiatives*' (Bhide 2000, p. 323, emphasis added). Another such obstacle to innovation is a company's desire 'to adhere to long-term strategies,' a reasonable goal, but one that dampens agility (p. 324). A third is the inability of a bureaucratized corporate structure to treat talented but temperamental or transitory employees differently than others (p. 325).

These are milder views on the rigidity of the established firm than Christensen's. When the smaller, more agile and innovative firm reaches a transition point and faces the challenge of growth, big companies offer one source of help, through alliances or other cooperative arrangements – or, of course, takeovers.

(3) What remains an open question is the flexibility and innovative capacity of the new generation of 'paranoid' mid-life giants like Intel, Microsoft, and Oracle (Grove 1996). While Chapter 16 described Intel's transition from start-up to world leader, that was but a single case.

The key was a leader, Andrew Grove, who acted like an entrepreneur throughout his sustained tenure at the head of the company. As noted, the defining moment in the company's evolution took placed when Grove asked Gordon Moore in 1985 what a hypothetical new CEO – brought in *as an outsider*, free of baggage and blinders – would do. Then the two went ahead and did it themselves, surrendering memory chips and redefining Intel around the microprocessor.

The question is whether that bold decision-making can happen in other corporate settings as well.

CULTURES AND CHANGE-MANAGEMENT

In a recent book the Silicon Valley marketer Geoffrey A. Moore assesses the strategic positions of the mid-life giants (Moore 2000, Chapter 6). He links the strengths and weaknesses of their corporate cultures to his 'technology adoption life-cycle.' We need not get into the specifics of either that model or his 'tornado' metaphor (which refers to the speed and breadth of change when a new IT standard is adopted by the mainstream market).

But his analysis of corporate culture offers a key to the puzzle at hand. Can the mid-life giants adapt to sharp changes in technological and market conditions better than the companies they displaced?

Who are the companies in question? A recent *Wall Street Journal* tabulation of the world's 100 largest companies by market valuation shows six of the global top 20 that fit the description (see Table 24.1). These are Intel (2), Cisco Systems (3), Microsoft (4), Oracle (12), Sun (18) and EMC

Table 24.1 IT giants among the world's 20 largest public companies, by market value (billions) as of August 15, 2000 (at December 31, 1999 exchange rates), as determined by the Wall Street Journal Market Data Group

2000 rank	1999 rank	Company (Country) (US IT in bold)	Market value ($)	Fiscal 1999 sales ($)*	Percent change from 1998	Fiscal 1999 profit ($)
1	2	General Electric (US)	562,937	111,108	11	10,725
2	8	**Intel (US)**	453,541	29,389	12	7,314
3	5	**Cisco Systems (US)**	432,357	12,154	44	2,096
4	1	**Microsoft (US)**	372,798	22,956	16	9,421
5	9/46	Exxon Mobil (US)[1]	281,469	185,527	9	7,874
6	18/76	Pfizer (US)[2]	265,664	16,231	20	3,199
7	69	Vodafone Group (UK)[3]	259,218	14,385	27	168
8	14	Citigroup (US)	249,292	82,005	7	9,855
9	--	NTT DoCoMo (Japan)	242,430	36,383	19	2,467
10	73	Nortel Networks (Canada)	233,625	22,807	26	-202
11	4	Wal-Mart Stores (US)	230,481	165,013	20	5,575
12	81	**Oracle (US)**	229,249	10,130	15	6,297
13	3	**IBM (US)**	219,918	87,548	7	7,703
14	7	Royal Dutch/Shell (Netherlands/UK)	215,164	149,706	8	8,584
15	13	BP Amoco (UK)	204,797	83,792	26	5,020
16	17	American International Group (US)	201,320	36,356	21	5,055
17	29	Nokia (Finland)	191,041	19,899	48	2,594
18	82	**Sun Microsystems (US)**	186,205	15,721	33	1,854
19	80	**EMC (US)**	182,560	6,716	69	1,020
20	10	NTT (Japan)	181,883	101,958	7	-663

* March 31, 2000, results are used for Japanese companies. 1. Figures reflect November 1999 merger of Exxon and Mobil. 2. Market value reflects June 2000 acquisition of Warner-Lambert, but results are for Pfizer only. 3. Figures reflect June 1999 acquisition of AirTouch.

Source: Wall Street Journal, September 25, 2000, http://interactive.wsj.com/public/resources/documents/wb00-100-public-2000-09-25.htm.

(19), although this last entry could still be considered 'an adolescent.' Also in the top 20 are GE (1), Wal-Mart (11), IBM (13), the oil companies and such non-US telecoms as Vodaphone (7), NTT DoCoMo (9), Nortel Networks (10), Nokia (17), and NTT(20).

Moore arrays four cultures in relation to two criteria. One refers to a company's preference for individual-versus-group decision processes. The other describes objective-versus-subjective standards.

Competence, Collaboration, Control, Cultivation

Then Microsoft and Intel display a *competence* culture, valuing objective performance indicators and individual decision. In contrast, Hewlett-Packard displays a *collaboration* culture, where the thematic question is not 'how?' but 'who?' A third variant, the *control* culture fits the older firms, IBM, Motorola, and GE, where group decision-making, hierarchy, and authority set the tone. At the other end of the age spectrum, *cultivation* is the culture of the start-up – an environment in which self-realization and creativity are prized.

Each of these four environments can be right for a given state of the market for IT products and services and wrong (less adaptive or competitive) for other stages. Moreover, each culture can stagnate, defaulting to rituals of context over productive activities.

In a section on 'aging cultures,' for example, Moore defines the 'parodies' that result when 'a culture loses its core resources to context tasks' (p. 263). Then the culture of cultivation can become a 'cult,' as at Apple after 1985. The culture of competence can rigidify into a 'caste' system, and that of collaboration a 'club.'

Bringing it all back home, the parody of the culture of control (the culture found at GE, IBM, or Motorola) is bureaucracy. When such companies succumb, 'the only way forward is to do an aggressive core-versus-context housecleaning with major outsourcing of context functions' (p. 266). This, one might surmise, is what IBM managed to do under Louis Gerstner in the 1990s. The source of the original problem, however, was that cultures of control are powerless in the face of disruptive technologies, in line with Christensen's *Innovator's Dilemma* (1997).

As to the Intel and Microsoft cultures of competence, Moore sees each company as facing a rocky future. Antitrust aside, each faces key challenges as the Internet shifts software functions away from stand-alone systems and hardware needs away from PCs. The implication is that the twin titans are approaching their own mid-life crises. The same can be said, in Moore's view, of H-P, the archetype for a culture of collaboration, but subject as a result to bureaucratic gridlock from the lack of bold decision-making.

The upshot, it would seem, is that *the only sure prescription for maintaining economy-wide innovation and adaptive capacity is to create an environment that leaves room for and encourages start-ups*. From among the next 1,000 flowers, as it were, some will flourish, and a handful may even succeed in the drive to great size and global reach.

DESIGNING A RESILIENT ECONOMY

In a similar vein of cosmic prescription, we conclude this chapter with a list of 12 recommended institutional arrangements for the design of a high-performance market-based economy (see Table 24.2). It comes from Michael Cox of the Federal Reserve Bank of Dallas. Most of the recommendations in the table, including in particular free trade, would be readily embraced by a large majority of American economists.

One less predictable feature of interest at this juncture is Cox's reference to government-supported infrastructure. The next chapter picks up on this theme, showing that both the productivity slowdown after 1973 and the upturn in the late 1990s can be linked to large-scale public infrastructure projects.

Table 24.2 Getting it right: policies for market-based growth

1. Establish and preserve property rights.
2. Create market-friendly institutions.
3. Maintain stable government policies.
4. Avoid protecting existing jobs, industries or businesses.
5. Keep taxes low and simple.
6. Abstain from excessive regulation.
7. Invest in infrastructure.
8. Maintain stable prices.
9. Nurture business credit, especially for entrepreneurs.
10. Focus unemployment outlays on retraining.
11. Make education a priority.
12. Promote free trade.

Source: Cox 2000 (http://www.dallasfed.org/htm.homepage/free.html).

25. Parables of productivity

> About once in 100 years, something really big happens, and this is it. (Stephen Slifer, quoted in Berenson 2000, p. 8)

The New Economy is real. Until recently that proposition remained a matter of faith: either one believed or not. But as the productivity gains of the late 1990s continued to roll in, some prominent unbelievers among economists saw fit to rethink the question (see Figure 25.1). This final chapter shows why.

Part I of the book surveyed three conceptions of the New Economy. We concluded that it is 'part micro, part macro, and all digital.' The acceleration of productivity growth highlights the interplay of the three dimensions.

We can begin in the realm of macroeconomic policy, where a rise in productivity growth by one full percentage point after 1995 allowed the economy to grow faster than most economists had thought possible.

BREAKING THE SPEED LIMIT

The macro drama turns on Fed Chair Alan Greenspan's decision after 1996 to let the economy expand at GDP growth rates of 4 percent or more a year.

As background, before Alan Blinder left his position as Vice Chairman of the Fed in January of 1996, he had made a case for 'opportunistic disinflation' (Donovan 2000, p. F1). To wit: Instead of targeting a zero inflation rate, the Fed should settle for low inflation and allow faster growth.

Until then the Fed and most other central banks in the industrial nations had concluded that their sole mission should be to fight inflation. Given the mandate to end the federal budget deficit, fiscal policy had disappeared as an instrument. In short, faster growth and lower unemployment were no longer to be pursued as policy goals. Blinder, it seemed, was a lone liberal voice crying out in the wilderness.

For his own reasons Greenspan followed Blinder's growth strategy when the latter left the Fed in January 1996. He decided an IT revolution was creating productivity gains that were raising the economy's 'speed limit.'

Why the Speed Limit Used to Be 2.5 Percent

At that point the US was thought to have a given natural rate of unemployment (a NAIRU, for 'non-accelerating-inflation-rate-of-unem-

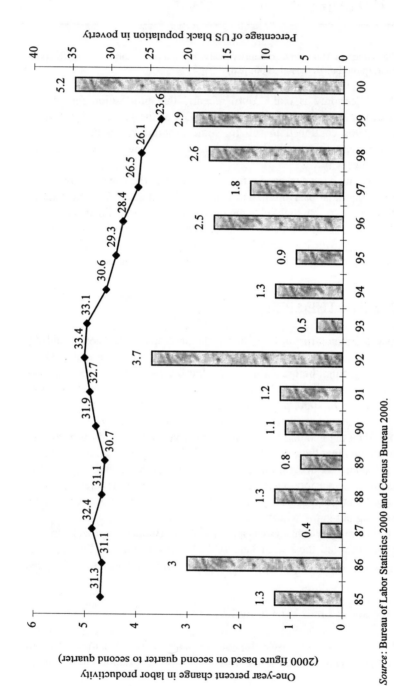

Source: Bureau of Labor Statistics 2000 and Census Bureau 2000.

Figure 25.1 Productivity surged and black poverty fell 10 points in the 1990s

ployment') of 5.5 percent. If GDP grew too rapidly, pushing short-term unemployment below 5 percent, inflation would increase. Labor shortages would allow unions to bid up wages in excess of productivity gains, raising production costs, forcing firms to raise prices.

By the same token, once the economy reached 'full employment' at the natural rate of unemployment of 5.5 percent, the Fed's task was clear. It should permit GDP growth no faster then the sum of (1) the rate of growth of the labor force and (2) the increase in productivity per worker. Since the labor force was growing about 1 percent and labor productivity about 1.4 percent a year, the speed limit for GDP was at most 2.5 percent.

In this prevailing view, then, growth above 2.5 percent a year would increase inflation, requiring a Fed clamp-down, leading in the usual sequence to a recession.

The $500 Billion Bonus

Instead Greenspan had gradually come to believe that in *The Weightless World*, bits were replacing atoms in ways that opened new methods of production and created faster productivity growth (Coyle 1998).

He and the Fed Board of Governors thus sat on their hands as GDP growth increased from 2.5 to over 4 percent a year. Not all the Governors were happy; some persuasion from Greenspan was needed to win over inflation hawks like Laurence Meyer, who wanted a measured inflation rate of zero. But Greenspan prevailed.

We saw the results at the beginning of the book, in Figure 1.1. Having reached nominal full employment in 1996, the economy went on to grow at rates averaging 4.2 percent for the four years 1996-99. In an $8 trillion economy, this difference of 1.7 percentage points (from 2.5 to 4.2) a year equaled over $500 billion from 1996 through 1999.

That was $2,000 extra per person in the US over the last four years of the century. Some of it went to people already working and some to new workers. Some went to governments – creating not only a federal budget surplus, but full coffers for states and cities. Most striking, the black poverty rate fell by 10 percentage points over the decade, as Figure 25.1 shows.

The US economy thus generated an extra half trillion dollars while shattering the speed limit through the last four years of the decade. Instead of rising, inflation edged down each year until 1999, when the consumer price index moved up slightly. Since unemployment was falling, too, the 'misery index' (the sum of the inflation and unemployment rates), reached its lowest level since the early 1960s – for which also, see Figure 1.1.

The explanation for the rise in the speed limit can be seen in the right-hand-side of the speed-limit formula,

$$\%dGDP = \%dLH + \%dLP$$

Here we replace the growth of the labor force by the growth in actual hours worked, denoted as $\%dLH$ (for 'percentage change in labor hours'). The reason for the replacement is that labor hours actually worked is a more easily measured quantity.

The Surprising Increase in Labor Hours

The equation says that the growth of real GDP is constrained by the sum of the growth of hours worked, LH, and the rise in labor productivity, LP. A rise in either of the two right-hand-side variables raises the speed limit. (A third issue – by how much official measurements understated LP growth – is irrelevant in this context because whatever the bias, it affects the left-hand-side variable, measured real GDP growth, as much as LP growth, leaving the perceived speed limit unaffected.) Both constraining variables grew faster than expected after 1995.

The first, LH, rose much faster than the normal growth from the entrance to the labor force of young workers or from immigration. As the economy reached 'full employment' of 5 percent by the end of 1997, tightening labor markets sucked successive waves of discouraged workers into (or back into) the labor force. They included midlife men downsized in the early 1990s, inner-city and minority workers, the handicapped, and, late in the decade, women making the shift from welfare to work.

In other words, job opportunities, not wage increases, induced further growth in the labor force. Newly flexible labor markets and the wave of cheap foreign imports after the Asian meltdown and currency devaluations of 1997 kept a lid on labor costs and on product prices.

In any case, the second boost to the speed limit was a jump in labor productivity growth after 1995 by about a percentage point. And that brings us to the paradox enveloping the enigma containing the riddle.

MICRO PARABLES

A New Economy explanation of the late 1990s productivity surge has to address the familiar 'productivity paradox.' To wit: The microprocessor was invented at Intel in 1971, the Apple II appeared in 1977, and the IBM PC in 1981. Yet dramatic productivity gains showed up only after 1995.

If they provide the explanation to the productivity surge, why did it take so long for the microprocessor and the PC to raise productivity growth? Or, was the acceleration after 1995 caused by the Internet – which was itself maturing during the same period? As to the context, why had productivity growth slowed after 1973?

One way to sort out these issues is to recall two persuasive parables about productivity, one a decade old, the other of more recent vintage.

The Dynamo and the Computer

In a 1990 paper, 'Computer and Dynamo: The Modern Productivity Paradox in a Not-Too-Distant Mirror,' Paul David explored parallels in the economic impacts of the two 'general purpose engines.' The account brings to mind Benjamin Franklin's reply when asked about the value of a new invention. 'What,' Franklin replied, 'is the value of a new-born baby?'

In the same spirit, David contends that when a revolutionary new 'general-purpose engine' like electricity or the PC comes along, its initial uses tend to be limited. Only over time will production systems gradually be reorganized to take full advantage of the new possibilities.

'In 1900 contemporaries might well have said the electric dynamos were to be seen "everywhere but in the economic statistics,"' wrote David, echoing Robert Solow's much-quoted observation about computers (David 1989, p. i). The reason was that it takes a long time for households and businesses to figure out what to do with major new technologies.

The story unfolds in the decades bracketing 1900, as electric power replaced steam. Edison's famous filament experiment met success in 1881, and electric lighting for cities found rapid adoption. Electric generators ('dynamos') soon became practical. By 1892 Edison Electric had become General Electric. By 1896 its patent-sharing agreement with Westinghouse cleared the way to new forms of power transmission. By 1907 the price of electric power to industrial users was falling rapidly.

However, as late as 1920 electricity was still being used to power factories in a 'doubling-up, or overlay of one technical system upon a pre-existing stratum' (David, p. 19).

Only during the investment boom of the 1920s were factories built from scratch around the new power source, as in the re-engineering of office systems around PC networks in the early 1990s. At that point continuous-process manufacturing took hold in such industries as petroleum, paper, and chemicals.

The upshot was 'a thorough rationalization of factory construction designs and internal layouts of production lines and materials handling techniques, thereby raising the measured efficiency of labor and capital inputs in many established branches of manufacturing' (David, p. 30).

In turn, the productivity evidence for the first three decades of the century mirrors this sequence. Initially, labor productivity rose only as a result of rising capital intensity. Not until the 1920s did total factor productivity respond.

The implication? Measured from either 1970 (the date he ascribes to Intel's microprocessor) or 1981, the year the IBM PC burst upon the scene, it might take 20 years before firms and households reorganized themselves around the prodigious new general-purpose engine.

Still, as to the Internet and its impact on productivity, we would do well to augment this story with a second parable – about another network. In other words, David's version of why the PC should take so long to boost productivity has now been complemented by a parable with a different spin, one that highlights the contribution of *public infrastructure*.

Two Highways Taken

Why did productivity growth slow after 1973? A new answer comes from John G. Fernald's 1999 article in the *American Economic Review*, 'Roads to Prosperity? Assessing the Link between Public Capital and Productivity.' As a starting point, and viewing the twentieth century as a whole, the rapid productivity growth of the 1950s and 1960s – the 'golden age' – had been an aberration from a slower long-term trend.

Fernald provides convincing evidence that the rise in productivity growth in the golden age reflected a massive public infrastructure project, the building of the interstate highway system. As he puts it,

> Construction of the interstate highway system peaked in the late 1950s and early 1960s, and was largely completed by 1973. The results suggest that this construction boom substantially boosted productivity. In particular, the estimates imply that public investments . . . contributed about 1 percentage point more to total factor productivity growth before 1973 than after. Hence, public investment can explain a substantial share of the 1.3 percentage-point slowdown in productivity growth. (1999, p. 620)

The argument gains force from the industry-by-industry link he finds between productivity gains and vehicle-intensity. (Vehicle-intensive industries included transportation, gas and electric utilities, communications and construction.) On average, transportation improvements led to the largest productivity gains in the most vehicle-intensive industries.

By extension, *the great slowdown after 1973 reflected the exhaustion of the payoffs from the project*. Accordingly, Fernald rejects the idea that the slowdown was mainly a statistical artifact, a result of measurement error. In addition, he advances an alternative explanation for the long lag before the

PC's productivity benefits showed up in the official measurements. It may be that such benefits did occur – but were swamped by the decreases from the tailing off of gains from the Interstate Highway System.

What are the parallels with the development of the Internet? In each episode – the 1950s and, with ARPAnet, the 1970s and 1980s – public infrastructure investment led to subsequent cuts in firms' costs of transportation or communication. In the first, the payoffs showed up sooner (in the 1950s and 1960s). In the second, the benefits develop later, with much private intermediation, as the Internet.

The point is not necessarily the economic foresight of the federal government. Both projects were packaged as essential to national security in the event of a nuclear war. The first would help decentralize productive capacity away from prime nuclear targets and population centers. The second was intended to decentralize decision-making capacity, so that a 'first strike' against Washington, DC, would leave an informed retaliatory capacity in the hinterlands (as well as undersea). That was the Cold War economy: worthy infrastructure or education projects dressed in uniforms.

The Falling Costs of Information in the 1990s

The surge in productivity growth in the late 1990s may reflect a similar sector-by-sector improvement from both the gradual absorption of the PC in the production process and the Internet's reduction in communication costs.

Consider how fast and far information costs have fallen in the 1990s. As Figure 25.2 shows, the costs of storing one megabit of digitized information (one million transistors) on a semiconductor chip fell from $7.85 to 17 cents between 1990 and 1999 – a continuation of Moore's law.

That was routine compared with the fall in costs for transmitting digitized data, from $90 per trillion bits in 1990 to 12 cents in 1999. Just as Moore's Law gives no sign of being repealed over the next decade, Gilder's Law of increasing bandwidth promises a similar pace in the journey to near-universal light-speed connectivity (Gilder 2000).

The New Economy interpretation is that such achievements provide one explanation for the productivity surge of the late 1990s.

THE EVIDENCE

The New Economy debate of mid-2000 turns on why labor productivity growth accelerated – and whether the faster pace will last.

A good introduction to the debate is 'The Resurgence of Growth in the Late 1990s: Is Information Technology the Story?' (Oliner and Sichel

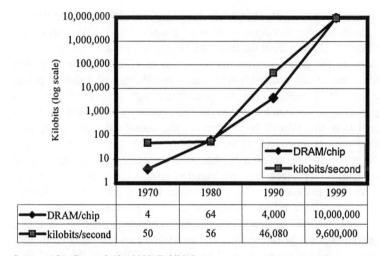

	1970	1980	1990	1999
DRAM/chip	4	64	4,000	10,000,000
kilobits/second	50	56	46,080	9,600,000

Source: After Cox and Alm 2000, Exhibit 3.

Figure 25.2(A) Moore's Law (for DRAM) and Gilder's Law

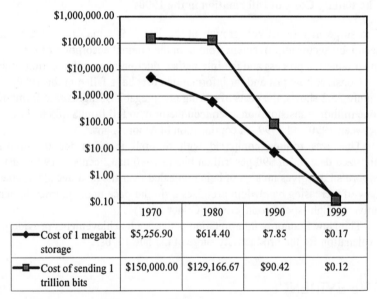

	1970	1980	1990	1999
Cost of 1 megabit storage	$5,256.90	$614.40	$7.85	$0.17
Cost of sending 1 trillion bits	$150,000.00	$129,166.67	$90.42	$0.12

Source: After Cox and Alm 2000, Exhibit 3.

*Figure 25.2(B) The falling costs of data storage and transmission,
1970-1999*

2000). Steven D. Oliner and Daniel E. Sichel of the Federal Reserve Board track the sources of real output and productivity growth since 1974. For reasons of data quality and availability, they track not total GDP but non-farm business output. This latter variable, which we will term simply 'output,' omits production in agriculture, government, and the non-profit sector. We recount their data and analysis now.

An essential framing point is that in an earlier study the two authors had found only weak evidence for a 'New Economy' effect on productivity growth (Oliner and Sichel 1994). As with some other recent productivity studies, however, the new data Oliner and Sichel analyzed changed their minds. (See also Jorgenson and Stiroh 2000, who come to similarly revisionist conclusions.)

The sequence for output growth, as Figure 25.3 shows, finds an average before 1990 of 3.06 percent a year. In the first half of the decade it slumped to 2.75 percent a year. From 1996 through 1999 it accelerated to 4.82 percent. Non-farm private output thus grew even faster in the latter half of the 1990s than total GDP, which averaged 4.2 percent over the same period.

Part of the reason for the higher output growth after 1995 was the increase in labor hours (*LH*) as a result of the tight labor markets. As Figure 25.3 shows, the increase in *LH* in the latter half of the 1990s raised the growth rate of output by some 0.7 percentage points relative to 1991-95. That is, the increase in hours worked had added about 0.8 percentage points to output growth in the first half of the decade, but 1.5 percent a year in the second half.

But the main source of acceleration of output growth was productivity per labor hour, as rendered in the other slices of the bars in the figure.

Three Components of Labor Productivity Change

Figure 25.4 shows labor productivity growth separately. As can be seen in the heights of the bars, the productivity slowdown lasted from 1974 to 1995. Labor productivity grew at a sluggish 1.37 percent from 1974 to 1990, then rose slightly to 1.53 percent from 1991-95.

Between 1996 and 1999 labor productivity growth jumped a full percentage point to an average 2.57 percent. This, in an economy that had been expanding for several years, when, as a cyclical tendency, productivity growth could be expected to slow.

In turn, the growth of labor productivity itself can be allocated to three sources. As Figure 25.4 illustrates, one is changes in *labor force quality* stemming from changes toward or away from experienced workers. Another is changes in capital intensity, as labeled '*capital deepening*' in the chart. This variable measures the capital back-up workers have, including

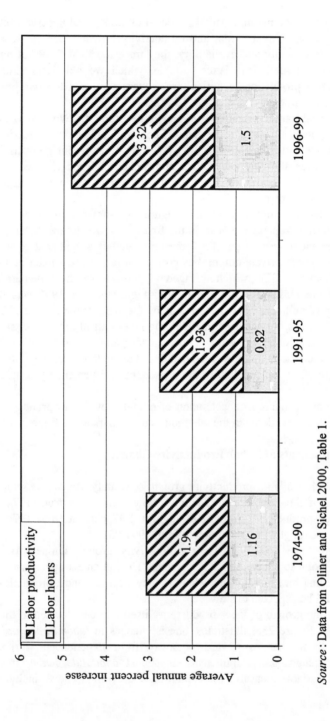

Source: Data from Oliner and Sichel 2000, Table 1.

Figure 25.3 Contributions to output growth, 1974-1999 (nonfarm business output)

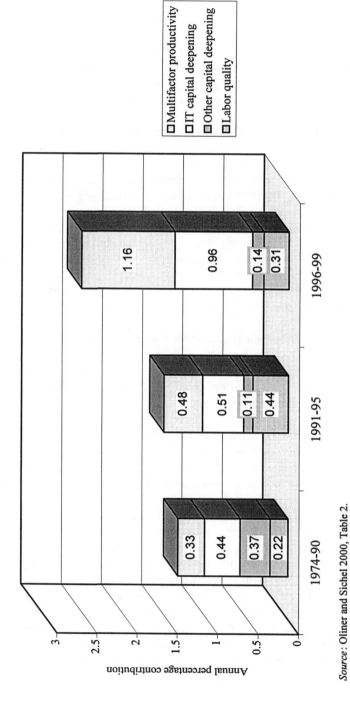

Source: Oliner and Sichel 2000, Table 2.

Figure 25.4 Contributions to labor productivity growth, 1974–1999 (nonfarm business sector)

not only traditional machinery (labeled 'other capital deepening') but also
IT equipment.

The third source is '*multifactor productivity*' (*MFP*). It is the component
of productivity growth that is not explained by the other two. (Statistically,
MFP is the unexplained residual in an equation that regresses changes in
labor productivity on labor force quality and capital deepening.)

IT and Labor Productivity: (1) Use Elsewhere and (2) IT Production

In this context, Oliner and Sichel view IT capital deepening as something
that raises labor productivity growth throughout the economy. That is, this
gives a measure of the productivity effects from the *use* of IT in the
economy.

In contrast, the rise in *MFP* is in part a measure of generalized
productivity gains in the *production* of IT equipment. This pertains to
computers, as in Dell's streamlined mass customization methods, for
example. But it is even more evident in semiconductors, where Moore's law
generates rapidly falling costs of production per chip, as memory and speed
double every 18 months through process improvements.

IT Accounted for Two-Thirds of the One Point Productivity Surge

What explains the one-point increase in labor productivity growth between
the first half of the 1990s and the second half? Figure 25.5 shows that
nearly all the part attributable to capital deepening is the 0.45 a year from
IT.

How much of the *MFP* improvement of 0.68 can be attributed to IT?
The conservative estimate is 0.26, *MFP* in computer production and
computer-related semiconductor production. (This is conservative in that it
omits gains in production of semiconductors for uses other than in
computers.)

That is, 0.45 of the rise reflects rising IT capital, a component Oliner
and Sichel identify with IT use in other sectors, and another 0.26 reflects
MFP gains in the production of computers and semiconductors. 'Taken
together, these factors account for about two-thirds of the speed-up in labor
productivity since 1995' (Oliner and Sichel, p. 17).

In sum, all this makes a strong case for a New Economy perspective on
the stellar macro performance of the US economy in the late 1990s. The
combination of (1) unending process improvements in the production of
semiconductor chips and (2) major new payoffs from rising computer back-
up for workers throughout the economy tells the tale. What has changed
most is (2), the IT capital backing up workers throughout the economy.

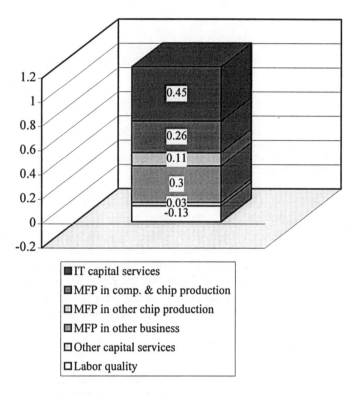

Source: Oliner and Sichel 2000, Table 5.

*Figure 25.5 Dissecting the one-point gain in labor
productivity from 1990-95 to 1996-99*

HOLDOUTS

Still, among academic economists there remains intense and informed resistance to the notion of a decisive break. Perhaps because they were so openly scornful for so long, Paul Krugman and the *Economist* magazine come to mind in this regard.

Consider, for example, Krugman's predictions on productivity growth in mid-1998, a few months after he had written a conclusive 'Requiem for the New Economy':

Productivity will drop sharply this year [1998]. Nineteen ninety-seven, which was a very good year for worker productivity, has led many pundits to conclude that the great technology-led boom had begun. They are wrong. Last year will prove to have been a blip, just like 1992. Inflation will be back. (Krugman, 'Why Most Economists' Predictions Are Wrong,' *Red Herring*, June 1998, p. 28)

Things turned out differently, and to his credit Krugman changed his mind. Nor was he alone. As the suddenly enthusiastic *Economist* observed,

> [O]utput per hour . . . rose by an annualized 5% in the second half of 1999, bringing the overall productivity rise for the year to a pretty impressive 2.9% for the year. This sterling performance comes hot on the heels of a 2.8% productivity rise in 1998, and a 2.7% rise in 1996. . . . Output per hour among manufacturing firms rose . . . 6.4% for the year [1999] as a whole. That is the fastest manufacturing productivity growth since the early 1970s. (*The Economist* 2000, p. 27)

The article concludes, 'as the years pass, it is becoming increasingly implausible to dismiss the productivity surge as simply a cyclical phenomenon.' That is, it must be secular, a new long-term trend. (We should add, however, that the magazine would later flip-flop on the issue.)

More resolute are such skeptics as Robert Schiller, author of *Irrational Exuberance* (2000). He views the stock market's bull run after 1995 as a bubble and the Internet as a toy relative to the great breakthroughs of the past. He and others point out that the business cycle will always be with us.

Gordon: Why the Internet Is Not a 'Great Invention'

A particularly vigorous critic of the New Economy thesis is the distinguished macroeconomic theorist, Robert J. Gordon. He debunks the thesis on two separate and unrelated fronts. First, he argues that the Internet falls far short of the 'Great Inventions of 1860-1900.' Second, and as a statistical matter, he contends that the increase in productivity growth from 1996 on is unsustainable and narrowly based (Gordon 2000).

On what basis, then, does Gordon downgrade the Internet? (1) It has not increased the demand for PCs, which displays the same unitary price elasticity now as before the Internet. (2) The cost savings in communication it brings represent not a radical breakthrough but a shift from other communication media. (3) The appearance of business advances is in part illusory, because some Internet forays are by established firms like Borders forced to defend themselves against newcomers like Amazon. (4) Paper use, as for mail-order catalogs, is rising, despite the rise of electronic media. (5) Some uses of the Internet entail increasing consumption while on the job.

In contrast, Gordon claims, the Great Inventions of the late nineteenth century were truly revolutionary. In the 'Second Industrial Revolution,' the coming of five clusters set the stage for the great advances of the twentieth century. These were electricity, the internal combustion engine, chemical advances, telecommunications, and indoor plumbing.

All this represents, one might venture, a false dichotomy. Its resolution lies in the understanding that the era in question was a 'new economy' in its own right, just as would happen again after 1945 from different wellsprings. So much at least was the argument of this book in Chapter 6, where we referred to the rhythm of roughly 50-year technology regimes that have marked US industrial history. In that sense it is fruitless to compare the importance of one new regime relative to another. In its own time, each drives the economy forward.

As to the central empirical question, too much of Gordon's econometric argument seems to depend on the way he has discounted some of the economy's productivity surge in advance by attributing it to unsustainable cyclical effects. His argument is that yes, there has been a surge in productivity growth in the late 1990s, but after you discount most of it as cyclical, not much can be ascribed to the New Economy. In Oliner and Sichel's view, 'In the face of this uncertainty, Gordon imposes a strong assumption that effectively pre-ordains his result' (p. 20).

CODA

In sum, the productivity surge of the late 1990s provides additional evidence for a New Economy. Dale Jorgenson, President of the American Economic Association, makes the point best. 'Economists have not been quick to jump on the New Economy bandwagon. After looking at it more carefully . . . I've become an enlistee in the army of people touting the New Economy' (Quoted in Liesman 2000, on-line).

As to the social payoffs, the productivity surge raised the economy's speed limit to 4 percent or more in the late 1990s. Tight labor markets then sparked a ten-point decline in the rate of black poverty between 1992 and 1999.

Returning to our larger theme – the role of newcomer entrepreneurs as creators – it would be hard to top Krugman's post-conversion comments in March of 2000:

> Indeed, to a remarkable extent America's new economy seems to be the creation of new men (and a few new women). Not only weren't they born to wealth; in many cases they are immigrants or the children of immigrants. . . . The old line that 'It's not what you know, it's who you know' has never seemed less true. So let's hear it for America, where our new technology starts are selling ideas, not connections and – who knows – might actually make money for their stockholders. ('Aristocrats.com,' *New York Times*, March 19, 2000, p. 4:15)

Bibliography

Abramovitz, Moses (1981), 'Welfare Quandaries and Productivity Concerns,' *American Economic Review*, **71**(1), March, 1-17.

Adams, John (1979), *International Economics: A Self-Teaching Introduction to the Basic Concepts*, 2nd edn, New York: St. Martin's Press.

Adams, Russell B. Jr. (1977), *The Boston Money Tree*, New York: Thomas Y. Crowell.

Aghion, Philippe and Peter Howitt (1992), 'A Model of Growth through Creative Destruction,'*Econometrica*, **60**(2), March, 323-51.

Alderfer, Evan and H.E. Michl (1942), *Economics of American Industry*, New York: McGraw-Hill.

Alexander Grant & Company (1982), *The Third Study of General Manufacturing Business Climates of the Forty-Eight Contiguous States of America: 1981*, Chicago.

Anderson, Kurt (1999), *Turn of the Century*, New York: Random House.

Apple, R.W. Jr. (2000), 'On the Road: Smiling Through the Mists at Life's Delights,' *New York Times*, 18 August, p. E29.

Atkinson, Robert D., Randolph H. Court and Joseph M. Ward (1999), *The State New Economy Index*, Washington, DC: Progressive Policy Institute.

Augarde, T. (ed.) (1991), *The Oxford Dictionary of Modern Quotations*, London: Oxford University Press.

Arthur, W. Brian ([1990], 1994), 'Positive Feedbacks in the Economy,' in *Increasing Returns and Path Dependence in the Economy*, Ann Arbor: University of Michigan Press, pp. 1-12.

Batzell, E. Digby (1979), *Puritan Boston and Quaker Philadelphia*, New York: The Free Press.

Barber, Benjamin R. (1995), *Jihad vs. McWorld: How Globalism and Tribalism Are Reshaping the World*, New York: Random House.

Baumol, William J. (1993), *Entrepreneurship, Management, and the Structure of Payoffs*, Cambridge, MA: MIT Press.

Beenstock, Michael (1984), *The World Economy in Transition*, London & Boston: Allen & Unwin.

Berenson, Alex (2000), 'Rising Productivity Challenges Notions on Limits of Growth,' *New York Times*, 10 September, p. E8.

Berners-Lee, Tim with Mark Frischetti (1999), *Weaving the Web*, San Francisco: Harper.

Berlin, Mitchell (1998), 'That Thing Venture Capitalists Do,' *Business Review* (Federal Reserve Bank of Philadelphia), January/February.

Bhide, Amar V. (2000), *The Origin and Evolution of New Businesses*, Oxford: Oxford University Press.

Blanchard, Olivier Jean and Lawrence Katz (1992), 'Regional Evolutions,' *Brookings Papers in Economic Activity*, **1**.

Blanton, Kimberly (1999), 'Intel Urges Tax Credit Extension,' *Boston Globe*, 9 June, p. D1.

Bluestone, Barry and Bennett Harrison (1982), *The Deindustrialization of America*, New York: Basic Books.

Bonn International Center for Conversion (1996), *Conversion Survey 1996: Global Disarmament, Demilitarization, and Demobilization* (http://bicc. uni-bonn.de/general/survey96/intro/intro_ex.html).

Booth, Douglas (1986), 'Long Waves and Uneven Regional Growth,' *Southern Economic Journal*, **53**, 448-60.

Borchert, John R. (1967), 'American Metropolitan Evolution,' *Geographical Review*, **57**, 301-32.

Boulding, Kenneth (1980), 'The Ripening Society,' *Technology Review*, June/July, 6-7.

Bowles, Samuel, David M. Gordon and Thomas E. Weisskopf (1983), *Beyond the Waste Land: A Democratic Alternative to Economic Decline*, Garden City, NY: Anchor Press/ Doubleday.

Branson, William H. (1980), 'Trends in United States International Trade and Investment since World War II,' in Martin Feldstein (ed.), *The American Economy in Transition*, Chicago: University of Chicago Press, pp. 183-257.

Branson, William H. (1981), 'Industrial Policy and US International Trade,' in Wachter and Wachter (eds), pp. 378-408.

Braudel, Fernand (1982), *Civilization and Capitalism: 15th-18th Century. Vol. 11. The Wheels of Commerce*, translated by Si-an Reynolds, New York: Harper & Row [French, 1979].

Bray, Hiawatha (2000), 'Pulling an Al Gore?' *Boston Globe*, 22 June, p. D1.

Brittan, Sam (2000), 'A Brighter Prospect for Europe,' *Financial Times*, 11 May, on-line at www.ft.com.

Brooks, David (2000), *Bobos in Paradise*, New York: Simon & Schuster.

Buderi, Robert (2000), *Engines of Tomorrow*, New York: Simon & Schuster.

Burns, Arthur (1934), *Production Trends in the United States Since 1870*, New York: National Bureau of Economic Research.

Business Week (1981), *America's Restructured Economy*, special issue, 1 June, 55-100.

Business Week (1982), *The Reindustrialization of America*, New York: McGraw-Hill (based on a special issue of *Business Week*, 30 June 1980, 55-146).

Carroll, Paul (1993), *Big Blues: The Unmaking of IBM*, New York: Crown.

Cassidy, John (1998), 'Annals of Enterprise: The Comeback,' *The New Yorker*, 23 February, 122-7.

Casson, Mark (1993), 'Entrepreneurship,' in David R. Henderson (ed.), *The Fortune Encyclopedia of Economics*, New York: Warner Books, pp. 631-5.

Castells, Manuel (1989), *The Informational City*, London: Blackwell.

Castells, Manuel (1996), *The Rise of the Network Society*, Oxford: Blackwell.

Castells, Manuel (1998), 'Dark Side of the Boom' (interview with Jay Ogilvey), *Wired*, 188-9.

Ceh, Brian (2000). 'Measuring Industrial Creativity in North America,' processed.

Chandler, A.D. (1959), 'The Beginnings of "Big Business" in American Industry,' *Business History Review*, **33**, Spring, 1-31.

Chesbrough, Henry (1999), 'Arrested Development: The Experience of European Hard Disk Drive Firms in Comparison with US and Japanese Firms,' *Journal of Evolutionary Economics*, August, 9(3), abstract, p. 287.

Chinitz, Benjamin (1961), 'Contrasts in Agglomeration: New York and Pittsburgh,' *American Economic Review: Papers and Proceedings*, May, 279-89.

Chinitz, Benjamin (1984), 'The Regional Transformation of the American Economy,' *American Economic Association Papers and Proceedings*, May, 300-3.

Christensen, Clayton M. (1997), *The Innovator's Dilemma: When New Technologies Cause Great Firms to Fail*, Boston, MA: Harvard Business School Press.

Cohan, Peter S. (1999), *Net Profit: How to Invest and Compete in the Real World of Internet Business*, San Francisco: Jossey-Bass.

Covey, Steven (1990), *The Seven Habits of Highly Effective People*, New York: Simon & Schuster Fireside.

Cook, W.J. (1992), 'Competitive Streak,' *US News and World Report*, 18 May, p. 14.

Cox, W. Michael (2000), 'Free Enterprise: Policies for Growth,' on-line at www.dallasfed.org/htm/homepage/free.html.

Cox, W. Michael and Richard Alm (2000), 'The New Paradigm,' in Federal Reserve Bank of Dallas,' *1999 Annual Report*, 3-25.

Coyle, Diane (1998), *The Weightless World: Strategies for Managing the Digital Economy*, Cambridge, MA: MIT Press.

Cringely, Robert X. (1993), *Accidental Empires: How the Boys of Silicon Valley Make Their Millions, Battle Foreign Competition and Still Can't Get a Date*, New York: Harper Business.

Crum, Rex (1998), 'Umass Study: IT Sector Is Transforming Economy,' *Boston Business Journal*, 16-22 October.

David, Paul A. (1989 [1990]), 'Computer and Dynamo: The Modern Productivity Paradox in a Not-Too-Distant Mirror,' Center for Economic Policy Research, July.

Dedrick, Jason and Kenneth L. Kraemer (1998), *Asia's Computer Challenge*, New York: Oxford University Press.

Dertouzos, Michael (1989), *Made in America*, Cambridge, MA: MIT Press.

DeVol, Ross C. (1999), *America's High-Tech Economy: Growth, Development, and Risks for Metropolitan Areas*, Santa Monica: Milken Institute.

Di Tella, Guido (1982), 'The Economics of the Frontier,' in Charles P. Kindleberger and Guido Di Tella (eds), *Economics in the Long View*, Vol.1, New York: New York University Press, pp. 210-27.

Donovan, William J. (2000), 'How Greenspan and His Board Manage the New Economy,' *Providence Journal*, 19 March, p. F1.

Drennan, Matthew (1999), 'National Structural Change and Metropolitan Specialization in the United States,' *Papers in Regional Science*, **78**(3), July, 297-318.

Drucker, Peter (1985), *Innovation and Entrepreneurship*, New York: Harper & Row.

Duca, John V. (1998), 'The New Labor Paradigm,' *Southwest Economy*, May/June, 6-8.

Eads, George C. (1983), 'Commentary,' in Federal Reserve Bank of Kansas City, pp. 157-67.

Echeverri-Carrol, Elsie L. and William Brennan (1999), 'Are Innovation Networks Bounded by Proximity?' in Manfred M. Fischer, Luis Suarez-Villa and Michael Steiner (eds.), *Innovation, Networks and Localities*, Berlin: Springer-Verlag, pp. 28-49.

The Economist (2000), 'Up and Up It Goes,' 12 February, 27.

The Economist (2000), 'A British Miracle,' 25 March, 57-9.

Equity Analytics (2000), 'Initial Public Offerings of Securities,' www.e-analytics.com/ipo/bplan8.htm.

Farrell, Larry C. (1993), *Searching for the Spirit of Enterprise*, Staunton, VA.

Federal Reserve Bank of Kansas City (1983), *Industrial Change and Public Policy: A Symposium Sponsored by the Federal Reserve Bank of Kansas City*, Kansas City.

Ferguson, Charles H. (1990), 'Computers and the Coming of the US Keiretsu,' *Harvard Business Review*, July-August, 55-70.

Fernald, John G. (1999), 'Roads to Prosperity? Assessing the Link between Public Capital and Productivity,' *American Economic Review*, **89**(3), June, 619-38.

Florida, Richard and Martin Kenney (1990), *The Breakthrough Illusion: Corporate America's Failure to Move from Innovation to Mass Production*, New York: Basic Books.

Florida, Richard and Donald F. Smith, Jr. (1992), 'Venture Capital's Role in Economic Development: An Empirical Analysis,' in Edwin S. Mills and John F. McDonald (eds.), *Sources of Metropolitan Growth*, New Brunswick: Center for Urban Policy Research, pp. 183-209.

Fogel, Robert William (2000), *The Fourth Great Awakening and the Future of Egalitarianism*, Chicago: University of Chicago Press.

Forester, Tom (1993), *Silicon Samurai: How Japan Conquered the World's I.T. Industry*, Oxford: Blackwell.

Foster, Richard (1986), *Innovation: The Attacker's Advantage*, New York: Summit Books.

Freeman, Christopher, John Clark and Luc Soete (1982), *Unemployment and Technical Innovation: A Study of Long Waves and Economic Development*, Westport, CT: Greenwood Press.

Freeman, Richard B. (2000), 'Single-Peaked Vs. Diversified Capitalism: The Relation Between Economic Institutions and Outcomes,' NBER Working Paper No. W7556, February.

Friedman, Thomas (1999), *The Lexus and the Olive Tree,* New York: Farrar, Straus & Giroux.

Galbraith, John Kenneth ([1967] 1985), *The New Industrial State*, Boston: Houghton Mifflin.

Galston, William A. and Elaine C. Kamarck (1998), 'Five Realities that Will Shape 21st Century Politics,' *Blueprint*, Fall, on-line at www.ndol.org/blueprint/fall/98/article1.html.

Garreau, Joel (1981), *The Nine Nations of North America*, NY: Houghton Mifflin.

Gendron, George (2000), 'The Origin of the Entrepreneurial Species,' interview with Amar V. Bhide, *Inc.*, February, 104-14.

Gilder, George (1989), *Microcosm*, New York: Touchstone.

Gilder, George (2000), *Telecosm*, New York: The Free Press.

Glaeser, Edward L., Jose A. Scheinkman and Andrei Schleifer (1995), 'Economic Growth in a Cross-Section of Cities,' *Journal of Monetary Economics*, 36, 117-43.

Gold, Bela (1964), 'Industry Growth Patterns: Theory and Empirical Results,' *Journal of Industrial Economics*, **13**, November, 53-73.

Gordon, Robert J. (1999), 'Has the "New Economy" Rendered the Productivity Slowdown Obsolete?' Working Paper, Northwestern University, 14 June.

Gordon, Robert J. (2000), 'Does the "New Economy" Measure up to the Great Inventions of the Past?' *Journal of Economic Perspectives*, forthcoming.

Gordon, David M., Richard Edwards and Michael Reich (1982), *Segmented Work, Divided Workers: The Historical Transformation of Labor in the United States*, NY: Cambridge University Press.

Grant, Charles (1997), 'Linking Arms: A Survey of the Global Defence Industry,' *Economist*, 14 June.

Greenspan, Alan (2000), 'Technological Innovation and the Economy,' remarks before the White House Conference on the New Economy, Washington, DC, April 5.

Gross, Daniel (2000), *Bull Run: Wall Street, the Democrats, and the New Politics of Personal Finance*, New York: Public Affairs.

Grove, Andrew ([1983], 1985), *High Output Management*, New York: Random House Vintage.

Grove, Andrew (1993), 'How Intel Makes Spending Pay Off,' *Fortune*, 22 February, 57-61.

Grove, Andrew ([1996], 1999), *Only the Paranoid Survive*, New York: Currency Doubleday.

Hafner, Katie and Matthew Lyon (1996), *Where Wizards Stay Up Late: The Origins of the Internet*, New York: Simon & Schuster.

Hall, Peter (1998), *Cities in Civilization*, New York: Pantheon.

Hansen, Alvin H. (1939), 'Economic Progress and Declining Population Growth,' *American Economic Review*, 29(1), March, 1-15.

Hansen, Niles (1997), 'Defense Conversion in Texas: Challenges, Responses, and Opportunities,' in R.D. Norton (ed.), *Regional Resilience and Defense Conversion in the United States*, Greenwich, CT and London: JAI Press, pp. 115-44.

Hansen, Niles (2000), 'The New Economy: Implications for Peripheral Regions,' paper presented at the Southern Regional Science meetings, Miami Beach, April.

Harberger, Arnold (ed.) (1984), *World Economic Growth: Case Studies of Developed and Developing Nations*, San Francisco: ICS Press.

Hayek, Friedrich A. ([1942] 1972), 'Socialist Economic Calculation: The Present State of the Debate,' in Hayek, *Individualism and Economic Order*.

Haynes, Kingsley E., Stephen Fuller and Li Qiangsheng (1997), 'The Northern Virginia Economy: The Changing Role of Federal Spending,' in R.D. Norton (ed.), *Regional Resilience and Defense Conversion in the United States*, Greenwich, CT: JAI Press, 145-61.

Healy, Beth (2000), 'Venture Funding Soars to $14.69B in 4th,' *Boston Globe*, 13 February, p. C15.

Heilbroner, Robert L. (1993), 'Socialism,' in David R. Henderson (ed.), *The Fortune Encyclopedia of Economics*, New York: Warner Books, pp. 161-65.

Heilbroner, Robert L. and Aaron Singer (1984), *The Economic Transformation of America: 1600 to the Present*, 2nd edn, New York: Harcourt Brace Jovanovich.

Heim, Carol (1984), 'Decline and Renewal in Britain and the United States: The Role of Less Developed Areas within Mature Economies,' processed.

Hekman, John (1979), 'Regions Don't Grow Old; Products Do,' *New York Times*, 4 November.

Henriques, Diana B. (1998), 'Sewing a Label on a Decade,' *New York Times*, 4 January, C3.

Hoffmann, Walther G. ([1931] 1955), *British Industry, 1700-1950*, New York: Augustus M. Kelley.

Holly, Brian P. and Audrey E. Clarke (1998), 'Regional Change in Computer Services in the United States,' June, processed (ISBN 0704419491).

Hoover, Edgar M. (1948), *The Location of Economic Activity*, New York: McGraw-Hill.

Howitt, Peter (2000), 'Endogenous Growth and Cross-Country Income Differences,' *American Economic Review*, September, 829-46.

Jackson, Tim (1997), *Inside Intel*, New York: Penguin Dutton.

Jacobs, Jane (1969), *The Economy of Cities*, New York: Random House.

Jacobs, Jane (1984), *Cities and the Wealth of Nations*, New York: Random House.

Jewkes, John, David Sawers, and Richard Stillerman, ([1958] 1969), *The Sources of Invention*, Second edition, New York: W.W. Norton.

Jorgenson, Dale and Kevin Stiroh (2000), 'Raising the Speed Limit: U.S. Economic Growth in the Information Age,' *Brookings Papers on Economic Activity*, **1**.

Kenney, Martin and Urs von Burg (1999), 'Technology, Entrepreneurship and Path Dependence: Industrial Clustering in Silicon Valley and Route 128,' *Industrial and Corporate Change*, **8**(1), March, 67-103.

Kerschner, Edward, Thomas Doerflinger and Michael Geraghty (2000), 'The Information Age Is Alive and Well,' 16 April, *Investment Policy*, New York: PaineWebber, 1-8.

Kindleberger, Charles P. (1953), *International Economics*, Homewood, IL: Richard D. Irwin.

Kindleberger, Charles P. (1961), 'Obsolescence and Technical Change,' Bulletin, *Oxford University Institute of Economic Statistics*, 23, August, 281-97.

Kindleberger, Charles P. (1962), *Foreign Trade and the National Economy*, New Haven, CT: Yale University Press.

Kindleberger, Charles P. (1973), Letter, *New York Times*, March 1.

Kindleberger, Charles P. (1974), 'An American Economic Climacteric?' *Challenge*, **16**(6), January/February, 35-44.

Kindleberger, Charles P. (1978), 'The Aging Economy,' *Weltwirtschraftliches Archiv*, **114**(3), 407-21.

Kindleberger, Charles P. (1980), The Economic Aging of America, *Challenge*, **22**(6), January/February, 48-9.

Kindleberger, Charles P. (1983), [review of Olson], *International Studies Quarterly*, **1**(1).

Kirchner, Jake (1997), 'The *PC Magazine*'s 100 Most Influential Companies,' *PC Magazine*, July, 213-45.

Krugman, Paul R. (1983), 'Targeted Industrial Policies: Theory and Evidence,' in Federal Reserve Bank of Kansas City, pp. 123-55.

Krugman, Paul R. (1991), *Geography and Trade*, Cambridge, MA: MIT Press.

Krugman, Paul (1997), 'Unmitigated Gauls,' 5 June, *Slate*, on-line at www.slate.com.

Krugman, Paul (1997b), 'Requiem for the New Economy,' *Fortune*, November 10, on-line at web.mit.edu/krugman/www/.

Krugman, Paul (1998), 'America the Boastful,' *Foreign Affairs*, **77**(3), May/June, 32-45.

Krugman, Paul R. (1998b), 'Why Most Economists' Predictions Are Wrong,' *Red Herring*, June, 28.

Krugman, Paul (1999), 'Want Growth? Speak English,' *Fortune*, 57.

Krugman, Paul (1999b), Why Germany Kant Kompete,' *Fortune*, July, on-line at web.mit.edu/krugman/www/.

Krugman, Paul (2000), 'Aristocrats.com,' *New York Times*, 19 March, 4:15.

Krugman, Paul (2000b), 'Going for Broke,' *New York Times*, 2 July, A:11.

Kuznets, Simon (1930), *Secular Movements in Production and Prices – Their Nature and Their Bearing upon Cyclical Fluctuations*, Boston, MA: Houghton Mifflin.

Kuznets, Simon (1940), 'Schumpeter's Business Cycles,' *American Economic Review*, June, 257.

Kuznets, Simon (1953), *Economic Change – Selected Essays in Business Cycles, National Income, and Economic Growth*, New York: W.W. Norton.

Kuznets, Simon (1959), *Six Lectures on Economic Growth*, Glencoe, IL: Free Press.

Kuznets, Simon (1971), *Economic Growth of Nations: Total Output and Production Structure*, Cambridge, MA: Belknap Press of Harvard University Press.

Lange, Oskar and Fred Taylor (1938), *On the Economic Theory of Socialism*.

Laughlin, James D. and Vincent A. Digirolamo (1994), 'A Market-based Approach to Development Finance: Case Study of the Capital Access Program,' *Economic Development Quarterly*, November, 316.

Lawrence, Robert Z. (1983), 'Is Trade Deindustrializing America? A Medium Term Perspective,' *Brookings Papers in Economics Act.,* 1, 129-71.

Lawrence, Robert Z. (1984), *Can America Compete?*, Washington, DC: Brookings Institution.

Leechor, Chad, Harindars S. Kohli and Sujin Hur (1983), *Structural Changes in World Industry: A Quantitative Analysis of Recent Developments*, Washington, DC: World Bank.

Leonhardt, David (2000), 'California Dreamin': Harvard Business School Adds Silicon Valley to Its Syllabus,' *New York Times*, 18 June, p. 3:1.

Levinthal, Daniel A. (1998), 'The Slow Pace of Rapid Technological Change: Gradualism and Punctuation in Technological Change,' *Industrial and Corporate Change*, June, 217-47.

Lewis, W. Arthur (1978a), *The Evolution of the International Economic Order*, Princeton, NJ: Princeton University Press.

Lewis, W. Arthur (1978b), *Growth and Fluctuations 1879-1913*, London: George Allen & Unwin.

Liesman, Steve (2000), 'New Economy Finds Converts in Two Skeptical Economists,' *Wall Street Journal Interactive Edition*, 1 August, on-line at www.wsj.com.

Lindbeck, Assar (1981), 'Can the Rich Countries Adapt? Needs and Difficulties,' *OECD Observer*, 108, January, 6-9.

Magaziner, Ira C. and Robert B. Reich (1982), *Minding America's Business: The Decline and Rise of the American Economy*, New York: Harcourt Brace Jovanovich.

Magee, Stephen P. (1980), *International Trade*, Reading, MA: Addison-Wesley.

Mahoney, Chris (2000), 'Report: IPO Market Had "Fabulous" Fourth Quarter,' *Boston Business Journal*, 7-13 January, 4.

Mandel, Michael (1999), 'Meeting the Challenge of the New Economy,' *Blueprint*, Winter (www.ndol.org/blueprint;winter98/thechallenge.html).

Markoff, John (1992), 'Mobile Computing Is All American,' *New York Times*, 23 November.

Markusen, Ann, Peter Hall, Scott Campbell and Sabina Deitrick (1991), *The Rise of the Gunbelt: The Military Remapping of Industrial America*, Oxford: Oxford University Press.

Marolda, Anthony J. (1997), 'Commercialization of Defense Technology: The Key Success Factors,' in R.D. Norton (ed.), *Regional Resilience and Defense Conversion in the United States*, Greenwich, CT and London: JAI Press, pp. 31-53.

Marshall, Alfred (1919), *Industry and Trade*, London: Macmillan.

Marshall, Alfred (1920), *Principles of Economics*, London: Macmillan.

Matthews, R.C.O., C.H. Feinstein and J.C. Odlingsmee (1982), *British Economic Growth, 1856-1973*, Stanford, CA: Stanford University Press.

Meeker, Mary and Chris DePuy (1996), *The Internet Report*, New York: Morgan Stanley.

Miara, Jim (1998), 'Economists Wrong but Offer Reasons,' *Boston Business Journal*, 25 May, p. 3.

Micklethwait, John (1997), 'The Valley of Money's Delight,' *Economist*, 29 March, survey insert.

Micklethwait, John and Adrian Wooldridge (2000), *A Future Perfect: The Challenge and Hidden Promise of Globalization*, New York: Times Books.

Mirmirani, Sam and H.C. Li (1997), 'Arms Export and Its Employment Impact on the United States,' in R.D. Norton (ed.), *Regional Resilience and Defense Conversion in the United States*, Greenwich, CT and London: JAI Press, pp. 55-68.

Moore, Geoffrey A. (2000), *Living on the Fault Line*, New York: HarperCollins.

Morris, Charles R. and Charles H. Ferguson (1993), 'How Architecture Wins Technology Wars,' *Harvard Business Review*, March-April, 86-96.

Moschella, David C. (1997), *Waves of Power: The Dynamics of Global Technology Leadership 1964-2010*, New York: American Management Association.

Mowery, David and Nathan Rosenberg (1998), *Paths of Innovation: Technological Change in 20th Century America*, Cambridge, UK: Cambridge University Press.

Murphy, Michael (1998), *Every Investor's Guide to High-Tech Stocks and Mutual Funds*, New York: Broadway Books.

Murray, Matt (2000), 'GE Posts 16% Rise in 4th-Quarter Net on Strong Results for Most of its Units,' *Wall Street Journal Interactive Edition*, 21 January.

Niedorf, Shawn (2000), 'New Yorkers Not Talk of Town,' San Jose *Mercury News* online, 7 March.

Nordhaus, William D. and James Tobin (1972), 'Is Growth Obsolete?' in Robert J. Gordon, *Economic Research: Retrospect and Prospect – Economic Growth*, New York: National Bureau of Economic Research, pp. 1-80.

Norman, Colin (1980), *Microelectronics at Work: Productivity and Jobs in the World Economy*, Washington, DC: Worldwatch Institute.

Norris, Floyd (1997), 'Ten Years Later, IBM Sets a New High in a Changed Market,' *New York Times*, 14 May.

Norton, Bruce (1984), 'Marxian Stagnation and Long Wave Theories: A Review,' processed.

Norton, R.D. (1979), *City Life-Cycles and American Urban Policy*, New York: Academic Press.

Norton, R.D. (1981), 'Regional Life-Cycles and U.S. Industrial Rejuvenation,' in Herbert Giersch (ed.), *Towards an Explanation of Economic Growth. Symposium*, Tübingen: J.C.B. Mohr, 1981, pp. 253-80.

Norton, R.D. (1986), 'Industrial Policy and American Renewal,' *Journal of Economic Literature*, March, 1-40.

Norton, R.D. (1996), 'The Westward Rebirth of American Computing,' in Norton (ed.), *New Urban Strategies in Advanced Regional Economies*, Greenwich, CT: JAI Press, pp. 93-115.

Norton, R.D. (ed) (1997), *Regional Resilience and Defense Conversion in the United States,* Greenwich, CT and London: JAI Press.

Norton, R.D. (1999), 'Where Are the World's Top 100 I.T. Firms – And Why?' in Manfred M. Fischer, Luis Suarez-Villa and Michael Steiner (eds.), *Innovation, Networks, and Localities*, Berlin: Springer-Verlag, pp. 235-56.

Norton, R.D. and John Rees (1979), 'The Product Cycle and the Spatial Decentralization of American Manufacturing,' *Regional Studies*, **13**(2), August, 141-51.

O'Brien, Virginia (1996), *The Fast Forward MBA in Business*, New York and Chichester: John Wiley.

O hUallachain, Breandan (1999), 'Patent Places: Size Matters,' *Journal of Regional Science*, **39**(4), 613-636.

Oliner, Stephen and Daniel Sichel (2000), 'The Resurgence of Growth in the Late 1990s: Is Information Technology the Story?' Processed.

Olson, Elizabeth (2000), 'Nations Cutting Aid to the Jobless, Study Says,' *New York Times*, 22 June, p. C4.

Palfreman, J. and D. Swade (1991), *The Dream Machine: Exploring the Computer Age*, London: BBC Books.

Peirce, Neil R. and Jerry Hagstrom (1983), *The Book of America: Inside 50 States Today*, New York: W.W. Norton.

Peppers, Don (1995), *Life's A Pitch Then You Buy*, New York: Currency Doubleday.

Peppers, Don and Martha Rogers (1997), *Enterprise One to One: Tools for Competing in the Interactive Age*, New York: Doubleday.

Perloff, Harvey and Lowdon Wingo (1961), 'Natural Resource Endowment and Regional Economic Growth,' in J.J. Spengler (ed.), *Natural Resources and Economic Growth*, Washington, DC: Resources for the Future.

Piore, Michael (1982), 'American Labor and the Industrial Crisis,' *Challenge*, **25**(l), March/April, 5-11.

Piore, Michael and Charles Sabel (1984), *The Second Industrial Divide*, New York: Basic Books.

Plessz, N. (1981), 'Western Europe,' in Christopher Saunders (ed.), *The Political Economy of New and Old Industrial Countries*, London: Butterworth & Co., Ltd, pp. 217-39.

Pollack, Andrew (1992), 'Fifth Generation Becomes Japan's Lost Generation,' *New York Times*, 5 June.

Pollack, Andrew (1994), 'Japan May Abandon Its System of HDTV,' *New York Times*, 23 February.

Pollack, Andrew (1997), 'Aerospace Engineers Are Turning to Hollywood,' *CyberTimes*, 10 October.

Pollack, Andrew (2000), 'Biotech Industry Flexes New Muscle,' *New York Times*, 24 August, p. C:1.

Pontin, Jason (1997), 'There Is No New Economy,' *Red Herring Magazine*, September, on-line.

Porter, Michael (1990), *The Competitive Advantage of Nations*, New York: Free Press.

Porter, Michael B. (2000), 'Location, Competition, and Economic Development: Local Clusters in a Global Economy,' *Economic Development Quarterly*, **14**(1), February, 15-34.

PricewaterhouseCoopers (2000), 'Western Europe Economic Overview,' on-line at www/pwcglobal.com.

Quinones, Eric R. (1998), 'Forbes' 400 Richest Include 189 Billionaires,' *Boston Globe*, 28 September.

Redding, S. Gordon (1990, [1993]), *The Spirit of Chinese Capitalism*, Berlin: Walter de Gruyter.

Reich, Robert B. (1982), 'Industrial Policy: Ten Concrete, Practical Steps to Building a Dynamic, Growing and Fair American Economy,' *The New Republic*, 186, 31 March, 28-31.

Reich, Robert B. (1983), *The Next American Frontier*, New York: Penguin Books.

Reich, Robert B. (1984), 'Small State, Big Lesson,' *The Boston Observer*, 3(7), July, 32.

Renaissance Capital: www.ipo-fund.com/topfive.htm.

Reynolds, Paul D, Michael Hay and S. Michael Camp (1999), *Global Entrepreneurship Monitor: 1999 Executive Report*, Kansas City: Kauffman Center for Entrepreneurial Leadership.

Ridley, Matt (2000), *Genome*, New York: HarperCollins.

Ritter, Jay (1999), 'Big IPO Runups of 1975-1999,' on-line at http://bear.cba.ufl.edu/ritter/ritterbi.htm.

Rogers, Everett M. and Judith K. Larsen (1984), *Silicon Valley Fever: Growth of High-Technology Culture*, New York: Basic Books.

Rohatyn, Felix (1983), '*The Twenty-Year Century: Essays on Economics and Public Finance*,' New York: Random House.

Romer, Paul M. (1986), 'Increasing Returns and Long-Run Growth,' *Journal of Political Economy*, **94**, October, 1002-37.

Romer, Paul M. (1993), 'Economic Growth,' in David R. Henderson (ed.), *The Fortune Encyclopedia of Economics*, New York: Warner Books, pp. 183-89.

Rorke, Marcia L., Harold C. Livesay and David S. Lux (1991), *From Invention to Innovation: Commercialization of New Technology by Independent and Small Business Inventors*, Rockville, Maryland: Mohawk Research Corporation.

Rosenberg, Nathan (1982), *Inside the Black Box: Technology and Economics*, New York: Cambridge University Press.

Rostow, Walt Whitman (1960), *The Stages of Economic Growth*, Cambridge, England: Cambridge University Press.

Sale, Kirkpatrick (1975), *Power Shift: The Rise of the Southern Rim and Its Challenge to the Eastern Establishment*, New York: Random House.

Saxenian, Annalee (1994), *Regional Advantage: Culture and Competition in Silicon Valley and Route 128*, Cambridge, MA: Harvard University Press.

Saxenian, AnnaLee (1996), 'Inside-Out: Regional Networks and Industrial Adaptation in Silicon Valley and Route 128,' *Cityscape*, **2**(2), 41-60.

Schiller, Robert (2000), *Irrational Exuberance*, Princeton: Princeton University Press.

Schlefer, Jonathan (1989), 'Making Sense of the Productivity Debate,' *Technology Review*, August/September, 28-40.

Schoonhoven, Claudia Bird and Kathleen M. Eisenhardt (1992), 'Regions as Industrial Incubators of Technology-Based Ventures,' in Edwin S. Mills and John F. McDonald, (eds), *Sources of Metropolitan Growth*, New Brunswick, NJ: Rutgers, pp. 210-52.

Schultze, Charles L. (1983), 'Industrial Policy: A Dissent,' *Brookings Review*, **2**(1), Fall, 3-12.

Schumpeter, Joseph (1934), *The Theory of Economic Development*, Cambridge, MA: Harvard University Press.

Schumpeter, Joseph ([1939] 1962), *Business Cycles: A Theoretical, Historical and Statistical Analysis of the Capitalist Process*, 2 vols, New York: McGraw-Hill.

Schumpeter, Joseph ([1942] 1962), *Capitalism, Socialism, and Democracy*, New York: Harper & Row.

Schumpeter, Joseph (1947), 'The Creative Response in Economic History,' *The Journal of Business History*, VII(2), November, 149-59.

Schwert, G. William (1999), 'FIN 423—Corporate Financial Policy & Control: Venture Capital,' and 'FIN 423—Corporate Financial Policy &

Control: Initial Public Offerings (IPOs),' slideshow online at schwert.ssb.rochester.edu/f423/f423ipo.htm.

Seattle *Post-Intelligencer* (1998), 'Washington State High-Tech Workers Are Highest Paid,' in San Jose *Mercury News*, 20 May, (http://www.sjmercury.com).

Shapiro, Carl and Hal R. Varian (1999), *Information Rules: A Strategic Guide to the Network Economy*, Boston, MA: Harvard Business School Press.

Shenon, P. (1997), 'Charleston Bounces Back after Closing of Base,' *New York Times*, 12 June, p. A16.

Slater, Robert (1999), *Jack Welch and the GE Way*, New York: McGraw-Hill.

Spinosa, Charles, Fernando Flores, and Hubert L. Dreyfus (1997), *Disclosing New Worlds: Entrepreneurship, Democratic Action, and the Cultivation of Solidarity*, Cambridge, MA: MIT Press.

Stanley, Alessandra (2000), 'Full-Moon Haircut Breaks Italy's Law: Commerce Is Changing, but Some Regulations Remain in Place,' *New York Times*, 18 June, p. E10.

Stevens, Benjamin H. and George I. Treyz (1983), 'Trends in Regional Industrial Diversification and Self-sufficiency and Their Implications for Growth,' processed.

Stevenson, Seth (1998), 'In Other Magazines,' *Slate* (on-line), 1 September.

Storper, Michael and Richard Walker (1989), *The Capitalist Imperative: Territory, Technology, and Industrial Growth*, Oxford: Basil Blackwell.

Suarez-Villa, Luis (1997), 'California's Recovery and the Restructuring of the Defense Industries,' in R.D. Norton (ed.), *Regional Resilience and Defense Conversion in the United States*, Greenwich, CT and London: JAI Press, pp. 85-114.

Surowiecki, James (2000), 'The Financial Page: Why Do Companies Like Company?' *The New Yorker*, 24 April and 1 May, 68.

Taylor, George Rogers (1949), *The Turner Thesis Concerning the Role of the Frontier in American History*, Boston, MA: D.C. Heath.

Taylor, Timothy (1996), *A History of the U.S. Economy*, Springfield, VA: The Teaching Company, p. 20.

Testa, William, Thomas Klier and Richard Mattoon (1997), 'The Midwest Turnaround: Internal and External Influences,' in R.D. Norton (ed.), *Regional Resilience and Defense Conversion in the United States*, Greenwich, CT and London: JAI Press, pp. 183-213.

Thurm, Scott (1997), 'High-Tech Catapults to No. 2,' San Jose *Mercury News*, 18 October.

Thurow, Lester (1980), *The Zero-Sum Society*, New York: Basic Books.

Thurow, Lester (1981), 'Getting Serious About Tax Reform,' *The Atlantic*, 247, March, 68-72.

Thurow, Lester (1984), 'Losing the Economic Race, *New York Review of Books*, September 27, 29-31.

Thurow, Lester (1998), 'Laws of Economic Relativity,' *Boston Globe*, 16 June, p. C4.

Thurow, Lester (1999), *Building Wealth: The New Rules for Individuals, Companies, and Nations in a Knowledge-based Economy*, New York: HarperCollins.

Tisdell, Clem (1999), 'Diversity and Economic Evolution,' *Contemporary Economic Policy*, 17(2), April, 156-65.

Uchitelle, Louis (1998), 'The Economy Grows. The Smokestacks Shrink,' *New York Times*, 29 November, p. 3:4.

Uchitelle, Louis (1999), 'Economists Reject Notion of Stock Market "Bubble,"' *New York Times*, 6 January, p. C2.

US Department of Commerce, Bureau of the Census (1990 and 1998), *County Business Patterns 1986 and 1987* and *County Business Patterns 1995 and 1996* (CD-ROMs), Washington, DC.

US Department of Commerce, Bureau of the Census, *Current Population Reports*, Series P-25.

US Department of Commerce, Bureau of Economic Analysis (1998), *The Emerging Digital Economy*, Washington, DC: US Government Printing Office.

US Department of Commerce, Bureau of Economic Analysis (1973), *Long Term Economic Growth, 1860-1970*, Washington, DC: US Government Printing Office.

US Department of Labor, Bureau of Labor Statistics (various issues), *Employment and Earnings*, Washington, DC: US Government Printing Office.

US President, Council of Economic Advisors (2000), *Economic Report of the President 2000*, Washington DC: US Government Printing Office.

Valencia, Matthew (2000), 'New Economy, Old Problems,' *The Economist*, 29 April, Survey insert 17-18.

Van Duijn, J.J. (1983), *The Long Wave in Economic Life*, London: George Allen & Unwin.

Varga, Attila (1999), 'Time-Space Patterns of US Innovation: Stability or Change?' in Manfred M. Fischer, Luis Suarez-Villa and Michael Steiner (eds.), *Innovation, Networks, and Localities*, Berlin: Springer-Verlag, pp. 215-34.

Vellante, David (1998), 'Business Review: They Said It,' *Boston Globe*, 16 June, p. F2.

Vernon, Raymond (1966), 'International Investment and International Trade in the Product Cycle,' *Quarterly Journal of Economics*, 80, May, 190-207.

332 *Creating the New Economy*

Vogel, Ezra F. (1979), *Japan as Number One*, Cambridge: Harvard University Press.

Von Mises, Ludwig (1935), 'Economic Calculation in the Socialist Commonwealth,' in Friedrich A. Hayek (ed.), *Collective Economic Planning*.

Warsh, David (2000), 'Boston's Place,' *Boston Globe*, 21 March, p. E1.

Weber, Max ([1905] 1958), *The Protestant Ethic and the Spirit of Capitalism*, London: Charles Scribner's Sons.

Weil, Frank A. (1980), 'The US Needs an Industrial Policy,' *Fortune*, 101, 24 March, 149-52.

Weinstein, Bernard L. (1997), 'Welcome to the New Economy,' *Perspectives*, 12(2), December, 1-4.

Wheat, Leonard (1973), *Regional Growth and Industrial Location: An Empirical Viewpoint*, Lexington, MA: DC Heath.

Winograd, Terry and Fernando Flores (1986), *Understanding Computers and Cognition*, Norwood, NJ: Ablex.

Wolf, Julius (1912), *Die Volkswirtschaft der Gegenwart und Zukunft*, Leipzig: A. Deichertsche Verlags.

Wolman, William and Anne Colamosca (1997), *The Judas Economy: The Triumph of Capital and the Betrayal of Work*, Reading, MA: Addison-Wesley.

The World Bank (2000), *Entering the 21st Century: World Development Report 1999/2000*, New York: Oxford University Press.

Wright, Austin Tappen ([1942], 1996), *Islandia*, LightYear Press reprint.

Yourdon, Edward (1993), *The Decline and Fall of the American Programmer*, Englewood Cliffs, NJ: Yourdon Press.

Zacharakis, Andrew, Paul D. Reynolds and William Bygrave (1999), *National Entrepreneurship Assessment: United States of America 1999 Executive Report*, Kansas City, MO: Kauffman Center for Entrepreneurial Leadership.

Zandi, Mark (1998), 'Musings on the New Economy,' *Regional Financial Review*, March, 4-10.

Zandi, Mark (1999), 'The Quality of Jobs,' *The Dismal Scientist*, 3 August, www.dismal.com.

Zuckerman, Mortimer (1998), 'A Second American Century,' *Foreign Affairs*, 77(3), May/June, 18-31.

Name index

Subject index